I0652547

FOURTEEN ON FORM

FOURTEEN ON FORM
CONVERSATIONS WITH POETS

William Baer

UNIVERSITY PRESS OF MISSISSIPPI
JACKSON

www.upress.state.ms.us

The University Press of Mississippi is a member of
the Association of American University Presses.

Copyright © 2004 by University Press of Mississippi
All rights reserved
Manufactured in the United States of America

Print-on-Demand Edition

Library of Congress Cataloging-in-Publication Data

Baer, William, 1948–
    Fourteen on form: conversations with poets / William Baer.
        p. cm.
    Includes index.
    ISBN 1-57806-671-9 (alk. paper)
    1. American poetry—20th century—History and criticism—Theory, etc.
2. English poetry—20th century—History and criticism—Theory, etc. 3. Poets,
American—20th century—Interviews. 4. Poets, English—20th century—
Interviews. 5. English language—Versification. 6. Poetry—Authorship.
7. Literary form. I. Title: 14 on form. II. Title.
    PS323.5.B34   2004
    811'.509—dc22   2004003584

British Library Cataloging-in-Publication Data available

CONTENTS

PREFACE

In past centuries, lovers of literature have surely asked themselves, "I wonder what Chaucer would have said about that?" Or Shakespeare? Or Pope? Or Tennyson? Fortunately, during the last half-century, it's become quite possible to hear what our best contemporary writers have to say about matters of artistic interest. The modern literary interview, in fact, developed rather quickly, reaching a high mark of excellence with *The Paris Review* interviews in the Sixties and Seventies. Soon afterwards, William Packard began his exceptional in-depth interviews for *The New York Quarterly.* For the first time, readers could hear contemporary writers commenting on a wide range of issues relating to the writer's craft.

The interviews in *Fourteen on Form: Conversations with Poets* have been conducted in the same spirit. They're relaxed but serious literary conversations with fourteen of the most distinguished poets writing in the English language. Although these poets come from a wide range of backgrounds, and write in their own unique styles, they do have at least two obvious things in common. Most of them are from our senior, Post-World War II literary generation, and all of them have remained consistently interested in matters of poetic craft and form. Although the interviews cover a wide range of topics—personal biography, poetic influences, education, mentors, methods of composition, specific poems, recurring themes, the teaching of poetry, academia, the contemporary poetry scene, etc.—it's relevant that all of these interviews were first published in *The Formalist*, a poetry journal with a special interest in poets committed to prosody and metrics. Whatever disagreements these opinionated writers might have, they all clearly believe that the traditional restraints of formal poetry, if used properly, can create poetic power and aesthetic beauty.

Despite writing for most of their careers during a time of free verse ascendancy, the poets interviewed in this book have all found ways to create significant and unique poetic voices that have been impossible to ignore. Their work has received countless literary accolades and prizes, and in the subsequent recognition of their work, they've all been out-spoken in their support of traditional craft. As a result, they've had a major impact on the younger poets of the "baby boom" generation who've initiated the current formalist revival. Many of these younger poets, the so-called "New Formalists," modeled their work on the poets in this book, and a number of them actually studied under these poets or developed special relationships with them. Brad Leithauser, for example, studied with Anthony Hecht; Rachel Hadas has known John Hollander most of her life; and Dana Gioia has co-edited a number of important textbooks with X. J. Kennedy.

From the late Sixties into the Nineties, there was a long period when it was very difficult for unestablished young poets to place their sonnets and other metrical verse in the vast majority of American literary journals. During that time, the senior poets in this book gave both inspiration and help to the slowly blossoming formalist revival that coalesced in the nineties around two highly successful poetry conferences (The Sewanee Writers' Conference founded by Wyatt Prunty in 1990, and the Exploring Form and Narrative Poetry Conference founded by Dana Gioia and Michael Peich in 1995); several literary journals (*The Formalist*, founded in 1989; the unfortunately defunct *Sparrow*, reformatted as *The Yearbook of the Sonnet* in 1994; *The Edge City Review* also begun in 1994; and *The Dark Horse*, founded in Scotland in 1995); and a number of anthologies (like Robert Richman's *The Direction of Poetry*, 1988, and Mark Jarman and David Mason's *Rebel Angels*, 1996).

When once confronted with the notion that a poem had "too much melody," Derek Walcott responded with some irritation, "I don't know any other culture in the history of the world that has ever said . . . [that a poem] has too much melody." Certainly, melodious sound, specifically reinforced by meter, is an obvious fact of all Western poetry from Homer to Dante to Shakespeare to Dickinson. A few poets in the past did, on occasion, try some non-metrical experiments, but it wasn't until Whitman and Henley in the late Nineteenth century that non-metrical poems were seriously written. Henley's poems, however, were generally uninteresting and considered insignificant, and even Whitman's free verse, despite the admiration of Emerson, had no real contemporary impact, and Whitman would only become a significant literary influence in the Twentieth Century. In France, the late Symbolists, specifically Mallarmé and Valéry, also experimented with *vers libre*, but, as Mallarmé put it, such verse was only to be seen as an experimental "side altar" in the great "cathedral" of metrical poetry.

It was really, of course, the American Ezra Pound, with his publication of *Des Imagistes: An Anthology* in 1914 (along with his influence, as foreign editor, at Harriet Monroe's *Poetry Magazine*) who initiated free verse into modern poetry. With the help of F. S. Flint and others, Pound was able to promulgate his dictum "to compose in the sequence of the musical phrase, not the sequence of the metronome," and *Des Imagistes* began a poetic trend that quickly accelerated and resulted in an avalanche of free verse poetry. Nevertheless, despite the natural attraction and excitement surrounding free verse during the first half of the century, most of the dominant poets were still skilled metrists: Yeats, Robinson, Hardy, Frost, and Auden—and even Pound and his influential protégé T. S. Eliot wrote metrical poems.

The more senior poets interviewed in this book arrived on the scene after World War II, several publishing their first collections in the late Forties and early Fifties. This was a period when metrical poetry, especially under the influence of Auden, had become respectable again. It was also a time when, as Maxine Kumin explains in her interview, "Young women were being discouraged by the literary editors, who had very different expectations for women writers." As Kumin points out, the American poet John Ciardi once admitted that there was a limiting quota placed on women poets at *The Saturday Review* where he served as poetry editor.

Although the same was true of other minorities, some women (like Elizabeth Bishop) and some African-American writers did write formal poetry at the time, although some (like Gwendolyn Brooks and later Adrienne Rich) would eventually move to free formats. Some literary critics have attributed such changes in literary style to political matters, claiming that progressive and marginalized writers will naturally tend to express themselves in more open formats. Although this might be true in a number of individual cases, it's certainly an inadequate generalization that can't explain why a Socialist like Auden was committed to forms, why several writers of the earlier Harlem Renaissance wrote exclusively in forms, and why the politically conservative Pulitzer Prize winning poet Peter Viereck wrote in free verse.

Beginning in the Fifties and continuing through the sixties, there was a vigorous reassertion of free verse in America due to the influence of such groups as the Beats, the Black Mountain Poets, the New York School, the Deep Imagists, and others. A few of the poets interviewed in this book did, on occasion, write in non-metrical or loosely-metrical formats, but none of them ever abandoned metrical forms. On the contrary, they constantly reengaged the tradition and promoted metrical verse.

I've mentioned these historical facts to illustrate the single overriding aesthetic interest that runs through all the disparate and distinguished poets interviewed in this book. Whatever their many differences of opinions about other subjects, these poets have all maintained a lifelong dedication to sound and prosody in contemporary English-language poetry.

In gratitude for the completion of this book, I would first like to thank my wife, Mona Baer, the Managing Editor of *The Formalist*, for all her help. She not only transcribed all the taped interviews, but she offered invaluable editorial suggestions and advice. I would also like to thank Wyatt Prunty, Director of the Sewanee Writers' Conference, for helping to facilitate my first interview with Richard Wilbur. Eventually, six of the interviews in this book would be conducted during the annual Sewanee Writers' Conference in Sewanee, Tennessee. Similarly, I'd like to thank Dana Gioia and Michael Peich, Co-Directors of the Exploring Form and Narrative Poetry Conference, who helped me arrange for three of these interviews to be conducted during the annual poetry conference in West Chester, Pennsylvania.

Finally, I would like to thank the fourteen generous and talented poets who contributed to this book. Now it's time to let them speak for themselves.

—William Baer

FOURTEEN ON FORM

RICHARD WILBUR

Richard Wilbur is not only, as *Book World* has put it, "the master crafts-man of our times," he is also one of the world's foremost contemporary poets.

Richard Wilbur was born in New York City, grew up in North Caldwell, New Jersey, and attended Amherst College. The year of his graduation, he married Mary Charlotte Hayes Ward, and began three years of military service as a cryptographer with the U.S. Army's 36th Infantry Division in Italy, France, and Germany.

After the war, he received a master's degree from Harvard University, and his first book, *The Beautiful Changes and Other Poems*, was published in 1947. Over the next ten years, he taught at Harvard and Wellesley, and, in 1957, his third collection, *Things of This World*, won both the National Book Award and the Pulitzer Prize for Poetry.

During the years 1957–77, Richard Wilbur was a Professor of English at Wesleyan University. In 1963, his verse translation of Molière's *Tartuffe* was the co-recipient of the Bollingen Prize for translation, and, in 1977, he received a second Bollingen Prize for his own poetry. From 1977–86, he was Writer-in-Residence at Smith College, and, in 1987, he was appointed the second Poet Laureate of the United States, succeeding Robert Penn Warren. The following year, he was awarded his second Pulitzer Prize for his *New and Collected Poems*.

This interview was conducted at the University of the South during the Sewanee Writers' Conference.

I'd like to begin, if I could, with a quote from Yeats that refers to many things about poetry but is very specific about the necessity of craftsmanship: "Alas

3

the inspiration of God, which is, indeed, the source of all which is greatest in the world, comes only to him who labours at rhythm and cadence, at form and style, until they have no secret hidden from him. This art we must learn from the old literatures of the world. . . . We have shrunk from the labour that art demands, and have made thereby our best moments of no account. We must learn from the literatures of France and England to be supreme artists and then God will send to us supreme inspiration." Do you think contemporary poets adequately learn their craft—or "trade" as Yeats put it in "Under Ben Bulben"?

RICHARD WILBUR: I think many poets nowadays do not, in fact, learn the trade, and I'm sorry about that. I agree with a large part of what Yeats says there. He's talking about those he refers to elsewhere as "sages standing in God's holy fire." We do need to be taught the essentials of our trade by the great things that have been done in verse in the past. There's no obligation to repeat exactly what has been done in the past, and I think it's a superstition of our day to suppose that the learning of lessons from the past will lead to repetition or copycatting. I recall William Carlos Williams, a marvelous man and poet whom I don't intend to attack, saying to me that it was not possible to write a sonnet nowadays without, in effect, making gestures of loyalty towards the court of Elizabeth I. That's simply not so. Had he looked about him with a less ideological eye, he would have seen people writing sonnets that are full of life and fully contemporary, poems that take present advantage of what the timeless contraption of the sonnet can offer to someone whose mind has been entered by inspiration.

Your wonderful and powerful poem, "The Writer," like the Yeats quote, is about many things. It's about love, it's about the relationship between a father and a daughter, and it's also about the intense, exhaustive, and exhilarating drama of the creative process. I wonder if you could read the section of the poem where the narrator, after hearing his young daughter struggling in "a commotion of typewriter keys" to write a short story, first wishes her "a lucky passage" and then recalls the incident of the "dazed starling"?

RICHARD WILBUR: Yes, certainly.

I remember the dazed starling
Which was trapped in that very room, two years ago;
How we stole in, lifted a sash

And retreated, not to affright it;
And how for a helpless hour, through the crack of the door,
We watched the sleek, wild, dark

And iridescent creature
Batter against the brilliance, drop like a glove
To the hard floor, or the desk-top,

And wait then, humped and bloody,
For the wits to try it again; and how our spirits
Rose when, suddenly sure,

It lifted off from a chair-back,
Beating a smooth course for the right window
And clearing the sill of the world.

It is always a matter, my darling,
Of life or death, as I had forgotten. I wish
What I wished you before, but harder.

It's a wonderful poem. And given the poem's intense feelings about the challenge of the creative process, I wonder what you make of the scene in the popular film Dead Poets Society *in which an innovative teacher not only cures a shy young man of his anxiety but actually turns him into a "poet" by haranguing him in front of the rest of the class?*

RICHARD WILBUR: I have only a vague recollection of that scene, but I can imagine the kind of therapeutic effect it might have to compel a shy young man to unburden himself somewhat by reciting the poetry of others. That's what he was doing, wasn't it?

Actually, he was being forced to create "poetry" on the spot. The teacher put the boy in front of the classroom, made him look at the picture of Walt Whitman, and made him "yawp." The teacher would "yawp!" And then the shy kid started yawping, and then he continued doing it for a bit, and then finally the kid just started spitting out stuff about a "blanket" that covers everybody . . . and the whole class was stunned by his marvelous "poetry." The idea was that everybody has an accessible poetry within them, and if they're sincere enough and just dig deep enough, they can suddenly become poets. There was absolutely no sense of craft. It seemed a very easy and simplistic way of portraying how poetry can come about, and I was curious what you felt . . .

RICHARD WILBUR: It's clear to me now why I had forgotten that scene. I doubt the value of that kind of enforced explosion of language. It seems to me that the way truly powerful words are produced is through a more complex circuit—the circuit, in fact, that Yeats is describing or implying in the remarks you quoted. A direct spillage of raw feeling is seldom of any use to us as art.

Unless it's carefully guided through the language and technical skills of the writer?

RICHARD WILBUR: Yes.

Your own method of composition is truly organic. An "unfolding" in Robert Frost's sense of the term. Could you describe it?

RICHARD WILBUR: Yes, well, I'm often thought of by people who themselves aren't frequent users of meter—or rhyme, or the other arrows in the formalist's quiver—as somebody who writes in old forms. But the fact is that I, like a number of other poets who might be classified as formalists, very seldom use such time-honored forms as the sonnet. When I do use the sonnet form it's because my developing argument has, as it were, reinvented it; and I don't hesitate to violate the supposed "rules" of the form. Now, what was I talking about? Where am I going?

Well, it was the unfolding idea, that you would get the germ of an idea, and maybe get a line or two, and then the stanzas would start forming.

RICHARD WILBUR: Yes, my practice is absolutely the reverse of saying, well let's write a sestina now, let's see if I can write a rondeau. I've never, never found myself doing that kind of thing. It's always a matter of sensing that something wants to be said, something of which, as yet, I have a very imperfect knowledge, and letting it start to talk, and finding what rhythm it wants to come out in, what phrasing seems natural to it. When I've discovered those things for a couple of lines, I begin to have the stanza of my poem, if I'm going to have a stanzaic poem. In any case, the line lengths declare themselves organically as they do, I suppose, for a free verse poet. The difference between me and a free verse poet is simply that I commit myself to the metrical precedents which my first lines set. I have found that though I don't know how a poem is going to end, I always have a pretty good advance awareness of how long the poem is going to be, what its tone is going to be, and thus can initially arrive at rhythms and line lengths which are going to be capable of repetition without troubling the flow of thought as it emerges.

This is a very slow process for you. Yeats once described his own writing process as "an intense unnatural labour that reduces composition to four or five lines a day." You also tend to write slowly and with meticulous care. Does this try your patience? And does it create other difficulties?

RICHARD WILBUR: My great fear, always, is that the slow, laborious way in which I compose is going to estrange me from the spontaneous conversational rhythms which should accompany the statement of the subject. I have to keep watching out for that, and going back and making sure that I've not lost track of what I'm loosely calling a natural, rhythmical development of the subject. It's not a surprise to me, since I've read about Yeats' compositional methods, that writing was for him a slow and difficult business. He began, it appears, with what amounted to a prose sketch of the poem to come, or at any rate, with roughly-set-down lines having few interesting words in them. For him, to work on a poem would have been a matter of striving to overcome the flatness of his original statements. That to me sounds extremely onerous. One reason why I move so slowly is that my words have to interest me a great deal before I'll set them down at all.

So you want to feel satisfied yourself with what you've already written before you continue on?

RICHARD WILBUR: Yes. I want the first draft to be the last draft, and that's why I'm so terribly slow. This isn't to say I don't make changes. I blacken the margins of every worksheet with alternatives, and I do a lot of shifting around of possibilities in the mind. There's a species of revision that goes on, in other words, in the making of a first draft for me. Everybody's going to be a little different, I think, in his way of writing, but I must say that I'm not ashamed of being a slow writer, and I wish that some other people were a little slower at it.

In the past, like your friend Howard Nemerov, you have often asserted that meter and rhyme are actually liberating. That they incite originality. Mr. Nemerov once said of rhyme that "It makes you think of things you would not be forced to think of—wouldn't have had a chance to think of— otherwise." You've also written on the subject and talked about it many times. Could you comment on this curious phenomenon of freedom within restraints?

RICHARD WILBUR: I think this is something that needs to be said again and again. I have said it quite often, and, of course, Howard Nemerov would say it. I've even heard people like James Wright say it, though he turned his back after a time on the helps and surprises that come of rhyme and meter. Towards the end of his life, Jim Wright made some sort of public statement to the effect that rhyme and meter are liberating through the arbitrary demands that they make on us and the unexpected notions they suggest to us. I've, I think, mentioned once or twice in interviews, a game that we used to play in my graduate student days. We called it "Lake/Rake." A group of us would sit in a circle and play this party game. Someone looking into the rhyming dictionary section of a general dictionary would throw at us two rhymes, "lake" and "rake," for example. And we'd be given a minute in which to contrive some relationship between the two words. It was forever surprising to see how the most unpoetic and unpracticed natures were forced, as it were, to come up with interesting figures, often with metaphors, but in any case, with interesting reconciliations or combinations of the two terms. Words that rhyme do want, in a kind of magical way, to gravitate toward each other. And they do. The problem for a formal writer is simply to be judicious about how far he lets this process carry him.

Yes. And in your own work, you're extremely conscious not only of rhythm and rhyme, but also of diction. You have, in the past, criticized the general tendency of the '60s to limit the language and to fear words that might be considered "elegant." Do you still feel that eloquence of language has a place in modern poetry?

RICHARD WILBUR: I think that, in principle, there's no possible limit we can place on the vocabulary of poetry, and I'm sorry that for a while in these latter decades many people have felt bound to exclude certain kinds of elevated speech. Much of the excitement for me, in writing poetry and in reading it, is to find words of very different kinds of tonality and status cohabiting in the same poem. That's not only exciting because of the surprise element, it's also valuable, I think, because a poem that convincingly makes use of a lot of different lexicons, more thoroughly represents us and our experience.

Relating to this subject, Auden once said that the most promising young writer is not the one with the "ideas" but the one with the fascination for words and language. During World War II, you served in the 36th Signal Company in Italy, France, and Germany as a cryptographer—and you've even told stories of practicing Morse Code on your honeymoon. Do you think there is any relationship between your work with codes and symbols, and the poetry you were writing during the war? Things like the power of signs, the power of compression, density, hidden meanings, mystery, or symbolism?

RICHARD WILBUR: Well, my interest in cryptography began well before World War II. I'd taken a government course in cryptography previous to the start of the war, so it was inevitable that I should find myself spending part of my time in that kind of signal work. My interest in cryptography always seemed to me to be related to my interest in words generally—and in languages. As William Empson once said, there's a puzzle element in all good poetry, and it's there not to defeat and discourage us, but to produce surprise, which, so far as I'm concerned, is inseparable from poetry that is good or great. Good or great poetry is always permanently surprising. Even when you know what "Lycidas" is going to say, it keeps taking the top of your head off. Am I making sense about this?

Yes, absolutely. I'd also like to ask you about occasional poetry, and I wonder if you could re-tell the story about the man who wanted to send you to Antarctica? Or the Arctic? Or wherever it was?

RICHARD WILBUR: I wish I could remember anything beyond the bare bones of that story. It seems to me that Howard Moss, when he was poetry editor of *The New Yorker*, wrote me and said that there was some higher-up in the U.S. Navy who wanted a poet of some ability to accompany him to the Arctic or the Antarctic, I think the latter, and, as it were, bring it back in words. It sounded to me like a marvelous assignment, but I declined because I felt that I could not offer that admiral any guarantees. I wonder if somebody else didn't take it on? I have a sense that Donald Finkel wrote a lot of poetry about one pole or another, and I wonder if he did it under that kind of sponsorship?

I'm not sure. But given that your own descriptions of nature are so powerful, both summer and winter, I wonder—assuming that you never did get to the poles—if you ever regret not having been there and had that experience because you might have found some excellent material for your poetry? I realize that you didn't want to do it at the time because you didn't want to be under the requirement of having to come up with something.

RICHARD WILBUR: Yes, it would have had to be a huge occasional poem, wouldn't it? And you can't guarantee in advance whether you can do a poem that rises to the demands of some subject or occasion. I don't know whether I feel any regrets about missing out on some good polar material, because an odd thing about poets is that they are very different in relation to the experiences they have. Some can consume almost anything that comes along, and turn it into a poem. There are some poets whom John Frederick Nims describes as "Polaroid poets," and such people—I don't mean to scorn them—have the ability to see something *en passant* and just plain set it down. For me it's very difficult to be sufficiently intense about anything unless I've been around it for a long time. It's getting to be a joke with me, or on me, that for more than a quarter of a century I've spent much time each year in Key West, and have still not in any poetic way responded to its flora or waters. Whereas it's the fields and forests of New England that seem to me to have a lot to say.

Speaking of New England, I wonder why, in your opinion, Robert Frost never won the Nobel Prize? I know that he was a friend of yours and somebody whose work you very much admired.

RICHARD WILBUR: Yes, I think many people rightly thought that he deserved it. It's hard to say who's deserving of that enormous prize, but Frost was deserving of anything that he might have been given. One reason, perhaps, why he didn't get it is that much of the time in recent years the prize seems to have been given to people of fully demonstrated, generous and liberal political sentiments. Frost, certainly during the New Deal period, was associated with a kind of cantankerous resistance to liberalism. That would be one reason. And another reason, I suppose, has to do with the kind of subtlety that one finds in his poetry—his hints and displacements, his concealed sophistication. It's very hard, I think, to translate Robert Frost successfully, and even when he's translated successfully, I'm sure that he's not as easy of access as many other American poets. Some of his virtues and attitudes and turns of phrase and tricks of language are not for export, even when the translator is someone like

Andrei Sergeiev, the wonderful Russian translator who knows his New England English so well and has worked so well with Frost.

Several years ago, you once spoke of being very moved by Ingmar Bergman's great films The Magician *and* The Virgin Spring.

RICHARD WILBUR: Yes.

You said at the time that you were particularly attracted to what you called the director's "areas of concern": "religion, morals, and the arts." These are also important concerns in your own work. In your deceptively simple poem "On Having Mis-identified a Wild Flower," a thrush, aware of the narrator's error, bursts into a song: "In a world not vague, not lonely, / Not governed by me only." And in your poem "The Eye," the speaker goes a bit further spiritually and asks St. Lucy, the patroness of vision, light, and writers, to: "Charge me to see / In all bodies the beat of spirit." Why is poetry such a natural medium for spiritual considerations?

RICHARD WILBUR: Well, I suppose that in our namings of the world we choose all the time between mere self-projection and objectivity, whatever that is . . . let's say it means according a full reality to things that lie beyond the ego. The little poem "On Having Mis-identified a Wild Flower" is most certainly about that subject. It's about the refreshment of escaping from one's subjective and erratic sense of things into a corrected view of some part of the world. I remember reading a book by Jonathan Bishop in which he talked about the pleasure of being wrong about some natural thing, and then finding out what the right answer is. If you are wrong about something, then there's a way to be right which does not depend upon you alone. So that little poem is talking about that kind of refreshment, that kind of escape from the mere self. Any use at all that we make of language is an effort to balance or reconcile these two domains that we have distinguished—the subjective and the objective. I don't believe we had those words before Coleridge. It seems to me that he was the inventor of at least one of those words.

But there must always have been ways of saying that we must not be too much in or too much out.

Continuing with this notion of the spiritual in poetry, you once said, when pressured in an interview, that if you were forced to dictate one book for the world to read it would be The Book of Common Prayer. *The same interviewer also asked which famous poems you most wished that you had written and you mentioned* The Divine Comedy *and "Lycidas." But you yourself have written many wonderful and serious poems that are charged with a real sense of the mystical underpinnings of the material universe: "Love Calls Us to the Things of This World," "A Christmas Hymn," "Matthew VIII, 28ff.," "Peter," "A Wedding Toast," and many others. You've also written several serious religious poems that maintain a real sense of humble humor. I wonder if you could read the ending of your excellent poem "The Proof" which begins, "Shall I love God for causing me to be?"*

RICHARD WILBUR: Certainly.

> Yet when I caused his work to jar and stammer,
> And one free subject loosened all his grammar,
>
> I love him that he did not in a rage
> Once and forever rule me off the page,
>
> But, thinking I might come to please him yet,
> Crossed out *delete* and wrote his patient stet.

Would you like to comment further on this question of the spiritual in poetry? You're so good at describing the world and its objects and giving them meanings for your readers—but in a lot of your poetry, you also have the sense of a part of the world that goes beyond just the material, and I think all of those poems that I've just mentioned, and others as well, have that sense?

RICHARD WILBUR: I think they undoubtedly do, and I do as a person have that sense. Probably I can, in a loose way, be classified as a religious poet. It's harder nowadays to write poetry that lies comfortably and coherently within the boundaries of some particular faith, than it used to be. There is nothing limited about George Herbert's poetry, but it is poetry which cheerfully accepts the whole vocabulary and vision of Anglicanism. I'm an Anglican, I guess, but because I'm three centuries after George Herbert, I don't write in an Anglican vocabulary, or always with a governed vision that specifically belongs to any one faith.

Yes. Now I wonder if I could change the subject quite a bit, and ask you to give your opinion about the proliferation of creative writing programs at the American universities?

RICHARD WILBUR: It's a loaded subject nowadays, isn't it? I taught creative writing courses, so-called, from 1950 until 1986, and so it would ill become me to speak ill of that kind of course. I also taught all kinds of other courses, which were more improving for me than the teaching of writing. But to teach writing was always a pleasure. I enjoyed my students, and enjoyed especially those who began to catch on and to do well. Everyone who's taught writing knows that there's only so much you can do for a student. You cannot make a poet out of someone who hasn't been given the abilities necessary. You can be encouraging. You can be urgent. You can tell people to get off their butts and work harder at it. You can tell young people that they seem to have this or that potentiality, and that they ought to work on those potentialities, develop those strengths. So one can be of some use to young writers, and if a student doesn't emerge from such a course as a potential poet, he may very well emerge as a potential critic or a better reader. And so one needn't have a sense of time lost when teaching such courses. I think they are of value. I very much question, however, the notion of students majoring in creative writing. That seems to me a great privation that the potential writer should not undergo.

When John Updike and I were on the visiting committee at the Harvard English Department one year, I recall that a number of students, and a few members of the faculty, were beating the drum for what they called a "creative track," by which they meant a major in creative writing. It was interesting to me that Updike and I, the two professional writers on the committee, were the people who opposed the idea. Updike said, quite vehemently, "Writers have to know something! They ought to study languages, and history, and philosophy and geology. They ought to know what the earth that they are standing on is made of." I don't know, actually, whether our opposition to the proposed creative track was fruitful or not. There may be such a thing at Harvard now, for all I know. If so, it's too damned bad.

Another reservation I have about creative writing courses is one I've heard a good many people express. I happen to know that it's a valid reservation, because of my many years as a writing teacher. In a creative writing class, you cannot continually say to the students: "You're not much. You do not have the abilities of Pushkin or of Goethe. You don't stand a chance of greatness." You can't beat people over the head with the greatness of the great in every class. That would be churlish and discouraging. And so you find yourself being overly kind—over-praising, very often, timid or facile work. And you may also find yourself, if you are yourself a poet of a certain persuasion, encouraging students to write a kind of standard creative writing poem. If a student does that during freshman, sophomore, junior, and senior year of college, and then goes on to an MFA program, and then becomes an MFA teacher, I think there's some danger of his being a dully conformist poet working in the prevailing free verse style.

And on the other hand, there's also the loss of actual time spent reading the great literature, isn't there?

RICHARD WILBUR: Yes.

This leads to a related subject that has been a major area of contention since the late '60s—exactly what should be taught at American universities. The so-called "relevance" of the '60s not only eliminated Latin, but it also damaged what used to be considered the cultural core. At the same time, it exalted the pop culture, and claimed it to be an appropriate subject matter for serious poetry. I wonder if you would comment on these often-discussed issues?

RICHARD WILBUR: Well, it's really a two-part question, isn't it? The first is about the curriculum?

Yes.

RICHARD WILBUR: Well, I must say that I find myself very much an irate senior citizen when it comes to tamperings with the curriculum. I've felt that way—about the degradation of the curriculum—since the '60s. I remember talking to a charming young girl student in the '60s, at a rather progressive college, who told me that she didn't think Chaucer "relevant" to her life and therefore was not going to study Chaucer. I said, "Have you ever read any of Chaucer?" And she said, "No." And I said, "Then how can you tell that Chaucer is not relevant to your life?" We conducted our discussion on that primary level, but in fact, the absurdity of the idea of relevance is fully revealed by a few little questions like that. How do you know whether Latin is pertinent to your life until you know some Latin?

What was going on in the '60s was, of course, that young people were, as always, doing what they did on the authority of others. They had simply chosen a new set of authorities, a new set of grown-ups who were telling them what things mattered or should matter to them. I hope that some of the old authorities will get back in the saddle and will be accepted when they tell young people that it could indeed profit them to study Latin. As for pop culture in poetry, for me there's no limit to what ought to be the subject matter of poetry. And I think that poetry which tries to fend off the inelegant, popular world is in danger of seeming prissy and stuffy. What I do lament sometimes in poems which have pop material in them is the descent of the poem itself to the level of pop culture. It's perfectly all right to write about country and western music, I think, but poetry written with the usual sensibilities—with the usual limitations of sensibility—that we find in country and western are not likely to be brilliant poems.

Yes. But I guess I was trying to ask something even more specific than that. In other words, there might be a poem about Odysseus, and we accept that we know who Odysseus is in our culture. But then there might be a poem that's maybe not necessarily about country and western music, but might be about a particular country singer and a particular song from a particular period which we don't really expect that the culture will maintain over time. Thus it's forcing a footnote on the poem. Is it a mistake, do you think, to write poems like that—unnecessarily condemning them to a short life span?

RICHARD WILBUR: I know that there are such poems. I know that there are poems which expect us to know all about Jimi Hendrix, and I'm afraid that in many such cases I can't be reached by the poetry because Jimi Hendrix—whatever his qualities were, and I don't know what they were—has a higher degree of perishability than Odysseus and many other references from the Greek culture. Similarly, I'm often irritated by things like the New Year's Eve television program that says, we are now going to take you back through the years. What they assume my years amounted to, was a series of movies and songs and television programs and athletic events. Now in a lot of cases I have experienced those things and cared about them, but the assumption that I will know all of those things, and that they constitute my life, is an arrogant one. And I don't think poetry does well to treat us that way either. If it does expect us to know more than we need to know about Madonna, then it's low-brow poetry, and asks too much.

That's what I was getting at. It's one thing—you mentioned sports—to write about an athlete dying young, but then if you pick out a particular athlete from the 20th century who might have been very popular for a while, there's no guarantee that anyone is going to know who this individual is down the road. It seems limiting to the poetry, even though it might be fashionable in its time and appeal to its own generation—as pop songs do.

RICHARD WILBUR: Yes, well, I don't think we need to rule out any subject matter. I think probably what we're talking about is not how to choose imperishable subjects for poetry, but how to handle the perishable in such a way as to give it some kind of value. It strikes me that in a Pindaric mood you could take the most unpromising player in the major leagues today and write a splendid poem about him which would make him memorable through the memorability and intelligibility of the poem. It's all in how . . . what was that song of my childhood?—it went, "it ain't what you do, it's the way how't you do it!"

Yes. And what about popular music? I know that you yourself have written lyrics for the Broadway theater and that, in the past, you've discussed the differences between song writing and poetry writing. I wonder if you could talk about that for a little bit?

RICHARD WILBUR: Well, I have the profoundest respect for good lyric writers, people like Yip Harburg and Ira Gershwin. To have written the lyrics for a song like "Paper Moon" or one like "Our Love Is Here to Stay," would make me deeply contented. Lyric writing is a different art altogether from that of poetry because poetry, even if written with a seventeenth century ear for vowel music and for the possibility of a musical setting, is going to be a denser use of language. Poetry can always permit itself a degree of intellectual and emotional complexity that is most inappropriate in song. When I tried my hand at Broadway lyrics, that was one of the first things I learned, that one has to be somewhat repetitive, that one has to be as simple as possible, and that what may appear an utterly corny utterance—"I love you," for example—is very often exactly what is wanted, given the proper musical complement. I think it was unfortunate that, about 20 to 30 years ago, a confusion between pop lyrics and poetry set in, and that it came at a time when pop lyrics mostly had slack language, adolescent emotions, and vile rhymes. I can remember one young man with a guitar telling me off in the '60s. He said, "We're going to wipe out you Wallace Stevens people"—as if the two arts were vying for the same audience, or as if one must die that the other live.

It was English professors that put this notion in a lot of their heads. There were articles being written comparing the Beatles to Shakespeare and that kind of thing.

RICHARD WILBUR: There were. The swinging, young assistant professors of yesteryear made many such strained comparisons, in hopes of being lively and relevant. I don't thank them for muddling matters as they did.

In the past, you've also been wary of a 30-year-old trend in contemporary poetry that is primarily grim, complaining, whining, and self-absorbed. It seems, on the other hand, that your own poetry attempts to substitute a true compassion for all the grumbling: as in "For the Student Strikers," where the students are reminded that those they see as enemies are people "not unlike you"; or in "Cottage Street, 1953" where Mrs. Ward dies, "The thin hand reaching out, the last word love." How important is charity in poetry do you think, or in your own poetry?

RICHARD WILBUR: I think this takes us back to the earlier question about subjective, objective. To perceive that other things and other people really are there is to be on the threshold of feeling a compulsion to be fair, and to give others the same kind of break and consideration that you give to yourself. I would say that I am impatient of the poetry of complaint and whining and accusation, because it lacks the complexity of perception that an urge to fairness can beget. I think we've come to the threshold, there, of talking about charity.

Yes. And your fairly recent poem "The Ride," which initiates your New and Collected Poems, *illustrates this sense of charity in your work in a most marvelous way. The narrator, within a dream, is magically guided and protected through a hostile landscape by a wonderful horse which eventually leads the narrator to the safety and warmth of the inn. But then, the narrator suddenly wakes up, but he still wishes that he could get back to tend to the horse which is now abandoned in his dream. I wonder if you could read the last two stanzas?*

RICHARD WILBUR: Yes.

> How shall I now get back
> To the inn-yard where he stands,
> Burdened with every lack,
> And waken the stable-hands

To give him, before I think
That there was no horse at all,
Some hay, some water to drink,
A blanket and a stall?

It's another wonderful poem, and one that will endure.

RICHARD WILBUR: I liked your summary of that poem. That is, I think, what happens in the poem. I've never said to myself in so many words what that horse is, and I don't think I want to really, but I have a feeling, because many people have responded to that poem, that I have, by happy accident, gotten a hold of a kind of universal feeling, a common feeling, in that poem, of gratitude to something. One knows not precisely what.

Well, your readers feel a great deal of gratitude for you and your powerful poetry. Thank you very much.

RICHARD WILBUR: Thank you.

MAXINE KUMIN

Maxine Kumin, who was born in Philadelphia, Pennsylvania, received her A.B. and her M.A. at Radcliffe College in Massachusetts. While at Radcliffe, she married Victor M. Kumin, and they eventually had three children. From 1958–61, she taught at Tufts University, and, in 1961, she published her first collection of poems, *Halfway*. Her fourth collection, *Up Country: Poems of New England*, received the Pulitzer Prize for Poetry in 1973.

Over the years, she's taught at many universities as a visiting professor, including Columbia University, Princeton University, and the Massachusetts Institute of Technology. For several years, she was a member of the faculty at the Bread Loaf Writers' Conference, and, in 1981–82, she served as the Poetry Consultant to the Library of Congress.

Maxine Kumin is also the author of four novels; a collection of essays, *In Deep: Country Essays*; and many books for children. Her most recent collection of poetry is *Looking for Luck*, 1992. She currently lives, as she has for many years, on a farm in Warner, New Hampshire, where she raises horses.

This interview was conducted at the University of the South during the Sewanee Writers' Conference.

In your essay "Recitations," you've described your mother's adept ability for nonsense rhyming and her youthful public recitation of the poem, "The Curfew Bell." Did she encourage you to read verse as a child?

MAXINE KUMIN: I wish I could answer yes, but the truthful answer is no. My mother was much more interested in appearances, social contacts, and upward mobility, than she was in literature. So it was a high point in my childhood when I learned about her youthful recitation prize because it indicated that, at some time in her past, she'd cared about such things.

In the fourth or fifth grade, one of your teachers encouraged you to memorize a large section of James Russell Lowell's "The Vision of Sir Launfal." You've described in your essay "First Loves," how you "reveled in the sound of it," and that the poem's descriptions actually gave you "goose bumps." Can you still recite it?

MAXINE KUMIN: Would you like to hear some?

Yes.

MAXINE KUMIN:

> And what is so rare as a day in June?
>   Then, if ever, come perfect days;
> Then Heaven tries earth if it be in tune,
>   And over it softly her warm ear lays;
> Whether we look, or whether we listen,
> We hear life murmur, or see it glisten;
> Every clod feels a stir of might.
>   An instinct within it that reaches and towers,
> And, groping blindly above it for light,
>   Climbs to a soul in grass and flowers;
> The flush of life may well be seen
>   Thrilling back over hills and valleys;
> The cowslip startles in meadows green,
>   The buttercup catches the sun in its chalice,
> And there's never a leaf or a blade too mean
>   To be some happy creature's palace . . .

And so on—it's stayed with me all these years.

In the same essay, you discussed the beneficial power of early memorization, "I think we internalize the poems we have by heart, and they operate by osmosis to influence the writers we become. I favor the iambic tetrameter line, instilled in me by James Russell Lowell and sharpened by my later infatuation with Auden." But in contemporary times, not many students are encouraged to memorize poetry.

MAXINE KUMIN: Yes, and I think it's a great shame. Whenever I'm teaching, my students are forced to memorize, even if they're graduate students. Sometimes they'll complain, "Why are we doing this? It's terrible!" and I tell them, "I'm doing you a personal favor. When you're taken political prisoner, you'll have an internal library to draw upon." Then they look at me with horror because they can't imagine caring deeply enough about anything to end up a political prisoner. These days, I'm teaching at New England College, and I'm delighted to report that all of our students have to recite a poem from memory that's been pre-approved by the instructor before each workshop.

When did you start writing your own poetry?

MAXINE KUMIN: I started very young. While it's true that my mother had other interests, and that she never specifically encouraged my interest in poetry, she never actively discouraged it either.

You've always been grateful to your high school English and Latin teachers for having you do so much memorization, and this continued at Radcliffe, where your Professor Theodore Spencer had you memorize a poem each week—and where all the young women were "closet poets" who would "spout poems to one another by the hour." But then, in a class with Wallace Stegner, you were discouraged from writing your own poetry.

MAXINE KUMIN: He thought I was writing romantic drivel, and indeed I was. I can still remember one of my sonnets that began:

> When lonely on an August night I lie
> Wide-eyed beneath the mysteries of space
> And watch unnumbered pricks of dew-starred sky
> Drop down the earth with quiet grace . . .

So you can imagine what Stegner thought of that, and you can also imagine what I think of it today! But at the time, I was only seventeen years old, and I was in love with the sound of poetry like that—and the rhymes. I think it's important to point out that Stegner was only twenty-four years old at the time, so I can still feel charitably disposed toward him. After all, he was just a kid himself. But it did teach me that I should never discourage a student because you never know what will happen—there's no way of predicting. In the past, I've seen some perfectly terrible poems written by poets who are quite distinguished today, poets of major stature.

Aside from poetry, another passion in your life is swimming, which began at day camp when you were eight years old, and, eventually, led you to compete on the varsity team at Radcliffe. In time, you began to see many parallels between your two obsessions which you've discussed in your essay "Swimming and Writing." Both activities demand discipline, insist on an economy of movement/expression, and allow for repetition/redundancy. Amazingly, when you took up distance swimming, you actually began to swim to the cadences of A. E. Housman. Do you still do that?

MAXINE KUMIN: Yes, I still recite poems as I swim. I try to work out every other day, just to stay limber, and nothing is more boring than swimming laps in a lap pool. So I recite the poems in my head as I'm swimming to make it more interesting.

When you were eighteen, you were such a good swimmer that you were offered a job with Billy Rose's Aquacade and his traveling synchronized swimmers—billed, ironically, as "poetry in motion." Apparently, you had a good relationship with your father, but he put his foot down and ended the idea. Was it very disappointing?

MAXINE KUMIN: It was a terrible disappointment! Terrible! I'd never really been away from home before, except to go to college which was a closely controlled environment, and I would have loved to travel. They were willing to pay me a hundred dollars a week, plus room and board, which was a princely sum back in those days, but I still remember my father saying, "Swimming for money? What kind of a job is that for a nice Jewish girl?"

In 1945, when you were a junior at Radcliffe, you met your future husband Victor, and you were married the following year after your graduation. You subsequently completed your Masters degree at Radcliffe in 1948, and five years later, when you were pregnant with your third child, you finally returned to writing poetry, mostly light verse which you began to publish. Then in 1957, you enrolled in a poetry workshop at The Boston Center for Adult Education. One of your classmates was Anne Sexton, and your teacher was Tufts professor John Holmes who would be very influential in your life. What was he like?

MAXINE KUMIN: He was a very taciturn man, and he always had his pipe which he used as a prop. While he'd be sorting through the pile of poems looking for the one we'd start discussing, he'd take out his little tool and clean out the pipe bowl and tap it over the ash tray and then re-pack it, and all the while we were waiting breathlessly, hoping that he'd pick our poem. John was definitely a man of few words, not given to either excessive praise or excessive damnation, although he was very harsh in his personal condemnation of Anne. He was very concerned that my friendship with Anne would ruin my life. John's first wife had killed herself, so I think he saw the handwriting on the wall about Anne's instability. But he was a terrific workshop instructor, and he helped me in all kinds of ways, including arranging for my teaching job at Tufts.

You've often described Anne Sexton's career as taking off "like a rocket," and yours escalating "gradually," but within six months, you both had poems accepted by The New Yorker, *which is pretty incredible. Nevertheless, as you described in your essay "Recitations," "In the early sixties, the published women poets could still be counted on the fingers of two hands." Why was that the case?*

MAXINE KUMIN: Young women were being discouraged by the literary editors, who had very different expectations for women writers. A number of young women started submitting under their first two initials, so that they wouldn't be recognized as women. It was the tenor of the times.

In "Recitations," you mentioned that the literary editors back then looked at women poets, "As if we were some rare species of flightless bird to be sighted on special occasions," and John Ciardi's candid admission at Bread Loaf supported that contention.

MAXINE KUMIN: Yes, John Ciardi, who was the poetry editor at the prestigious *Saturday Review* back then, admitted in public that he would have loved to publish one of my poems in the upcoming *Saturday Review*, but since he'd just published a woman in the last issue, he'd have to wait a few months before his senior editor would consider printing one of my poems. That's the way it was.

You've also discussed that the women poets of your generation—Plath, Sexton, Van Duyn, Rich, and Kizer—didn't find useful female models for their work. But why not? Earlier in the century, there was Marianne Moore, H.D., Edith Sitwell, Edna St. Vincent Millay, Sara Teasdale, and, more recently, Elizabeth Bishop?

MAXINE KUMIN: H.D. wasn't really in the canon at that point, and Edith Sitwell was too idiosyncratic to be a model for anybody. Millay was seen as excessively romantic and passionate, and even Marianne Moore wasn't much help unless you were writing in syllabics. As for Elizabeth Bishop, there was something very classical and distant about her work that we only came to appreciate much later. So even though I could admire certain things about all those poets, they never really inspired me. I was inspired by Karl Shapiro and Auden and Yeats and Durrell. I was moved by their poetry and intrigued by their subject matter. And it was by studying Auden's poetry that I really learned about metrics.

After the writing course in Boston, you were part of a small workshop with Anne Sexton, John Holmes, George Starbuck, and Sam Albert.

MAXINE KUMIN: Yes, in 1960 we started meeting in one another's homes, rotating from house to house. We were all compatriots back then—all in it together—so there was no holding back. We definitely spoke our minds, and then the next day, an angry flurry of letters would start arriving in the mail saying things like, "I think Anne talked too much yesterday" or "Anne drank too much," and so on. At the time, John was a recovered alcoholic so he didn't drink at all, but the rest of us did, and the workshops got very noisy and long. Sometimes my poor kids would complain and then go off to sleep in the room above the garage to get away from the noisy poets. At the time, John was an especially good critic and a great help with "problem" poems, suggesting possible changes of direction and appropriate levels of diction. Anne also appreciated his comments. We all did.

Your seventeen-year friendship with Anne Sexton involved constant workshopping, and you even workshopped one of her poems together on the day she died. You once said that "Sexton and I were both formalists, loving the challenge of working in meter and rhyme and finding in the rigidity of a chosen form the permission to tackle emotionally charged or difficult topics."

MAXINE KUMIN: Anne was more immediately open to the expression of personal feelings in her poetry, whereas I was still withdrawn and careful and much more academic. When I look back at the diction in my first book, I see just how Latinate my work was at the time. Also, in terms of the subject matter, I certainly wasn't as ready as Anne to be more "confessional." You have to understand that Anne was a natural rebel and exhibitionist, and both of these traits related to her anxieties. I personally believe that her exhibitionism was counter-phobic. If Anne came to a street that was marked "one way," she would fell a strong impulse to drive down the street the wrong way—to prove that she wasn't afraid. In my opinion, many of Anne's best poems came out of her need to expose her counter-phobia. So our impulses were definitely different, and we helped each other. She helped me "open up" more, and I helped Anne pay more attention to the metrics.

In a 1975 interview with The Massachusetts Review, *you commented that the "curious thing for me is that rhyme makes me a better poet." Other writers like Howard Nemerov and Richard Wilbur have spoken about this phenomenon, and I was wondering if you could attempt to describe it.*

MAXINE KUMIN: Well, first of all, for me, there's the "play" element of writing in form that's really delicious. For example, I've got a double villanelle in *Looking for Luck* about the nuns and childhood, and it was such a lucky poem to come up with. The great fun of writing that poem was finding the different rhymes that go around "bramble." So there's that aspect which drives you forward, and then there's the question of knowing how to get out of the poem, where it should end. If you're writing a sonnet, that's predetermined for you, or if you're working in terza rima, you know that you have to turn it around at the end to close it off. And I find that very helpful. Then there's also the "permission" that a formal constraint provides. If you're working in a metrical pattern, or a rhyme pattern, stanzaic pattern, whatever, it seems, paradoxically, to free me to say the things that are hard to say—the things that are painful to say. I'm thinking of a poem "The Man of Many L's," one of those elegies I wrote for my brother. It rhymes quite formally, although the lines are pretty relaxed, but there's a distinctive rhyme pattern, which at the very end, just came to me out of the form, and it was a stroke of munificence on the part of the muse to give me that ending where instead of using different rhymes, I repeated key words. It's a poem that's probably better to see on the page than to read because it often plays on various misspellings with the "L's." It ends:

> O man of many L's, brother, my wily
> resident ghost, may I never spell
> these crowfoot dogbane words again
> these showy florid words again
> except I name them under your spell.

So, you see, having a formal rhyming pattern enabled me to do that at the very end. It wouldn't have occurred to me to do that without it.

That's what Howard Nemerov used to say, and Richard Wilbur as well, that rhyming helps you do things that you would never have done otherwise.

MAXINE KUMIN: Yes, and it also elevates your language because you are—at least I am—enabled to come upon surprising figures of speech, metaphors in particular, that I think I wouldn't have been capable of if I hadn't been pushed into them by the extraordinary effort of rhyming. Also, the rhymes have to be unobtrusive. They can call attention to themselves after they're there, but you can never wrench the normal word order to get to them, and you can't use poetic archaisms. So they place many constraints on you. Stanley Kunitz says that his best poems are, and I'm just paraphrasing here, written as if he were conversing at a fairly high level with an intelligent friend. That's the level of diction that I think I'm trying for. I don't want it to be showy or florid, but I want it to be sprightly enough. I want it to be surprising yet apt. When you work in form, you often get surprising yet apt conjunctions of words, and you realize you're very blessed.

Yes. I remember that you once said, in a review of one of Philip Larkin's books, something about how effectively he employed the technique of poetry but without letting it show.

MAXINE KUMIN: Yeah, he was really a master.

And, as you mentioned earlier, you learned a lot from Auden.

MAXINE KUMIN: Yes. Isn't that surprising? There was another woman poet who had the same experience . . . her name's just flown out of my head . . . oh, I know, it's Jane Cooper. She's a wonderful poet, and she said in an interview that when she was learning her craft, she shamelessly imitated Auden. Well, it was that way for me too. I was very fortunate in my college education that Auden was made accessible to me, along with Spender and Louis MacNeice, and Eliot, and Pound, and so on. But there was something about Auden's tetrameter and trimeter lines that excited me. I think that between Auden and Karl Shapiro I discovered that you could write poems about contemporary subjects and make them work—and that you could also mingle metaphor with fact. This is something Nemerov always did magnificently well. In fact, what does he say about metaphor? It mediates between a thing and a thought. And that's exactly what metaphor should do, when it's working well. And Auden, of course, taught us that. "In the nightmare of the dark / All the dogs of Europe bark. . . ." So that's where I cut my teeth, really. I just adore Auden. To this day I still love to read his poetry.

Continuing with this idea of influences, I'd like to discuss the regional aspect of much of your work. In your essay "A Sense of Place," you've mentioned several New England writers that influenced you—including Thoreau, Robert Frost, and John Holmes. I wonder if you're conscious of Frost at all when you're writing?

MAXINE KUMIN: Frost is kind of the benign shadow that stands behind me, that stands behind John Holmes, that stands behind Wesley McNair, and so many of us. He's always there. And we write, perhaps not consciously with him in mind, but he's still the benevolent grandfather.

Given your lifestyle, you actually deal with some of the same subjects as Frost. When I read your wonderful poem "Hay" about baling hay and so forth, it's hard not to think of Silas and "The Death of the Hired Man." Even though it's a quite different poem, the subject matter, at least in part, is similar. I wonder if you have any particular Frost favorites?

MAXINE KUMIN: When we lived in Newton, Massachusetts, which is where our kids all went to school, I remember that we had a tiny breakfast room with rough walls that I'd covered with a kind of paint that you could write on with chalk. Often, I would write poems on the walls, and then not say anything about them—just leave them there, hoping that by osmosis my kids would acquire something. And I remember two specific Frost poems that I wrote on that wall: one was "The Oven Bird," and the other was the one that begins "The great Overdog, / That heavenly beast / With a star in one eye, / Gives a leap in the east." And my kids really did learn those poems. Nothing was ever said about it, or about the process of memory, but I have since heard them kiddingly recite each of those poems, saying, "Oh yeah, when we were kids, my mother put these poems on the wall and we had to memorize them, and we couldn't have dessert until we knew them." Which is all a canard; it's just not true! But "The Oven Bird"— "There is a singer everyone has heard"— is a gorgeous poem about what to make of a diminished thing. It gives you great pause. It's a poem to sit and think about. In truth, I like virtually everything of Frost's. I can't think of a single poem of his that I don't like.

Did you ever meet Robert Frost?

MAXINE KUMIN: Yes, I did, three or four times. The first time was when John Holmes had been given a large endowment to bring some poets to read at Tufts when I was an instructor there, and Frost was one of them, and John Crowe Ransom was another. Afterwards, the Holmes always had a party back at their house, and Frost sat there and sort of held forth, and we all sat at his feet and ate fish chowder, and everyone drank a great deal and it was a marvelous evening. I may have actually seen him once before that at Bread Loaf. Maybe the first year that I went to Bread Loaf which would have been in the early sixties. He was a tower; he was the emperor of the mountain.

As with Frost, the New England rural life in your poetry is never sentimentalized. I can't help thinking of your poem "How It Goes On," about the little lamb, "tied to the seat / with baling twine," who's being traded for "two cords of stove-length oak." Is there a temptation to sentimentalize a poem like that?

MAXINE KUMIN: Not in my world because we have a working farm, and everything we do is reality-based. Recently, we lost an old dog, and I grieved mightily over that, but you try not to be sentimental about it. Also, I really don't feel that those poems are "pastoral" poems—they're just as anti-pastoral as they are pastoral.

Yes, you certainly don't portray the rural life as an idyllic refuge. In one of your essays from In Deep, *you point out that life on the farm does not "provide 'peace of mind,' an opiate once very much in vogue." Could you comment on that?*

MAXINE KUMIN: Well, the rural lifestyle is obviously not for everyone. People have a kind of grandiose, removed, and romantic notion of what it would be like to be awakened by the birds, tra la. But you have to factor into that getting up very early, the hot summer morning, the horses out in the pasture desperate to come into the cool shade of the barn, the black flies biting, and so on. Every morning I have a quarter-mile hike up to the pasture to get the horses to run to the barn. It's very hard work, and by the time I get them into the barn and feed them and get the fans on and the shutters closed, the "magic" has gone out of the early morning. I'm ready for coffee and breakfast and the refuge of the indoors for a while.

You've written that animals are your "confederates," and that they "help define who I am." "Credo," the opening poem of Looking for Luck, *says of animals, "I believe in myself as their sanctuary." This idea echoes your poem "Nurture" and many others. Is this the essence of one's relationship with animals, a kind of responsibility to them?*

MAXINE KUMIN: For me it is, yes. I happened to be in a situation where my children grew up and left home, and I acquired animals to take their place, and I consider myself the custodian of those I've taken on. Specifically, we breed horses. Some of them we sell, but we now have four that we're planning to keep forever. So it's really as though I have four children who live in the barn instead of the house. In some ways they're less trouble; in other ways they're more. In some ways, of course, they're not as rewarding, but in some ways they're deeply rewarding.

"Credo" states, "I believe in the gift of the horse, which is magic."

MAXINE KUMIN: They *are* magic. Aesthetically, they're magic to look at, and they're so powerful, and it's contained in such a beautiful package. I think one of my favorite sights is to see my horses galloping across ten or twelve acres of pasture. Now I know they're not completely free, but they're pretty close to being free since they've got about as much room to run as they could comfortably use—they're as little contained as a domestic animal can be. And they're very beautiful, especially when the weather turns and it's crisp, especially in winter during a snowstorm or just after a fresh snowfall. It's a ballet; it's absolutely gorgeous to behold, and it still gives me goosebumps to watch it. I love to watch young horses at play. It's magic.

Many of your other poems deal with family concerns and relationships, and you seem to find a kind of logical tie between place, nature, and the personal life. In your book In Deep, *you write of the natural order of things that the "sense of place underwritten by private history is part of that natural order." It seems to me that this is also true of Frost's poetry. Why is it that these things work so naturally together? Does it have to do with isolation?*

MAXINE KUMIN: I think so. I think it's that feeling of being enclosed and having almost a private dynasty. We're only two miles from town, but we're at the top of a dirt road, and it's a dead end, and once you get up that last couple hundred yards, it's as though you're on an island. So you do have this extreme sense of privacy, and maybe that intensifies the human relationships.

Again like Frost, you have a lot of delightful eccentrics in your poems. I think immediately of Henry Manley, who in one poem breaks his hip, sets himself up as "the sage of yesteryear," and then finds his home invaded by porcupines and other creatures.

MAXINE KUMIN: Henry Manley is sort of a composite, but there was a wonderful old guy who was our nearest neighbor, and he did acquire a telephone in the way described in the poem. We used to love it when he'd call, and the phone would ring and you'd pick it up and say, "Hello?" and the voice at the other end would launch right in and say, "Well, I just put up seventeen quarts of green beans, and I'm so tired." And you'd say, "Henry, is that you?" And then you'd continue with the conversation, but there was that wonderful faith on his part that he'd "connected" the minute he opened his mouth, and that you'd know exactly who it was. Also, another nice thing about living where your nearest neighbor is half a mile away, is a special sense of neighborliness. People definitely help each other out. There's a kind of natural interdependency.

You certainly didn't grow up in such an environment.

MAXINE KUMIN: That's right. I grew up in suburban Philadelphia in a very middle-class household with very urban expectations. My mother's idea of a good day was one in which she took the train into town wearing her hat and gloves and went shopping with her confederates. So I don't really know where my love for the earth and its creatures stems from, but I really think it was innate. I mean I was always that way, even when I was a young child.

In the past you've often written about New Hampshire when you were away from home. Has that changed?

MAXINE KUMIN: Well, I used to have problems writing about it when I was home because I was packing so much into the limited hours that I had there. But we've now been living in New Hampshire year-round since 1976, so maybe I've gotten over that. I've also now structured my life so that I can have three or four hours every day that I can spend at my desk. But you're absolutely right. For many, many years I could only write about New England when I was off somewhere doing "po-biz," making a living.

Let's talk a bit about your process of composition. How does it start?

MAXINE KUMIN: For me, poems can start anywhere, and they always begin totally unbidden. Since I never know where I'll be when an idea occurs, I always try to keep a notebook around so I can scribble down the new idea or line or phrase. These days, of course, I'm computerized, and that has changed things a lot since it's so fast and easy. But I also realize that there's a real danger in writing on a computer since it can make us very glib if we're not careful. In the old days, I'd always begin in longhand, and then type it out on the typewriter to see how it looked. Then I'd do a series of typed drafts, always keeping all the changes. But with a computer, you seldom save all your changes, and that can be a detriment.

Do you still do drafts as you revise?

MAXINE KUMIN: Yes, even though I'm not saving every single change made at the computer, I'm still doing a series of drafts that let me see the progression of the poem.

Do you still prefer to write in the mornings?

MAXINE KUMIN: I'm still a morning person. I think Donald Hall and I probably share the world record for poets getting up in the morning. For me, it's usually 5:30.

Do you work on a number of poems at once? Or do you try to finish a poem before moving on to the next?

MAXINE KUMIN: I'm generally working on a number of poems at the same time—many in different draft stages.

It's interesting that, in "The Porch Swing," the writer in the poem is defined as "a species of liar."

MAXINE KUMIN: Yes, all writers are a species of liar.

The writer in "The Porch Swing" uses the lives of her family—their "where-abouts, / squabbles, sexual habits"—in her work. Is there something uncomfortable about that?

MAXINE KUMIN: Well, I think I'm poking a little bit of fun at myself, but yes, there is a little discomfort in it. This comes from the fact that when family members see what you've written, they're always very quick to say to you, "but it didn't happen that way. She didn't live there, she lived on Atlantic Avenue, or some other avenue, and that such and such isn't true, or that it was five years later that. . . ." So that's why I'm kind of defending myself against the truth tellers.

Over the years, you've taught at many universities and conducted many poetry workshops. What goals do you set for yourself and your students in such classes?

MAXINE KUMIN: When I teach workshops, I have only one goal: to help students write better poems. I do make them read more widely and deeply than they're used to, and I must say, parenthetically, that I'm generally appalled by what I see in many of the MFA programs. Most of those students couldn't tell a trochee from a tree limb, and they've never even heard the word caesura! Most of them are only interested in writing poems, and very few of them do much reading. So, in general, I'm consistently horrified by the abysmal level of ignorance of many of the students in most of our MFA programs.

You learned prosody in high school from your English teacher Dorothy Lambert, but, as you've just pointed out, most contemporary students have no awareness of metrics. So how do you deal with it?

MAXINE KUMIN: Well, I have to stop class and teach them prosody. We could never imagine a serious artist who'd never studied anatomy! Unfortunately, most of these young people feel that all they need to do is put some words down on the page just as they occur to them, and then everything'll be fine. But nothing could be further from the truth.

What else do you recommend to young poets?

MAXINE KUMIN: Imitation is often very helpful, and I encourage it with my students. I have them imitate both older and more contemporary poems.

You mentioned "po-biz" earlier, how do you feel about the contemporary scene?

MAXINE KUMIN: I tend to be optimistic and side with those people who find it vibrant and diverse. Certainly compared to what was going on when I was first learning my craft, it's extremely vibrant and immensely diverse! I feel quite encouraged by the many books that come across my desk, especially the first books. And I'm particularly pleased by the number of talented young women writers, and I try to be supportive.

Do you think anything can be done about the fact that so few people actually read poetry anymore?

MAXINE KUMIN: To be honest, it doesn't bother me very much. I think that poetry, of all the art forms, is the most arcane and the most difficult to comprehend. It takes more of a commitment. Many people go to symphony and listen to the music, even though they can't tell Beethoven from Brahms. Or they go to some art exhibit because it's the fashionable thing to do, even though they can't tell a Picasso from a Matisse. And the same is true of ballet and the opera, and even, to some extent, the theater. But you can't do that with poetry. You have to bring a lot with you. You have to bring your ear and your eye and your brain; otherwise, it's meaningless. So I think the audience for poetry will always be reasonably small since it demands so much. On the other hand, I do think the public audience has been increasing during my lifetime. When I was in college, we didn't even have poetry readings. They really got started after World War II, and now there's all kinds of readings, even slams, and although I'm not a fan of the slams, I still think they're good for poetry overall.

You once had a "poetry" stalker. What happened?

MAXINE KUMIN: It started when I was still living in suburban Boston. I'd get invited to give a reading in the area, and this woman, whom I'd never met before, would occasionally show up and disrupt the reading.

One time, she jumped up in the middle of my reading and called out, "You're an impostor! This is not the *real* Maxine Kumin! I refuse to stay," and then she left. Then she started sending me mutilated copies of my books in the mail. One, for example, had an icepick through it. It got quite scary, and it made me afraid to give readings in the Boston area. Then she would mail me demented fragments, explaining, "I want you to get this published for me." So it went on like that for many years, and I thought it would never stop, but it finally did. I'm certain that she was hospitalized a number of times, but I don't know what finally ended it. Maybe she outgrew her psychosis, or maybe she died, or maybe she was committed somewhere. I really don't know.

Did you ever talk to her?

MAXINE KUMIN: I did confront her one time after one of my readings when I saw that she was hanging around. I told her that I didn't appreciate her letters and that I didn't want to hear from her anymore. But she seemed terribly hurt and bewildered, and she wondered if we could go out and have tea together, as if we were best friends or something. It was very awkward and unnerving. Poets aren't supposed to get stalked, that's for actors and rock stars.

In your collection of essays, In Deep, *you wrote that your poetry had become "more despairing over the past decade," but your subsequent book,* Looking for Luck, *contained many many relaxed and comfortable poems.*

MAXINE KUMIN: Yes, I think the poems in *Looking for Luck* are much more hopeful. The poems have pretty much come to terms with the world that I know, and with the aging process, although that's been a hard sell. It's really hard to grow old, but I now feel more divorced from the struggle.

You once said that "the distillation of everyday life experiences is exactly what I'm trying to particularize and order in poetry." Your poetry continues

to succeed in doing exactly that. I think of the last few, beautiful lines
of "Hay":

> where unspectacular people secure
> their bulky loads and drive away at dusk.

> Allegiance to the land is tenderness.
> The luck of two good cuttings in this climate.
> Now clear down to the alders in the swale,
> the fields begin an autumn flush of growth,
> the steady work of setting roots, and then
> as in a long exhale, go dormant.

Thank you for your time and thoughts and poems.

MAXINE KUMIN: Thank you, Bill.

DEREK WALCOTT

In 1992, Derek Walcott was awarded the Nobel Prize for Literature. As Peter Balakian has written in *Poetry* magazine, Walcott's verse "has already taken its place in the history of Western literature."

Derek Walcott was born in Castries, St. Lucia, in 1930, and he was educated at St. Mary's College in Castries and the University College of the West Indies in Mona, Jamaica. His first collection, *25 Poems*, was published in 1948 at Port-of-Spain, and his first produced play, *Cry for a Leader*, was performed in 1950 in St. Lucia.

From 1947 to 1955, he taught at various schools in St. Lucia, Grenada, and Jamaica, and he also wrote articles and drama criticism for *Public Opinion*. In 1959, he was co-founder of the Trinidad Theatre Workshop. Seven years later, he became a fellow of the Royal Society of Literature, and he received a Guggenheim Award in 1977 and a MacArthur Fellowship in 1981.

Since 1985 he has been a Visiting Professor at Boston University, and he's also taught at Harvard and Columbia. He currently lives in Trinidad. His numerous poetic works include *In a Green Night: Poems 1948–1960* (1962), *Collected Poems 1948–1984* (1986), *The Arkansas Testament* (1987), and his long poem *Omeros* (1989); and his many plays include *Dream on Monkey Mountain* (1970), *The Joker of Seville* (1978), *Remembrance* (1980), and *Three Plays* (1986).

This interview was conducted at the University of the South during the Sewanee Writers' Conference.

I'd like to ask you a few questions about your excellent and powerful poem "Eulogy to W. H. Auden," which you first read at the Cathedral of

St. John the Divine in 1983. Were you commissioned to write this poem by the church?

DEREK WALCOTT: No, not by the church. What happened was that Joseph who was a friend of Auden's—Joseph Brodsky—wanted a commemoration of Auden in New York City. I remember him telling me at some point, this is going to be done in the church, and that I *had* to write something. So I said, "Joseph, you're crazy, I can't do that," and he said, "Well, no, you *have* to." So I did it, with a great deal of concern. And I remember when I showed him something close to a final draft—or what I thought was a final draft—and he said, "Well, you know, it's okay, but it has to go 'up' at the end." Meaning it had to get, at some point, a bit seraphic at the end. Which I did. Not making it too sublime—but trying to balance something between the sublime and the ordinary.

How long did you have to do it, since it was being done for a specific event?

DEREK WALCOTT: I don't remember exactly, but it was quite difficult in terms of finding the appropriate structure—as well as the responsibility of actually doing it. I decided to use a model—Auden's tribute to Yeats—and I think that's what happens in all eulogies or tributes to poets who are master poets and whom one admires. For instance, if you take Auden's tribute to Yeats, it's very Yeatsian. Even in Shelley's tribute to Keats, Shelley picks up some of the flavor of Keats. Something unique happens, I think, in the writing of the actual tribute. You get absorbed in the person whom you're paying tribute to, and you also get absorbed into the sound of that person. Thus Auden got absorbed in the sound of Yeats because that's part of the tribute—the surrendering of oneself to the melody of the person whom you're commemorating. So the design of my own poem is obviously Audenesque. And the less one's presence is there in the poem, the better. You must accept it as a sort of acknowledged debt, especially with a master like Auden.

Then, once the shape is settled on, the tribute also acquires the diction of the poet. I don't think of it as pastiche; I think of it as homage. I think that what, in our time, a lot of people call derivative or maybe pastiche or imitation, is not something that bothered people in previous centuries. There were guilds of painters who were not really imitators—but who were continuing a kind of a style. And I think it's only the success of the identification of individuality in the author that makes people rear up at the idea of, say, writing in the same tone of someone to whom you're paying tribute. Yet even in the little tribute of Eliot to De la Mare, there's an attempt to try to express the quality of what De la Mare is all about. So the writer of a tribute must subdue his own style and individuality to what the sound of the person is. For instance, Joseph's poem on Lowell is very much like a Lowell poem.

Yes, it enhances the tribute.

DEREK WALCOTT: Yes, and I think any other way means that the ego of the person mourning is superior to the subject.

Did you know W. H. Auden?

DEREK WALCOTT: I didn't know him. I only met him once—very, very briefly. It was outside an elevator in Berlin, and I thanked him for his poetry, and he accepted it very graciously. Of course, Auden didn't know Yeats very well either, but I think the proximity of Auden and Yeats was something much closer. Even though I know an enormous amount about Auden—who doesn't?—there wasn't anything personal or close about it, but I did know how much Auden had done for Joseph. When Joseph had to get out of Russia, and, later, when he had nothing, he turned to Auden, and Auden was extremely kind to him. Thus Joseph's affection and respect for Auden is a very personal one. So when I was asked to do the poem, it was a personal request, and I felt extremely honored that Joseph would ask me to do it for a writer of that stature. That he should think that I could in any way do justice to Auden's memory was a tremendous burden. And a tremendous honor.

A lot of poets have difficulty with occasional poetry. They feel uncomfortable having to write for a specific event. How did you feel about that?

DEREK WALCOTT: Well, I wouldn't want to turn into a sort of MC, or a guy, you know, you could book him for a eulogy—a sort of George Jessel of the cemetery, or something like that. And I don't think I'd do it again. The thing about eulogies and elegies is that they're sometimes very suspicious because they so often focus on the person writing them rather than on the subject. "How do I feel about the subject," that kind of thing. But I remember when Joseph asked me to write the poem, and I thought to myself, this is a tremendously painful responsibility because I—as an admirer of Joseph—needed to somehow translate his gratitude and love of Auden into the poem, even though I don't mention Joseph within it. So it was more than an occasion, and it was not a typical occasional poem in that sense. It was something much more responsible, I think, than that.

And very personal, even though you only met Auden very briefly.

DEREK WALCOTT: Yes. And I do mean really briefly. I'm talking about a nod, you know.

Yes, I see. In Section II of the poem you talk about reading Auden's poetry in your youth: "when strict as Psalm or Lesson, / I learnt your poetry." Do you remember those early encounters with his work?

DEREK WALCOTT: Yes, I remember Auden being revealed to me through a man who died, a beautiful man called James Rodway—I've, just recently, given a memorial prize in his honor in the Caribbean. And Rodway had a collection of a lot of Faber books, a lot of modern poetry, and I'd often show him my work—my poems. He was an education officer from Guyana who lived in St. Lucia and also wrote verse. And I remember, during that period, reading Auden with a tremendous amount of elation, a lot of excitement, and discovery—everybody knows what I'm talking about. And some of the stimulating aspects of his work were there in Eliot before, but they became much more immediate in Auden— expressions like "arterial roads," or even a line like—and maybe it hit me harder than most readers—"August for the people and their favourite islands." That sort of thing. The freshness of his poetry was tremendously exciting, and it induced you to model yourself on Auden, or on the other Pylon poets, but obviously they themselves had been influenced by Auden, whether it was MacNiece or Spender or Day Lewis.

What one heard reading those books—even in the Caribbean, in another climate and another culture—the distance doesn't count, really—was the vigor and wit and freshness that was there in those poems. They were really tremendous. You see, I think Auden actually dared a lot more than either Pound or Eliot. I think that his intellect was far more adventurous, far braver, far stronger, and far more reckless than either of them—plus, of course, there was also that tremendous intelligence behind the poetry. There was so much to amaze you: the casual astonishments of certain descriptions of things that were happening, the strangeness of some of the words, the Anglo-Saxon derivatives that he used, the landscapes as they were described, and so on. It all created a new vocabulary. In a way, Eliot's vocabulary felt—as poignant as it was—a little jaded in the sense that it seemed as if it were looking at the world much more wearily and warily. But Auden took on the challenge of the phenomenally ordinary. In the vigor of Auden's work, there was no sort of poignancy or nostalgia. And there was no elegiac note. If it was elegiac, it was politically vigorous, it wasn't simply elegiac. And that was very exciting.

Even the books themselves made a tremendous impression on me at the time—the actual physical book, the Faber editions of Auden. You can't overestimate how a characteristic print—or font—affects you. When I first printed my own books, I modeled the print on the Faber type, because I felt, well, I'd like to have a book that looked like Auden's. It gave me the confidence of feeling that I was also, in a way, though not their equal, a contemporary poet. There was something in the actual font of the print that made it feel as if it were up to date, as if it were immediate and fresh. It didn't have that cursive, authoritative kind of lettering found in other, older editions, so you felt like it was fresh off the typewriter. You could hear the clatter of the typewriter in the language. And there were so many great poems.

Auden is a poet you go back to all the time, and, especially as you get older, you look and admire him more and more, and you see how tremendous his technical skill really was. That's what I mean in terms of the daring—the technical daring that goes beyond, I think, Eliot and Pound.

I have another question about the form of your poem. Edward Baugh in The Art of Derek Walcott *suggests that the meter and quatrain structure of Section 11 is based on the Wesleyan hymns that are mentioned in the poem. Did you have a sense of that, and keep that in mind?*

DEREK WALCOTT: Definitely. When you think of the experience of reading Auden, you think of a sort of fountain sound—of something that's like a very cold mountain spring. That's the feel of it: something way back in time. It comes out of the poetry itself, or the sound itself. And that sound, that kind of running clarity that's there—it's as if the line is also moving over the stones at the bottom of the stream, very fast, but you can still see the stones as the stream—or line—moves past. This is very much like the King James version of the Bible because the rhythm of the King James has a phenomenal clarity and still a tremendous depth. So when I'd go to church, the Methodist church, I'd hear those passages of Elizabethan poetry—which is what it really is if you're listening. And then, by the time I got to Auden, I could again make the same association to the sound of that running brook. Auden's work had the clarity that I'm trying to describe and even the same kind of language, plus the rigidity that's there in the design of the Methodist hymns—in the great poems by people like John and Charles Wesley, Bunyan, and others. The Methodist hymns were also sung in a very clean manner—there was no adornment in the chapel—just some flowers and a very simple altar. So the concentration was on the words and the music and not on the ritual. The whole experience was essential, and very clear. You directly addressed the very rigid stanzas of song that were there in the hymnbooks. Finally, there was also the pastoral aspect of the hymns that often occurs in Auden—pastoral in the sense of a pastor talking. Auden's poems often reflect the fact that he sometimes thought of himself as some kind of old vicar somewhere. That might seem slightly comic, but it's still perfectly appropriate.

As you've been discussing, your tribute to Auden—like other poems in The Arkansas Testament—*is very concerned about the craft of poetry. Edward Baugh in the collection of essays mentioned earlier says that, "Walcott's sustained engagement with the quatrain in* The Arkansas Testament *is an expression of his insistence on the notion of poetry as discipline, a craft which one has to learn, and work at, and 'get right.' " Given these concerns, do you feel that younger, contemporary, aspiring poets work as hard as they should at learning the fundamentals of their craft?*

DEREK WALCOTT: No, obviously not. I'm a teacher, and I find it very irritating that so many of the younger poets just read their contemporaries' poems. It's a dangerous and terrible thing in this country that poetry has become a very competitive and "contemporary" business. It's become a kind of career. It's become emphatically so in some young women who think that to be a woman now—to be a woman poet— means that you have the right to utter all kinds of dangerous things. It can happen to any group. It can happen to young black poets, and it can happen to feminist poets. It also astonishes me that in this country the usual complaint is that anything before William Carlos Williams is dated—or that American verse is something emphatically different from the world tradition. And not only are so many young writers ignorant of the tradition, but they've also been taught to write verse which takes total anarchy with the individual imagination—which, at any age, you really can't do. In truth, all you can really do at a young age is apprentice yourself to the craft. And the total absence of that apprenticeship in this country has made most of the verse unbearable.

And the young are constantly being misadvised. The greatest horrors in my teaching life have occurred when young students have repeated what other teachers have told them: "this thing has too much melody," "this thing has too much rhythm," "you shouldn't use rhyme," and so on. I mean, I don't know any other culture in the history of the world that has ever said that to anybody—that poetry has too much melody! I don't know on what basis this is founded. I think when a democracy gets over-assertive it becomes very fascist. It turns authoritarian in its insistence on freedom.

That problem doesn't seem to be going away.

DEREK WALCOTT: Yes, and I think that there are a lot of people, especially young students, who would have liked to have learned the craft, for all the difficulty that the craft presents. I try to explain to students that the difficulty *is* the joy, and that if you don't find the difficulty an elation, then there's no point in trying to write poetry—go and write something else, or do something else. But you can't separate the two. Just look at the terribly mediocre consequences, including the books that are published, one book after the next, like a little factory.

That reminds me of Larkin's little essay "The Pleasure Principle." That concept's certainly been lost. People don't think of poetry as something that should provide pleasure; it's just something that if you write it and you're "sincere," that's enough.

DEREK WALCOTT: Yes, but I had a nice experience last night. This house I'm staying in is full of books, but a library can be like a morgue sometimes, with all those names up there. So I'm looking through the books and I'm getting more and more abashed staring at all these books that I've never read. And I'm thinking, "What would I *really* like to read?" Then I saw Betjeman, and I thought, wait a minute, don't tell me I'm going to pick this book up, above all the others that are here, whether it's Melville or Hemingway or anybody else. Why am I picking up Betjeman? But I picked the Betjeman, and I began to read it, and I was reading it with complete delight and much more respect and fun, you know, than all the other guys on the shelves—very few of them have any fun . . .

Yes, he's remarkable . . .

DEREK WALCOTT: And Auden also had a lot of fun. That's the great thing about Auden, there's a lot of humor, a lot of wit, and a lot of fun.

Yes, always with that wit. Some of those ballads are very serious, but they're also very funny at the same time. Your own poem seems to reflect Auden's clever lines, "I cannot settle which is worse, / The Anti-Novel or Free Verse." In your poem, you say . . .

DEREK WALCOTT: I don't know that couplet. What did you say?

It's from one of the late poems, "Doggerel by a Senior Citizen." It goes: "I cannot settle which is worse, / The Anti-Novel or Free Verse."

DEREK WALCOTT: I didn't know that. That's very good.

You seem to echo it . . .

DEREK WALCOTT: But I couldn't really echo it because I didn't know it! That's hilarious, that's wonderful, funnier than anything I've ever said.

But what you did say is very excellent and interesting: ". . . but you, who left each feast at nine, / knew war, like free verse, is a sign / of awful manners."

DEREK WALCOTT: Yes. I think it's very Audenesque to think of war as bad manners, which it is in a way because war is based on a disrespect for another religion, culture, identity, race, whatever, or even territory. And in a sense, wars begin with a kind of indiscipline. They begin as a concept of some kind of indiscipline, with the promise of a reward of some kind. Some order is disestablished, to be reorganized aggressively. Thus the poem makes an analogy with free verse, which is sort of an expression of unrestrained free will, as opposed to subjugation to a kind of order superior to the idea of the individual artist. But that order really exists.

Yes, and it comes out of a long and valuable tradition. I also wanted to ask you about one of the most famous phrases in Auden's "In Memory of W. B. Yeats." He writes that "poetry makes nothing happen," yet, in the same poem, he concludes with a plea to Yeats to "persuade us to rejoice" and to "Teach the free man how to praise." What do you make of Auden's remark about the limits of poetry?

DEREK WALCOTT: You know, I've heard Joseph talk about it, and I've heard various interpretations of it, and I think that people are often too quick—we always quote half of the phrase—and forget that it continues into an image of poetry as a river which "flows south / From ranches of isolation." And I think if you said to a river, "What do you do for the world?" the river's answer would be, "I don't make anything happen." Nature doesn't make anything happen. As human beings we've certainly suffered the loss of awe, the loss of sacredness, and the loss of the fact that we're not here—we're not put on earth—to shape it anyway we want. So Auden's comment is actually an urgent reprimand, and not a resignation. It says, you want something to happen with poetry, but it doesn't make anything happen. So then somebody says, "What's the use of poetry?" Then you say, "Well, what's the use of a cloud? What's the use of a river? What's the use of a tree?" They don't make anything happen.

So it's more a description of its fundamental nature?

DEREK WALCOTT: That's exactly what it is. It goes beyond the simple, ordinary, human temptation of saying, "Well, you'd better do something, poetry." And those who demand it are tyrants—tyrants would naturally demand that it do something, right? They always do.

Let's take a parallel idea in Aimé Césaire when he talks about the black raising himself up, and he says "Hooray for those who have not invented anything." So if the accusation is, "What have you invented?" and the answer is, "Nothing," that's a profound answer. Because nothing that's ever been invented has ever cured a single evil. Perhaps the highest tribute that one could pay to one's creator would be to do "nothing." Maybe the beginning of trying to do "something" was the cause of the fall of man—doing something different than simply being in Eden, you see what I mean? That "do something" attitude leads to all kinds of consequences, so I think that Auden wanted to put poetry in another category—in the same category as, well, not exactly prayer, but beyond that. And I think that to take his phrase as a cynical comment of resignation—which people often claim it to be—is not enough. As a matter of fact, poetry does make something happen because in the flow of the river which he talks about, the river touches many things as it passes by.

Yes, and then the poem ends by asking Yeats to show us how to "rejoice" and "praise."

DEREK WALCOTT: Exactly right.

In your collection The Arkansas Testament, *the eulogy to Auden is the initial poem in the "Elsewhere" section which represents European culture, as opposed to the earlier poems about Caribbean culture that comprise the "Here" section. The eulogy refers to both the "Empire" and the "colonial streets," and it also talks about reconciliation. You use terms like "communion," "one mouth to speak for all," and "the gift of peace." These ideas relate directly to your long poem* Omeros, *and also to a comment you made in your* New Letters *interview with Rebekah Presson: ". . . the easiest thing to do about colonialism is to refer to history in terms of guilt or punishment or revenge, or whatever. Whereas the rare thing is the resolution of being where one is, and in doing something positive about that reality." Do you feel that this sense of a hope for some kind of reconciliation is one of the predominant themes in your writing? In other words, people always talk about your personal "search for identity," but it seems to me to go beyond that—that there might be one voice "to speak for all."*

DEREK WALCOTT: Yes, that process of a search . . . it's not really as simple as just a search for identity, but let me begin there because I think the process is an important aspect of English literature right now—whether it's Ondaatje, or Rushdie, or Naipaul, or anyone. It's a process, a post-empire process, which has to be historical, and which also has to be, eventually, spiritual in a sense.

For example, say you're not English but you're working in the English language, and you're writing in the best possible way you can. And though the language belongs to England—still there's no distinction between someone in Ceylon who's a young poet, and someone in England who's on the same level of talent or whatever, enjoying the language.

But what tends to happen is that things get divided up politically. An English critic might say, well here's a young guy from Ceylon who's certainly learned something about the English language and is doing "very well." Now that's a patronizing attitude that never goes away because people are protective about what they think is their language. I once had an Italian ask me, "What are you doing messing around with Dante?" As if to say, "He's our poet exclusively." I mean you often get that kind of stupidity. On the other hand, you can get the local stupidity which says that you must stick to local subjects and expressions—so you get into a battle on either side. And if you're not careful, you find yourself drawn in two—and a target for both sides.

And that's not to deny that there are real crises of resolution, and conflicts and ironies, about the fact that you're writing in English. For example, you can't just think of Sir Walter Raleigh as someone who was simply an adventurer, someone who exploited—even if you're inclined to use that kind of historical postmortem on Raleigh. You can't let it cloud the fact that Raleigh is a superb, a great poet. A more recent example is the Larkin controversy. Whatever his prejudices might have been, his poems remain pure because real poetry doesn't permit such prejudices. It purges itself of that. It's a kind of a grace that's bestowed on the serious and talented poet. Now one could, for example, write a kind of verse that might be very vigorous about, let's say, get the "niggers" out of Britain, and he could make it rhyme, and it could be funny, and it could be skillfully done. But then you ask yourself whether such a vitriolic, bitter—even anti-Semitic in the case of Pound—effort could really be poetry? No, I don't think so. I think that poetry—no matter how well it's done—must still achieve a supreme compassion and tenderness.

Now if that's the center of real poetry, then it really doesn't matter what the time or place or race of the writer. So no matter what the clever arguments, the English critic has no right to patronize somebody on their "efforts." And the local critic has no right to accuse someone of "betrayal." Unfortunately, all these various problems can exist inside the writer himself, and are externalized by these conflicts. And this complicated process affects writers from India, from Canada, or from anywhere else. But it's a conflict that makes a drama, and it's a conflict that makes the exercise, you know, the endeavor, dramatically and historically interesting. So, I guess, I've drifted away from a direct answer to the question, but I don't think that the options for the contemporary poet should be so harshly dramatized: that he has to make a choice, one or the other. That's what tyrannies say, vote for me—you can't choose. But that's not the territory of poetry.

Well, you did get to that important notion about the heart of poetry being compassion, and that leads into my last question about the "Eulogy" being a reaffirmation of the need for human kindness, as in the hopeful lines, "that the City may be Just, / and humankind be kind." Do you think that contemporary poetry deals enough with this concept? In other words, are we too afraid to come out and talk about charity and compassion and so forth? We certainly make a lot of noise about it, but does poetry really deal with it as much as it should?

DEREK WALCOTT: My answer to that question is this: aren't you, yourself, astonished, and in a way, disappointed, that the rein of American verse is so tight, that it's so small, so provincial, and that all it takes in is the neighborhood, the next farm, or the next street? Especially for a country of this size, whose responsibility in the history of the world is, as you know, the greatest responsibility any country has ever faced, in terms of conscience, and in terms of justice. Yet its poetry—if you looked at it generations down the road—you'd say, "What the hell were those people thinking about?"

Do you see what I'm saying? You pick up a contemporary poem and you say—apart from certain poets—that it's diminished; it's something so small and positively boring to hear about—all the little, anguished egos that are represented in all those little poems. No one dares to write a capital letter word like Pity, or Love . . . contemporary poetry doesn't exalt, it doesn't condemn, and it's all very muted. The limited scope of contemporary thought, and the narrowness and the confines of even young poets is astonishing. In the past, the average young poet was someone who was shouting inside himself. There was an exaltation, and there was a sort of daring. But today in America what you get is such timidity that it's astonishing. It could have come from a corner of the most remote little village somewhere. But it's what comes out of New York, and out of Boston, and out of Chicago.

It seems that to exult is to be embarrassed. Who can write something in the pitch of exultation like "The Windhover" or Dylan Thomas's poetry—because it becomes embarrassing to sound so . . . well, happy! I mean a lot of great poems are happy poems, poems of joy.

Well, "Eulogy to W. H. Auden" is a beautiful and masterly poem that's not afraid to remind us about Hope—one of those capital letter words—as in the last quatrain:

> *and the mouths of all the rivers*
> *are still, and the estuaries*
> *shine with the wake that gives the*
> *craftsman the gift of peace.*

DEREK WALCOTT: I should end by saying that the figure that one has of Auden at the end of the poem—keeping in mind that Auden was a religious poet in the nature of Herbert—is of this guy shambling along somewhere down lower Manhattan, almost looking like a bum in the way that he's going by, but containing within him a tremendous concern for others. All those big words. Auden could write them because he was a great poet. He could write Pity with a capital "P," and he could write Justice, and the Just. Maybe the authority to write of such emotions and qualities with a capital letter is gone now. But Auden was entitled to do it, and he believed in doing it. So the final scene of the poem highlights the fact that he contained so much love and concern within him—and also within an industrial context, not simply in a pastoral setting, not sitting outside the city brooding on the rocks, but in New York City.

Your own poetry has the same power to express the large and significant aspects of our lives. Thank you very much.

DEREK WALCOTT: Thanks a lot. I enjoyed it very much.

WILLIS BARNSTONE

Willis Barnstone was born in Lewiston, Maine, and received his B.A. at Bowdoin College. He then studied at the University of Paris and the School of Oriental and African Studies at the University of London before completing his M.A. at Columbia University and his Ph.D. at Yale University. In 1949 he married the painter Helle Phaedra Tzapoulou, and they eventually had three children.

Dr. Barnstone is currently Professor of Spanish, Portuguese, and Comparative Literature at Indiana University. In the past, he has taught at the Anavrita Academy in Greece, served as a Fulbright Professor in Buenos Aires, and taught at the University of Peking.

Willis Barnstone's numerous writings include translations, poetry, fiction, memoirs, and literary criticism. The following is a brief selection of his overall achievement: *From this White Island* (Twayne, 1959—finalist for the Pulitzer Prize); *Greek Lyric Poetry* (Bantam, 1962); *The Poems of Saint John of the Cross* (Indiana, 1967); *A Day in the Country* (Harpers, 1971); *China Poems* (Missouri, 1972—finalist for the Pulitzer Prize); *With Borges on an Ordinary Evening in Buenos Aires: A Memoir* (Illinois, 1993); *The Poetics of Translation: History, Theory, Practice* (Yale, 1993); and *Six Masters of the Spanish Sonnet* (Southern Illinois, 1993).

This interview was conducted at Indiana University.

David Wojahn has written of your recent book, Six Masters of the Spanish Sonnet, *that it contains "over one hundred bedazzling translations—all strictly rhymed and metered, and yet amazingly free of the awkwardness we have come to expect from such attempts at equivalent renderings." I wonder if you could give us a sense of your practical methodology—how did you approach each translation?*

WILLIS BARNSTONE: When I find a sonnet to translate, I, first of all, not in an arrogant manner, think of it as another poem that I might have written—not to impose my personality on it, but to impose my dedication and value to it. I also see, obviously, the problem of meter and rhyme, and I like those problems, as I like all obstacles in art. Obstacles are like the plot of a play which you may be given, as Shakespeare was given them, which you conform to and alter. Now the reason I like these obstacles is very simple. You can be very easily seduced by the obvious when you translate. If there are restrictions, instead of finding one solution, you find fifteen or twenty, and then surprisingly, the fifteenth or the twentieth is much closer than the original, seductive, obvious one—the surface, literal one—would be. And I've discovered that I like to be as *close* in meaning to the original as one can be—I know that's a very loaded word—and at the same time, add to the closeness by adding a musical, rhythmic, affinity. The advantage of using rhyme, which I don't recommend to people who can't do it well when translating, is that you can reproduce something which sounds, at least musically, more like the original.

This whole question of *how* do we do things, is the one people always ask of a translator, and I think the loveliest and most useful response relates to something I read in Edwin Honig's book *The Poet's Other Voice*, in which Robert Fitzgerald talks about going down to see Ezra Pound in his looney bin in Washington at St. Elizabeth's Hospital and telling Pound he was going to do Homer, and asking how he should do it. Now, of course, Pound begins *The Cantos* with his own Latin translation into English of an 11th or 12th Century Latin version of Homer. How obscurely far from a direct translation can you be?—especially since he combines Anglo-Saxon thoughts and rhythms—yet it all led to the glorious beginning of *The Cantos*. So in response to Fitzgerald, Pound, instead of saying, "Do as I do," said "Let Homer speak." I love the idea of what Pound said, "Let Homer speak," and I think that Fitzgerald is probably the best 20th Century translator of Homer.

Let me ask you some practical questions. Do you do prose translations first? Do you run the poem over and over in your head as you compose? Do you recite it out loud to yourself? Do you always work at a certain time of day? Things like that.

WILLIS BARNSTONE: Well, I don't do prose translations, and I hardly ever read ahead in the work because I like the notion of surprise. I once translated with my wife a modern Greek novel, and I loved it so much that I didn't want to read the end of it until we finally finished it, and I think that was very wise. As for writing, I work at any time of day, and I don't care where I am—in an airplane or standing up eating someplace. I work all the time—with the joy of something pleasant in my mind, whether it's a poem or fiction or translation.

I wanted to ask you about "literary accuracy." In your other recent book, The Poetics of Translation, *you clearly take issue with the translation "literalists" like Nabokov and Benjamin, and state that "The translation is loyal to the spirit, not the letter." How much latitude is allowed to the translator?*

WILLIS BARNSTONE: I have my own opinion about how much I should allow myself. Primarily, I always want to let the author come through so I always try to be "close." Yet when I teach translation, I tell the students that all translation is original writing. As Octavio Paz and countless other people have said, every translation is original, and every original thing is a translation—a translation in the larger sense of "moving something about." We do it in our thoughts, in our reading, in everything; we're always transforming and translating. The opposite of translation is death—no movement. Nevertheless, as I tell my students, if you want to convey the *voice* of another poet, you must make a partnership with that writer in which the original poet has the majority percentage of the stock, and you should not try to take over the firm. If you do, it's fine, provided you acknowledge it. As long as you say that this is "after" the original, or this is an imitation, as Robert Lowell very clearly does, I think it's perfectly legit. What I don't feel is helpful, is when a translator suggests that we're reading, say, George Seferis, and the "translation" really gives us himself.

Given my preferences, the two people that I would love to see do Dante are—and I know many people are doing the *Commedia*, including Robert Pinsky, and what I've seen of his is marvelous—W. S. Merwin and Richard Wilbur. I think, if either one would be willing to spend five years of his life doing Dante, we'd have a great picture of that voyage.

Yes, we would. You yourself did Canto I for The Chicago Review *about ten years ago, and you stuck to the terza rima. A lot of people don't, and I understand the difficulty.*

WILLIS BARNSTONE: Well, I find it more difficult not to.

You have an amazing facility with rhyme.

WILLIS BARNSTONE: In my mind I don't remember anything unless it echoes something else. I've also learned to work at it. One day Borges's editor Carlos Frías knocked at my door after I'd finished translating Borges's sonnet about Walt Whitman called "Camden, 1892." Frías pointed out that I hadn't really found the right rhyme in English for "Whitman," which is pretty hard, I would say—especially since not too much rhymes in English anyway—so I made all kinds of defensive remarks like, "Well, Borges is great, but maybe he doesn't understand off-rhyme, slant rhyme—because in English it's more common than in Spanish, and more modern," but I was soon interrupted by Frías who said, "Borges says try a little harder." And when I tried a little harder, I found it was just as easy to do the sonnet with complete, full rhyme. So that's my present attitude about rhyme.

You certainly pulled it off in that poem.

WILLIS BARNSTONE: Thank you.

As you know, many well-known contemporary poets translate from languages in which they have no facility—generally with the close assistance or collaboration of a native speaker, if not a language scholar. What is your opinion of such enterprises?

WILLIS BARNSTONE: Obviously there's an advantage to knowing the original language. But the real, *indispensable* qualification for a translator is to be a poet at the moment of translation—not necessarily outside the act of translation—and this qualification is not dependent on knowing a foreign language. Very often, especially with the more obscure languages—Russian, Arabic, Chinese, Japanese, etc.—it's very rare that you find someone who is truly a poet at the moment of translation. So it's much better to combine a conscientious, honest, talented poet, with an informed scholar or native speaker. That's what happens when, for example, you put Richard Wilbur with a native speaker. Wilbur readily acknowledges that he might not know the language fluently, but his translations are absolutely fabulous.

He seems to do them marvelously whether working with a language he really knows, like French, or with a language in which he needs assistance.

WILLIS BARNSTONE: That's right, and I must tell you that there's a certain freedom one feels in *not* knowing the language. Since a translation must have its own authority, sometimes ignorance is helpful in establishing that authority.

I know of your very high opinion of the translations of Robert Fitzgerald, Richmond Lattimore, Richard Wilbur, and your friend Anthony Kerrigan— I wonder how you feel about the future of American translation, especially with the younger generation?

WILLIS BARNSTONE: I think that my students in translation have been wonderful. But, I must say, that I have had very few students who've been able to handle form in any strict, even minorly strict, manner. And I think that has to do with the fact—although there is clearly a return to form in our eclectic age—that very few people are able to do it.

Don't you think that has a lot to do with the fact that there are many young people who, even before they get to translation, simply do not understand the metrical aspects of our language and poetry?

WILLIS BARNSTONE: Yes, I think that's the reason. We're still fighting battles which were fought in 1912 when Pound and Hulme invented European modernism, and when Braque and Picasso wiped away much of the past by inventing Cubism. We still think that it's a great feat of avant-garde enlightenment to reject the past, but it's no longer such a wonderful feat. We're wearing out our old modernist tricks.

That's very true, and it's something that young people often have difficulty understanding. Now I'd like to return again to Six Masters of the Spanish Sonnet, *and ask you why Spanish language poets avoided the English variation of the sonnet up until J. L. Borges? Was it that they could handle the more difficult rhyming of the Italian form? Or was it something else?*

WILLIS BARNSTONE: Well, it is obviously true that there are more rhymes in Spanish than in English, but I think that, like the English, the Spaniards are wonderfully parochial, and thus less inclined to the English variation. I think that's it.

And why do you think that it appealed to Borges—was it his Anglophilia, or was it something to do with the final couplet?

WILLIS BARNSTONE: Well, I think Anglophilia was one of the reasons— and also that Borges always did whatever he wanted.

In the Preface to Six Masters, *you mention that in 1975 and 1976 you collaborated with Borges "on rewording his sonnets into English." I was wondering, as you compiled this most recent book—which includes some of those same poems—whether you made any significant changes. I noticed only small changes like your substitution of "The gods who guard" for "Numens who rule" in "The White Deer"—which seems to enhance both the meaning and sound of the poem.*

WILLIS BARNSTONE: I don't remember any major alterations, though I always like to go back and tinker. But I'm also very lucky in that, as I've gotten older, I usually get things close on the first draft, and I end up rejecting very few things, in contrast to when I was much younger. It generally seems to come close the first time.

In J. L. Borges's "An Autobiographical Essay," he discusses how his blindness encouraged him to return to poetry and especially the sonnet, and he describes composing them while walking down the street or riding in a subway and then dictating them to friends or relatives. Given your close relationship with the poet, I wonder if you were ever with Borges when he was composing in his head?

WILLIS BARNSTONE: Well, yes. It happened on a plane from the Argentine city of Córdoba back to Buenos Aires. As we often did, I was reading him poetry on the plane, and I read him "Birches." He always liked to hear poems which he knew and he would talk along with them. It was impossible, for example, to read him Kipling because he knew them all by heart. So I was reading him "Birches" and afterwards I said, "You know, that childhood memory of being ten or eleven years old and bending down birch trees in New Hampshire or Vermont may be more an older man's imagination than an actual memory, even though it's artistically posed as a first person recollection, because Frost was born in California and he grew up in a mill town in Massachusetts." Then I added something like, "I think it's wonderful, but it was probably an impossible memory." And Borges immediately said, "Impossible memory! I think I have a poem!" I asked, "How long is it?" And he said, "I think it'll be 35 or 40 lines." And I said, "What will it consist of?" And he said, "Well, it will consist of my 'impossible memories.'" Not more than a week later, he gave the poem to the editor, Jorge Cruz, and I think it was called—I can check on the title— "Elegy of an Impossible Memory."

Did he ever compose his sonnets—or anything else—in English?

WILLIS BARNSTONE: He wrote two poems which are not very good. They're really not bad, but they're not very good. Borges had impeccable English, and he'd read much more in English than he had in Spanish, but he was smart to know what his language was.

In your book With Borges on an Ordinary Evening in Buenos Aires, *the poet reveals his high regard for the poetry of Robert Frost, and his equally strong distaste for Ezra Pound whom he calls "the Fraud." Was Borges's argument with Pound simply personal or political, or did the charge of fraudulence extend to Pound's work?*

WILLIS BARNSTONE: Oh, I think he was concerned with his work. Pound was apparently—from everything people have told me—one of the most generous people in the world. Despite his despicable politics and so forth, he helped people get Nobel Prizes, etc., and his Jewish, loyal friends were defending him in Washington while he was still blurting nonsense. But I can't tell you how many times Borges said something disparaging about Pound. I think he sensed—what I also feel about Pound—that he was a tremendous mixture of old-fashioned Edwardian speech mixed with the best modernity that the century has produced. He was the poet who had the greatest concept of a great work, namely *The Cantos.* Yet at the same time, I feel that he's a writer of fragments, and that there's hardly a single poem which holds up, despite the wonderful lines, and even though he probably wrote five times as many wonderful passages as most other equally well-known poets have done. But Borges was really put off. I think he also suspected that Pound's scholarship was razzle-dazzle and specious, and Borges's scholarship was never specious. He was, in fact, incapable of forgetting anything he learned. Once, after I'd read him the first 30 to 40 lines of Gerard Manley Hopkins' "The Wreck of the Deutschland," he came back the next week and said, "Do you recognize this?" and he recited all those lines. He absolutely didn't have that book in his house, and I'd only read them once. I asked him, "How could you remember that, you monster?" And he said, "There are some lines which are harder to forget than to remember."

It sounds like his character Funes, the Memorious?

WILLIS BARNSTONE: Yes, he *was* Funes. And Borges acknowledged it—Funes, *c'est moi!*

In the Preface to Six Masters, *you talk lightheartedly about the sonnet as "a persistent anachronism [which] doesn't know it's dead" and about its "tyrannical form." Yet, as you point out, it has attracted many of the best-known poets of the 20th Century including Borges, Lorca, Thomas, Wilbur, Neruda— and, of course, we could add many others: Hardy, Frost, Robinson, Millay, Nemerov, and even Yeats. How would you describe the persistent attraction of the form? Why is it so irresistible?*

WILLIS BARNSTONE: People have always done variations on the sonnet, such as Meredith whose *Modern Love* sequence had 16 line sonnets, and I've experimented, and I've always dreamed of coming upon some new form, but I don't know, 14 seems to get you. If I write a sonnet, and it turns out I've only written 13 lines or have written by mistake 15, I always find that it dramatically improves the poem to add the missing line or compress it and take out the extra line. It always gives me something better. I'm not persuaded that it's inherently magical, but there must be an arbitrary reason for it.

Yes, and most of those diverse writers I mentioned earlier were writing quite regular sonnets. There might be some experiments here or there, and of course you can find people like Lowell doing all kinds of different things, but for the most part, those major 20th Century writers were writing very regular sonnets. You've obviously enjoyed the challenge of the form for many years: there are sonnets in your early books Poems of Exchange *and* From this White Island; *you've written a short sonnet sequence,* Ten Gospels and A Nightingale; *there are several sonnets in* Five A.M. in Beijing; *and you now have a 501-sonnet sequence,* The Secret Reader, *coming out next year. In what ways do you feel your own sonnet writing has changed or developed?*

WILLIS BARNSTONE: In my last book of poems, *Diary of the Dog,* as well as in the recent sonnets, I've aspired to the notion that, although the form is absolutely strict, it should only be overheard, rather than heard. I like it to be as invisible as possible.

It seems to me that in your more recent sonnets, without any metrical sacrifice, you've developed a kind of remarkable movement and inventiveness within the line. I think of your excellent sonnet "Wang Wei and Snow" which appeared in the first issue of The Formalist *and ends with the meditative Chinese poet giving advice to one of his suffering friends:*

> *he tells a friend to walk the idle hills*
> *alone, to swallow failure like the ageing*
> *year, to dream (what else is there?) of snow.*

In poems like these, you employ all kinds of ingenuity within the line that make it interesting, yet not distracting—like the parenthesis and the question in the final line. I've also noticed in many of your more recent sonnets that there's a flow—a very smooth but almost quick movement— throughout the whole sonnet.

WILLIS BARNSTONE: During the last six or seven years, in addition to my prose books of criticism, I've also written books of memoirs, a novel, and a book of short stories, and I feel that the fiction, especially, has helped my poetry in terms of fluency—just as poetry has always helped me in scholarship and fiction—in the sense that it gives me both a flow and a precision, and I think those very qualities which you cite have their source in my fiction writing.

Aside from an increasing facility with the form of the sonnet, is there any other kind of interaction between writing your own sonnets and translating the sonnets of others?

WILLIS BARNSTONE: Definitely. I've learned more from translation than anything else. And by that I mean all kinds of translation. When you translate, *you* are the "other" poet, and if that doesn't teach you, nothing else will.

Well, in Six Masters of the Spanish Sonnet, *you've certainly captured, in a truly amazing way, the various moods and modes of the great Spanish-language sonneteers, and your readers look forward to all your future writing projects. Thank you very much for your time.*

WILLIS BARNSTONE: Thank you, Bill.

ANTHONY HECHT

Harold Bloom has discussed, at length, what he calls the "high artistry of Anthony Hecht," and Michael Dirda has suggested that the Pulitzer Prize-winning poet "may be the most accomplished master of technique since Auden."

Anthony Hecht was born in New York City, and he graduated from Bard College in 1944. After three years service in the U.S. Army during and after World War II, he studied at Kenyon College and eventually received his Masters Degree from Columbia University in 1950.

Recently retired from his position as Professor of English at Georgetown University, Anthony Hecht had previously taught at a number of American colleges including Kenyon College, University of Iowa, New York University, Smith College, Bard College, and Rochester University. He also served as a Fulbright Professor in Brazil, 1971, and as Poetry Consultant to the Library of Congress, 1982–84.

Anthony Hecht's books of poetry include: *A Summoning of Stones*, 1954; *The Hard Hours*, 1967; *Millions of Strange Shadows*, 1977; *The Venetian Vespers*, 1979; *The Transparent Man*, 1990; and *Collected Earlier Poems*, 1990. Among his other books are a collection of essays, *Obbligati*, 1986, and *The Hidden Law: The Poetry of W. H. Auden*, 1992.

In 1983, Anthony Hecht was awarded the Bollingen Poetry Prize, and his book *The Hard Hours*, 1967, won the Pulitzer Prize for poetry.

This interview was conducted at The University of the South during the Sewanee Writers' Conference.

Harold Bloom has accurately praised your poetry for its "emotional intensity and formal power," and it's clear to your readers that you take meticulous care in the creative process. I'd be very grateful if you could describe your own personal methods of composition.

ANTHONY HECHT: I wish it were easy to do. I write, roughly speaking, laboriously, and it takes me a lot of time. Some of my poems are elaborately patterned, some are in blank verse, and a few are in free verse, but not many. Generally, I can't tell ahead of time what's going to happen, although you can anticipate a few things. You can see, for example, that there are certain kinds of material that lend themselves to a short form like the sonnet, so that you wouldn't attempt to make an epic poem out of them, and vice versa. But I can't really say that I proceed with a specific method, and this might account for the fact that my output is really rather slight as compared with many others.

Do you have particular times you like to write, or do you have a special place?

ANTHONY HECHT: No special place, but what I need is a degree of silence. I cannot, for example, in the way that Hart Crane could, write with music going on. I find that completely distracting. I'm at my best, in my own mind—I once had the folly to say this out loud to a group of my students—in the early morning when I can get up and feel that I'm clear-headed and capable of assimilating things and bringing everything I need together. Then, when I'm a little fatigued in the afternoon, I'm prepared to teach. The students were not entirely pleased by that.

Your friends Richard Wilbur, Howard Nemerov, and many others have discussed the "liberating aspects of rhyme and meter." But sometimes this seems a paradox, especially to beginning writers, that constraint can lead to liberation. I wonder if you could comment a little on that?

ANTHONY HECHT: I think it probably has something to do with personal temperament, but it may be more than that. In the course of experience, you learn to be able to work within limitations, and these limitations invite invention on your part in order to be able to satisfy the laws that you impose upon yourself. This, unquestionably, can be carried too far, and I think of Merrill Moore who became so deft in writing fourteen-line poems in sonnet form that eventually they became rather effortless exercises. A poet has got to guard against such total mastery of a form that it becomes negligible for him. The form has got to be vital. It has to play a really serious part in governing his imagination, and if it does that, then the poem can work—but there's no way of guaranteeing that it will.

On the other hand, I believe firmly that there are an awful lot of poets who, discouraged by an initial inability to turn out a good poem in a formal pattern, decide that it's not worth the candle and just abandon it and never try again. I find myself, for example, not at all sympathetic with Galway Kinnell's declaration in his introduction to his translation of François Villon that rhyme and meter are a kind of old-fashioned thing and not really essential to poetry. He believes that it's only important to convey a poet's images, and so, if Kinnell is faithful to the images of Villon, then he's done everything that's necessary. But that seems to be absolutely wrong because the joy of reading François Villon is enjoying his marvelous aptitude for writing within very careful and demanding poetic forms.

In your wonderful tribute "To L. E. Sissman, 1920–1976" you affirm that Sissman's "ars" and "craft" give his poetry a lasting, permanent quality:

> And will be ringing in some distant ear
> When the Mod-est, last immodesty fatigues,
> All Happenings have happened, the Little Leagues
> Of Pop and pop-fly poets disappear
>
> To join, with all their perishable lines,
> The Edsel, Frug, beau monde of Buzzard's Gulch,
> The wisdom and the wit of Raquel Welch,
> "And connoisseurs of California wines."

Yet despite all the good humor in the poem, it also seriously highlights the "lasting" qualities that meter can give to a poem: rhythm, order, mnemonic enhancement, and a tap into the great tradition because so many writers in the past have used it. Why do you think so many contemporary poets ignore this potent tool?

ANTHONY HECHT: In some cases I think it's simply that they find they can't do it. It's just too hard. So they rationalize their inabilities into a wonderful set of self-congratulating convictions that they're being "original." Sometimes they are, but often they're not. It seems to me that no point or concept can be wholly original. Poems are only written because people have read other poems, and no one today would dream of inventing poetry. It's a traditional form, and even the wildest kinds of it have become part of the tradition. Whitman was certainly an inventor of forms, yet some of his best poems, like the great elegy for Lincoln, "When Lilacs Last in the Dooryard Bloom'd," is, in fact, really quite classical in its design.

For many years, up until recently when you retired, you've been teaching at Georgetown University and conducting writing seminars here at the Sewanee Writers' Conference each summer. What goals do you set for yourself in a poetry writing workshop? What is it that the teacher can do—or should do?

ANTHONY HECHT: That's not easy to say because suddenly you confront, as you always do when you have a class, a group of strangers. At Sewanee they happen to range in age and experience much more widely than they do in an undergraduate class or even a graduate class. And since they come with all kinds of strange, sometimes improbable, expectations and anxieties, and since they're only going to be there two weeks, it's imperative to deal with them with great care and kid gloves. Yet despite my efforts, I've twice had people break into tears, and I don't think of myself as a ruthless critic or commentator.

So I set no specific goals, to go back to your original question. What I do, and what I think students are looking for, is for someone to point out the problems in the poem, such as faults in construction. Very often these things are obvious to me, but not to the writer. There might be errors in syntax or grammar, or sometimes something might be done very deftly but the rhyme either interferes with what the poet's purpose is, or the poem has been coerced by the rhyme into saying something that the writer really doesn't want to say, simply to oblige the sound pattern. Things like these can be pointed out, but I think the setting of loftier goals is not really appropriate for a course that only lasts two weeks. You really can't hope for very much, yet, most often, I find that the people in my classes are genuinely grateful for having all these things pointed out to them. So I've tried to console myself when past students—there have only been two, I'm glad to say—have broken into tears when I thought I was being very delicate and gentle with them. And sometimes I'd recall Howard Nemerov who once had a student who turned in a sestina to him, and when Howard finished looking it over, he told the student, "I've never written a sestina, and neither have you."

Yes, Mr. Nemerov was very blunt and very honest. Continuing with this subject of teaching workshops, I'd be very interested to know your opinion concerning the proliferation of creative writing programs. Do you think that it's good in that it creates excitement about creative writing or has it reached the point of overkill?

ANTHONY HECHT: I don't have strong feelings about it. I know that some people have complained bitterly, and say it's corrupting—Dana Goia, I believe, has objected to it. But I don't think it's done any harm. It's like having knitting clubs. People learn how to knit. I don't think that's going to corrupt society. It may lead some people to think that they're better poets than they actually are, but I don't think in the long run that's going to be very harmful. Surely, even if they don't turn out any good poetry, one of the positive things it will probably do is to encourage them to actually read some poetry and buy some poetry books. And that, in a sense, is all to the good. So I don't see any danger in it.

On the other hand, I don't imagine that enormous good is going to come from it. One of the problems with contemporary poetry, I believe, has to do with the fact that there's a very, very latitudinous sense of what it actually is. Given Bill Moyers' poetry series on television, it's clear that his notion of poetry is essentially that of a performer's art. He likes poets that are good on TV, and he likes them to be easily accessible. He also likes them to be entertaining, and all that sort of stuff. And some poets indeed are, but not all. I don't think you could make a good case for some of the metaphysical poets being successes by Bill Moyer's standards.

Relating to these difficult questions of teaching poetry and what poetry really is, Derek Walcott has long been a vocal proponent of imitation for the apprentice writer—picking a notable poet from the tradition and writing in imitation of his work. Walcott believes that it's invaluable for developing craft and that it also helps to keep the ego in check. I wonder if you ever use that method in your workshops?

ANTHONY HECHT: I don't, but I entirely agree with Derek about that. It seems to me a very sound idea. One of the things that distinguishes his own poetry is the ability to employ whole ranges of different kinds of voices, with different lilts: his own Caribbean, and even within the Caribbean region, several different modes of speech; and then, in ordinary English, all the high, grand, rhetorical levels of heroic poetry down to plain colloquialism. It takes a careful, thoughtful and trained ear and a lot of practice to be able to do that, and I think his poetry, obviously, exhibits all those merits. Naturally, all young, struggling poets have a narrow range of voice—and it's certainly not wrong or wicked that they do—but what Derek Walcott has done is to enlarge his own range of voice so that he can accomplish all kinds of things in his poetry. Thus it's not surprising that Derek encourages his students to practice poetic imitation.

By the same token, and probably for the same reason, Joseph Brodsky likes to assign his poetry students to memorize a thousand lines of poetry. Memorization, like imitation, has gone way out of fashion and most students resist it vigorously. They resist many things. I even had— and I find this very shocking—a graduate workshop in which the students refused to read Paul Fussel's hundred-page book called *Poetic Meter and Poetic Form*. They simply wouldn't read it. They felt it was irrelevant to what they wanted to do. Now these were graduate students at a university! I find that shocking. And it's equally shocking that most students do not want to memorize poetry. They want to write it, but they don't want to learn any of it by heart. Think of what this would mean to a musician. A good concert pianist knows reams of Mozart and Beethoven by heart, and when he gives a concert he usually plays without a score. But these guys and gals don't want to trouble themselves with learning anything by heart.

Yes, it's very unfortunate. When I was an undergrad at Rutgers our Shakespeare teacher made us memorize large passages of the plays. So even in the literature courses of the past, you'd often find considerable memorization. Since this subject of memorization relates directly to the matter of influences, I'd like to ask you about that. We all know of your admiration for Auden, Eliot, Shakespeare, and the Metaphysicals. Were there other poets that had a major impact on your thinking or writing?

ANTHONY HECHT: I don't know that I can point out anyone mysterious in the background. By the time somebody gets to my age they've read so many poets of such a scattered variety and admired so many of them. I don't know. I think I first began reading John Donne with admiration, and only later came to George Herbert. But I've also been influenced, like almost all poets, by more immediate contemporaries as well. Wilbur surely is one of them. Merrill is another. Elizabeth Bishop is surely one too. And John Crowe Ransom was one of my teachers. The first thing I did when I got out of the Army after World War II was to go to Kenyon College as a special student and study with Ransom. And I later studied with Tate as well. So in fact I'd been to Sewanee long before this conference ever began. I came to visit Tate when he lived right near the Inn where you are staying, just next to the golf course.

Both Ransom and Tate were major literary figures, and, it seems to me, neither gets the appropriate attention he deserves. Thinking of Ransom, and, in particular, his sometimes curious diction, leads me into another subject that I wanted to discuss. The diction in your poetry, as with your deft rhyming and skillful metrics, has often been described as "elegant." Although you often make use of the contemporary and colloquial in your works, you have, like Richard Wilbur, firmly insisted on a place for a grander diction as well. The trend, of course, seems to be against that, and in a sense you are trying to enlarge the language or at least maintain it. I wonder if you could comment on this important subject?

ANTHONY HECHT: I've thought about this thing in a very imprecise way. Certain twentieth century poems really reach for an elaborate kind of rhetorical mode of speech—Miltonic, sometimes, in its pretensions—and I think this is attempted in order to enlarge the space that's available. I personally wouldn't want to write all my poems in a flat, declarative, ordinary voice. It would become tedious after a while. A number of my poems that are dramatic monologues are written in a subdued voice that's generally colloquial, but what I've tried to do is move, in my poetry, between the two poles: the ordinary mode of speech and the more elaborate and enriched one.

Given the complexities of your work—technical precision, bold diction, wit and irony, and Biblical and literary allusions—how do you guard against opacity or inscrutability?

ANTHONY HECHT: This subject might bring us back to Bill Moyers who would expect any poem to be instantly accessible. Recently, I've been reading the discourses of Joshua Reynolds about painting, and he says it's only on the lowest and least interesting level that art is immediately apprehensible—and that almost any other level of art requires education and learning. And Reynolds is talking about painting, which, after all, is not full of quotations. Though it is in subtle ways, in different ways.

I've spent my whole professional life as a teacher in the academy, and that may be a bad thing from somebody's point of view, but I write a kind of poetry which does often require some kind of special knowledge or annotation. So when I give poetry readings, I try very hard to supply those notes in advance—to elucidate unfamiliar words. This afternoon, for example, I'm going to be reading here at Sewanee, and I plan to annotate several unusual words in the poems because they're comparatively unfamiliar. So I certainly don't feel that I'm forbidden to use such words when I'm writing my poems, and I would resent anybody who said you could only use simple words in poetry. I think that poetry ought to be enriched by as large and inventive a vocabulary as the poet wishes to command. And I think that many of the poets whom I greatly admire, including, offhand, Ransom, T. S. Eliot, Wallace Stevens, and Pound—all of these people use unfamiliar words, and, some of them, unfamiliar languages. I see nothing wrong with that.

In Alone with America, *Richard Howard had high praise for your first two volumes, and described selections in* The Hard Hours *as "among the most agonizing poems to have appeared in America." He suggests that your poetry was undertaking a* via negativa—*an effort to deal with the dark and suffering aspects of human history and especially contemporary life. This focus in your work has continued through your most recent collection of poems,* The Transparent Man, *yet there is not, it seems to me, a despairing aspect to your poetry. The truth of the suffering is always tempered by compassion, humaneness, appreciation of life, and even occasional humor. How conscious are you of the dangers of falling into nihilism when dealing with contemporary horrors? Do you guard against that consciously?*

ANTHONY HECHT: No, I don't think I guard against that consciously, nor do I think of it as a possible temptation. Nihilism seems to me, in fact, sort of lax. It's like lying down and saying, "I'm not even going to bother to write this damn poem." That would be nihilism. No, I think that what Richard Howard points to and what I recognize in myself is a kind of very strong, almost embarrassing, Puritan streak in myself which feels that it's impossible to look at existence, even at its most joyful, without remembering that there are other people who are suffering at the same time—and keeping that double vision in mind is difficult. It often prevents any kind of free and spontaneous happiness untainted by that knowledge, because the knowledge is always at least unconsciously there, and in my case, very often consciously there. My poems often try to take all that worst part of existence into account and then try to find something redemptive in it.

Yes. There are many dark and terrifying visions in your poems: the dark birds in "Crows in Winter" who sit like "morticians in our trees," or the ravenous doves in "Birdwatchers of America" who've plucked the eyes out of a corpse; or the awareness of the Jewish father in your well-known, powerful poem "It Out-Herods Herod. Pray You, Avoid It." who, observing his young sons watching a western on television, suddenly realizes his impotence to protect them in certain circumstances:

> *Who could not, at one time,*
> *Have saved them from the gas.*

Nevertheless, there are also many moments of "alleviation," if not "redemption," in your poems. For example, the thirty-year-old leukemia victim in "The Transparent Man" who finds a certain contentment in his observances of the trees outside his window; the Biblical Joseph in "Exile," who despite his betrayal and subsequent bondage in Egypt, is welcomed by the animals; and even the narrator of "The Venetian Vespers" who finds periodic solace at a small alley shrine of "Saint Mary Paregoric, Comforter." Such moments not only seem true to life, but they also offer respites of comfort and hope within the tragedies of life.

ANTHONY HECHT: Yes. I've often wondered how some writers like Elie Wiesel and others who've actually gone through the Holocaust have managed to view the world as possibly redemptive when they've endured sufferings the like of which I would have difficulty even understanding. There's a scene in *Crime and Punishment* in which Sonia meets Raskolnikov for the first time and, just looking at his face, is overcome and falls down on her knees in front of him because he's suffered so much. And Sonia, of course, has already suffered in terrible ways. One has difficulty understanding how people endure, and how they are able to avoid nihilism. And I myself think regularly, constantly, of people whom I know who've gone through this kind of horror—it's more than misery, and it's more than terror and tragedy; it's something so depriving to the human spirit that you can't imagine how anyone could survive and go on hoping and living. And yet these people do. I don't know that I can explain it. On the other hand, I know as a real fact that I could not in honesty ignore it and pretend that it doesn't exist.

Your use of the word "endure" makes me think of Faulkner's summation of Dilsey in the Appendix to The Sound and the Fury: *"They endured." Along with your well-known darker poems, you've also written many excellent humorous poems—such as "The Dover Bitch," "Samuel Sewall, "The Ghost in the Martini," "Application for a Grant," and "Naming the Animals." You're also the co-inventor with Paul Pascal of the demanding Double Dactyl. I wonder how seriously you and John Hollander really attempted to keep track of the Double Dactyl "canon" —or was that all tongue-in-cheek?*

ANTHONY HECHT: It was tongue-in-cheek.

So does the form have much of a future? Or is it just too demanding? Maybe now with computers, people could somehow find the appropriate words.

ANTHONY HECHT: I don't know. It was a lot of fun to do, and we got a lot of people involved. People are still writing them, and I occasionally get some in the mail, and I'm sure John does too. I think the nicest tribute we've ever had to the form is that Auden wrote some Double Dactyls in one of his later works that was set to music by Hans Werner Henze. But it was all done for fun.

That notion of "fun" in poetry is something that I wanted to get to, or at least "enjoyment." In your introduction to The Essential Herbert, *you cite Eliot's belief that "We must enjoy the poetry before we attempt to penetrate the poet's mind; we must enjoy it before we understand it, if the attempt to understand is to be worth the trouble." Eliot's, of course, talking about serious and dark poetry as well as humorous verse. And years later, Philip Larkin wrote his well-known little essay "The Pleasure Principle" dealing with this same subject. But it seems to me that many poets have forgotten this aspect of poetry, that there should be pleasure or enjoyment for the reader.*

ANTHONY HECHT: Well, I think Eliot was talking about his own poetry as much as he was talking about George Herbert, and the truth is he's quite right about this. Before his poetry was understood, people were absolutely struck by things that stuck in the memory and the mind and couldn't be gotten rid of. For example, "When the evening is spread out against the sky / Like a patient etherised upon a table" —even people who hated those lines could not dismiss them, and I think Eliot was talking about lines that cannot be dismissed. Now that can lead to all kinds of abuses. There are poets now who simply think that what you do to write a poem is to think up a lot of astonishing lines and then just place them one after another. But that's not poetry. T. S. Eliot was a good poet who could astonish and surprise, and, quite often, it took his readers a long time before they understood his meanings. And this is exactly what he's saying about George Herbert, and he's right about Herbert too. So I've translated your word "pleasure" into astonishment. But, whatever you call it, it's something that stops you in your tracks and gives you great pleasure.

As for Philip Larkin, he writes a kind of colloquial poetry. He was part of that gang of writers—John Wain was one. . . .

The Movement? Conquest and Gunn?

ANTHONY HECHT: Yes, the Movement. And they were a revolutionary force in some ways in trying to take poetry out of the hands of academia and out of the hands of intellectuals and out of the hands of high-falutin types and bring it down to elementary, often lower middle-class concerns. Kingsley Amis, I guess, was one of them too. And that's good. But certainly poetry can't address itself always to lower middle-class concerns. It would be very boring if it did. What Larkin did, he did extremely well, and always with a wonderful sense of irony and vigor and comedy, and in that sense he aimed to give poetic pleasure. And he did.

I think that one of the reasons is that they tried not to take themselves too seriously. Certainly, Larkin was able to poke fun at himself, and that approach can alleviate the typical moaning and groaning about oneself that we see in some of his poetry and in a lot of contemporary poetry.

ANTHONY HECHT: Yes, and if you read his collected poetry you can see—I haven't read the letters or the biography, but I guess he did feel pretty sorry for himself—that the irony in his poems, when it really works, is a protection against what he must have realized was a tendency to feel sorry for himself.

Yes, that's right. —At the end of your introduction to the Herbert volume, you wrote that "Introducing me to the works of certain poets has been one of the greatest services that a few other poets, teachers and friends have done me, and I should be proud to have done as much for others, and not least for total strangers." Is there any poet—maybe one who's somewhat neglected—who you'd like to recommend to your readers?

ANTHONY HECHT: I've been appointed, within the last two or three years, to write articles for *The Wilson Quarterly*. Is that a journal you know?

Just by chance, I recently read Joseph Brodsky's piece on Evgeny Rein in last Fall's issue, but I don't see it regularly.

ANTHONY HECHT: Well, I write in the same series as Brodsky, and what I'm invited to do is recommend to the reading public poets whose works I think have been neglected. Over the years, I've recommended a wonderful poet named Katherine Hoskins whose work is virtually unknown, even though she died very recently. I mean, she's not an Eighteenth Century poet or anything of that sort. She was a contemporary of mine, and Robert Lowell and William Meredith both thought very highly of her work. I've also written about L. E. Sissman, George Starbuck, John Crowe Ransom, and a few others. I can't remember all of them. But I do this from time to time for *The Wilson Quarterly*, trying to point out poets whose work I think has been undeservedly ignored.

It's a wonderful idea. I'd like to finish up today by citing Ted Hughes's observation that your work includes "some of the most powerful and unforgettable poems at present being written in America." I'd like to thank you for those poems and also for the opportunity to talk with you this afternoon.

ANTHONY HECHT: Well, thank you very much.

DONALD JUSTICE

Donald Justice has been described by Mark Strand, a recent U.S. Poet Laureate, as "one of the century's superb poets, one of the writers of genius that our country has produced."

Donald Justice was born and raised in Miami, Florida, and he received his bachelor's degree in English from the University of Miami. Later, he did graduate work at the University of North Carolina, Stanford University, and the University of Iowa. After receiving his Ph.D. from the University of Iowa in 1954, he taught in the Iowa Writers Workshop for much of his teaching career, although he was also a professor at Syracuse University, the University of Florida, and a number of other universities.

His books of poetry include *The Summer Anniversaries*, 1960; *Night Light*, 1967; *Departures*, 1973; *Selected Poems*, 1979; *The Sunset Maker*, 1987; and *New and Selected Poems*, 1995. He's also edited *The Collected Poems of Weldon Kees*, 1960 and 1975, and, with Alexander Aspel, *Contemporary French Poetry*, 1965.

In 1991, Donald Justice received the Bollingen Poetry Prize, and in 1980 his *Selected Poems* was awarded the Pulitzer Prize for poetry.

This interview was conducted at The University of the South during the Sewanee Writers' Conference.

You grew up in Miami and have written about the city and your youth there in many of your poems. I wonder if you could discuss the uniqueness of that Southern city in the thirties and forties?

DONALD JUSTICE: Yes, Miami *was* a unique city back then, and it still is, though in a different way now. As I recall it, the city always had a bilingual, bicultural life to it, but certainly much less so when I was a kid than now. It was a much smaller town too—but not that small, 110,000 to 130,000, I believe—and the area I grew up in, the Northwest section, was very Southern. Most of the residents there had come down from Georgia during hard times on the farms, and they were very glad to be in the city, where they had a decent chance of finding work. That was certainly the case with my father and other relatives who'd followed this common migratory pattern.

In those days, Miami was still sort of a raw town, not fully formed, and it could have gone in several directions. In the winter time, of course, it really came alive because of all the tourists coming down—lots of rich people, as we thought of them—coming down from the North. I think the city's culture was probably unlike that of anywhere else in the country, and it was a beautiful place to live—with a wonderful climate except for the heat. And as children, we didn't know that it wasn't hot everywhere, so it seemed perfectly okay to us. And then there was the ocean as well.

I've often thought, looking back, that Miami was an ideal place to grow up, though not without some reservations. The most important lack was the absence of any artistic culture to speak of. There was a public library, thank God, but beyond that there wasn't a whole lot. There was some music, very little art, some theater, and movies, of course. I had a happy childhood, partly owing to the city itself. At the time, it may have seemed like an unhappy childhood to me, but I know better now.

In your 1987 collection, The Sunset Maker, *you began writing specifically about the South, even citing Quentin Compson's powerful lines from Faulkner's* Absalom, Absalom!: *"I dont! I dont hate it! I dont hate it!" I know that over the years you've been quite ambivalent about considering yourself a Southern writer. Why is that?*

DONALD JUSTICE: Well, the "Southernness" of poets and their subjects, as I came to recognize it in adolescence, was associated for me with the Fugitives, the Fugitive Agrarians. I became fascinated by their work and their ideas and even did my master's thesis on that subject. But it gradually became clear to me, I remember, that the Fugitive attitudes were those of a sort of Southern aristocracy, though not represented as such. Whether the old South had actually existed in the manner it was imagined to have existed—well, I'm doubtful about that. In any case, it seemed alien to my own Southern experience, which was that of the transplanted farm boy in Miami whose relatives were all poor farmers from Georgia.

And didn't you spend part of each year in Georgia?

DONALD JUSTICE: Yes, we'd visit Georgia every summer for as long as my father could get away from his job, and sometimes with my mother I would stay a bit longer, several weeks anyhow. Which I didn't like very much. I was a city boy, but I did get a good sense of how it was to live in the underclass in the South. So, years later, when I put my own experience side by side with the Southernness I was reading about in the poetry and prose of the Agrarians, there was quite a gap, and I realized that I was a Southerner in a very different way. There were, of course, other things about the South, such as the situation of the black people, that did not seem right and that already bothered me. So in late adolescence I left, and yet I kept coming back. My experience of being a Southerner is to go away and then to come back.

Even though you've often cited Baudelaire and Stevens as the poets who've influenced you the most—and others have suggested Auden as a possible influence— I think that your work also has many traits in common with John Crowe Ransom: careful craftsmanship, elegance of language, a deep concern for the common tragedies of life, and the evocation of mood. Given that you did your Masters thesis at the University of North Carolina on the Fugitives, I wonder if you feel, in any special way, affected by the work of Ransom?

DONALD JUSTICE: More by Ransom than by the other Fugitives. I certainly respect greatly the poetry of Ransom and Tate, poetry I learned to appreciate very early on, and it's not that I haven't continued to like their poetry, it's just that their view of the South seems to me such a strange one.

I wonder if we could talk a bit about Thomas Hardy since I know you admire his work so much. Larkin, of course, felt that Hardy was the major poet of the twentieth century.

DONALD JUSTICE: I wouldn't be that bold, but he's clearly one of the best and most steady-going poets—underrated for a long time. You can always return to Hardy and find something new and startling. Frost is a worthy competitor, if it's a competition. And then there's the whole very different line of major work represented by Pound and Eliot in the early part of the century.

And Yeats.

DONALD JUSTICE: And Yeats somewhere in between those two. And a number of other poets that I've liked a lot. You mentioned Stevens earlier, and I would add Williams, when he's going good, of the older generation. I do believe that it's mostly an older generation that influences a poet, rather than one's contemporaries, though there must be exceptions to that. The Fugitives themselves, I believe, would be an exception since they influenced each other. But ordinarily it's the older generation that has the most impact.

Another poet whom you've greatly admired—and very much helped to promote by editing his poetry—is Weldon Kees. I wonder if you could tell the story about your finding his work, writing "Sestina on Six Words by Weldon Kees," and then being contacted by the poet's worried father?

DONALD JUSTICE: I'd read some of Kees's poems in various magazines, and we'd even appeared in the same issue of *Furioso* in 1952. But I hadn't read him with any concentration until I casually picked up *The Fall of the Magicians* in the Miami Public Library one winter evening and took it home and read it through in one sitting, and was, as they say now, "blown away" to see all those unique poems written in that plain but semi-formal style that seemed so convincing—and on such believable and unpretentious subjects. It seemed like I'd experienced the work of a real person writing real poetry. That's not well put, but Kees's poetry was certainly different from the other poetry I'd been reading at the time. It was, it seemed to me, uniquely honest.

So one day, casting about for things to write, I borrowed six words from a Kees sestina and worked out one of my own. Later I was surprised to find that Bertran de Born had done much the same thing with Arnalt Daniel's sestina, the very first ever written. When my "Sestina on Six Words by Weldon Kees" came out in *The Hudson Review*, I planned to send the finished poem to Kees himself—to say how much I admired his work and that the sestina was a tribute. But a friend who'd just been in San Francisco, and who knew Kees slightly, told me that Kees had disappeared, that nobody knew where he was, and that he may have jumped from the Golden Gate Bridge. And there was no point any longer to sending the poem.

But a month or so after the *Hudson Review* publication, I got a letter from the poet's father asking about the meaning of the six words. Apparently he thought that they were part of a conversation I'd had with his son before Kees disappeared, and he hoped that the words might, in some mysterious way, reveal his son's whereabouts. So I wrote back explaining that, regretfully, I'd never known his son, and that the sestina was based on such and such a poem and that I'd only borrowed his son's end words. As a result, we had a small correspondence over the course of the next several years. And then a friend in Iowa City, who was just beginning to start up a hand press, was looking for something to print, and I suggested a *Selected Kees*. The printer already knew some of Kees's work, and he thought it was a good idea, but his teacher and predecessor—Harry Duncan, who'd done those beautiful Cummington Press books—said, "Why stop at a *Selected*? Why not do a *Collected*?"

So Harry talked us into this rather mammoth project for a hand press—which was actually the first normal-sized book that my friend, Ken Merker, and his partner, Raeburn Miller, ever printed. They devoted a whole year of their lives to putting the book together, and Kees's father became very interested in the project. He thought that, through the book, he might somehow re-establish contact with his missing son. It was his consuming interest, and he'd even hired a private detective to try and track the missing poet down, without luck, of course. We planned, at one point, to use a photograph of Kees in the book because the father had suggested the idea—thinking that it might help locate his son. But, of course, a limited edition of 250 copies or whatever number it was, wasn't going to help much, even if Kees had been among the living, which was highly unlikely.

The story seems to imply that, in his relationship with his son, the father knew that Kees could be intentionally mysterious or cryptic—that Kees could be, at the very least, difficult to figure out in some ways.

DONALD JUSTICE: I hadn't thought of that, but yes, I expect you're right. I don't know whether Kees's father ever accepted the idea that his son was dead, or probably dead. He certainly remained interested in his son's work, and he deposited the papers he had at the Lincoln, Nebraska, Public Library. I've seen some of them there. And I believe he gave Kees's paintings and drawings to the Sheldon Museum of Art in Lincoln, and he later arranged for the paperback edition of the *Collected Poems* with the University of Nebraska Press. In other words, he was loyal and devoted to his son's memory.

Did you know about the—I don't know what to call it—the celebration of Kees in Beatrice, Nebraska, his birthplace?

I've only heard about it.

DONALD JUSTICE: It was about seven years ago, if I remember correctly. A number of people interested in Kees gathered in Beatrice—that's said with the accent on the second syllable—on the invitation of a high school teacher there, and it was really an odd and touching occasion. Beatrice turned out to be a very nice midwestern town, and the people that we met there, who'd once known Kees, were very smart and sophisticated, decent people. The most bizarre aspect was the two tour buses!

You've done a lot to get an important poet before the public—one of the most talented of his generation.

DONALD JUSTICE: I always thought he belonged up there. By now I've added two or three more to my canon of the best of that generation, but I still like Kees very much, and I'm glad that others have learned to like him too. He's still not a darling of the critics, but a lot of poets like his work, a point Dana Gioia keeps stressing, properly.

Speaking of critics, I wanted to ask you about Yvor Winters. After you finished up at North Carolina, you went to Stanford where you audited a number of classes with the influential critic. I wonder if you could describe being in Winters' class and the kinds of things he taught his young students?

DONALD JUSTICE: Although I wasn't one of Winters' circle—I was on the periphery of it—I admired and respected Winters a great deal. He was an autocrat in the classroom, and in all of his classes, he used his own book, *In Defense of Reason*, a combined printing of his earliest three books of criticism with an additional essay. No matter what course he was teaching—"Chief American Poets," "Chief American Historians," "Modern Criticism," etc.—he used *In Defense of Reason*.

So the book had everything in it!

DONALD JUSTICE: Indeed. I already knew the book very well, and since his method of teaching was generally to read from *In Defense of Reason* I didn't necessarily have a lot to gain from attending his classes. But he did often add valuable asides and digressions, sharp with insight, so you never knew what to expect—and it was usually worth waiting for. Winters was an excellent explicator of poems, especially of difficult poems. I once asked what was going on in a Stevens' poem—I believe it was "The Revolutionists Stop for Orangeade"—and he told us. Unfortunately, I've forgotten now what it was. Winters was also a great reader of verse in the classroom. The recordings of his readings are not truly representative of his power as a reader of poetry. I've never forgotten a reading of Wordsworth's sonnet to Milton on an otherwise ordinary day in the classroom. His voice would drop by about a perfect fifth—a way of announcing that he was reading a poem—and you wouldn't think that you would like this, but it was quite effective. Poetry was never spoken with greater dignity and honor. Winters, of course, had very strong opinions, and he didn't care much for dissent or negative discussion. But I remember that as he was reading that Wordsworth poem—and so beautifully— he paused at the line, "Thy soul was like a star, and dwelt apart," and wondered aloud how that could be, since Milton was an argumentative, aggressive, political secretary, and a revolutionary. That may not be exactly how he put it, but that was the point he was making, and I timidly raised my hand and observed that Wordsworth did say it was his "soul" that was like a "star" and not Milton himself. Winters, as I recall, accepted that as a possibility, which was a small triumph of sorts. I don't believe he was convinced at all—and perhaps he shouldn't have been.

When you eventually went to the University of Iowa for your Ph.D., you studied in the workshops with an amazing group of fellow students— W. D. Snodgrass, Henri Coulette, Jane Cooper, Philip Levine, and others— and studied under visiting professors like Robert Lowell, Karl Shapiro, and John Berryman. Was there a sense, at that time, that something really important was happening? That the future of American poetry—and even how American poetry would be taught—might be affected by what was going on there?

DONALD JUSTICE: Actually, I don't remember thinking about how we might come to matter to American poetry in the future, but we did think we were pretty good. We thought we knew the answers, which turned out not to be the case, but there was a good spirit of friendly competitiveness and a desire to be as good as we could be, according to our own lights. We naturally appreciated the attentions that the somewhat older poets like Lowell and Berryman gave us, and we felt that we were, let us say, the crew of a ship sailing off into the future. It was exciting, but we weren't really aware of the implications you might read back into the situation now, stretching a little. Mostly, we were just a bunch of friends trying to learn how to write as well as we could, and having some confidence that we would eventually do something that would turn out well.

85

In a recent APR *interview, you said that "University life was much more humane then than it has now become. Less doctrinaire, less 'correct,' more open-minded. Fewer intellectual fascists about." Why do you think this has happened? Especially given that "liberal" thinking dominates the academy, and really has since Trilling made that statement back in the fifties. What in your opinion has created this environment? What went wrong?*

DONALD JUSTICE: Well, since I retired, I'm no longer really in touch with what's going on in the universities, but I did see, before my retirement, what I thought were a number of terrible things happening. My own explanation, which may just be simple-minded, is that the humane people in, say, English departments—that's what I know most about—naively, in a sort of blind liberalism, welcomed the barbarians through the gates, and these barbarians turned out to be true barbarians who were soon demanding exclusive rights to all privileges—and even to the possession of all ideas that were now going to be adopted by forced conversion. I really do think it was like the barbarians getting in through the gates and taking over—barbarians who no longer had any regard for humane principles, yet spoke as if they were even *more* humane than everyone else.

The moral superiority bit.

DONALD JUSTICE: It was an amazing thing. I was quite innocent myself, and too many of my friends and colleagues were as well. We too easily laid down our arms. Now is the time of the occupation and the resistance.

Of course, at the time you couldn't have imagined what would happen.

DONALD JUSTICE: I certainly didn't, but within the course of about two or three years, I saw conditions change drastically at Florida, and since I was hearing tales from friends at other schools of similar invasions, I knew the same thing was happening elsewhere. It was as if there was a massive conspiracy, which there wasn't—at least, not to the best of my knowledge—but it actually seemed as if that were the case.

And it happened very quickly.

DONALD JUSTICE: Yes, during a few years in the eighties.

*When you finished your Ph.D. at Iowa, you began teaching in the Writers'
Workshop, and it's believed by many that you've been the most influential
poetry teacher in America over the past few decades. Your students have
included Mark Strand, Robert Mezey, Marvin Bell, Charles Wright, Jorie
Graham, David St. John, and many others, and it's a fact of history that many
of your students, after leaving the Iowa Writing Workshops, set up or took part
in similar writing programs at other universities across the country. I'd first
like to ask you about what kinds of things—especially in regard to craft—you
believe can be taught in writing workshops, and then I'd like to ask your opinion of the current proliferation of writing programs at U.S. universities.*

DONALD JUSTICE: In the fifties, when I was first a student and later
first began teaching in the Iowa workshops, it was impossible to foresee
the eventual multiplication of such programs. One of the pleasures of
the early Iowa workshop that we've spoken about—which included
Coulette, Levine, Snodgrass, and others—was that there weren't many
other programs like it in the country. It wasn't that our situation was
totally unique, but it was close to that. We felt ourselves to be a small
group of dedicated souls. Nowadays, however, it's hard for me to believe
statistically—despite the growth of the country's population—that there
are enough poets to support this many writing programs. And are there
really enough teachers who write and think well enough to conduct
all these workshops? There's naturally been some kind of dilution. I realize
that it's common for people who've reached my age to look back and see
this kind of worrying shift in history. But it does seem to me that the
proliferation of workshops has become like a pyramid scheme. It's bound
to collapse at some point. There can't be that many great poems being
written, and there can't be that many great classes or teachers or magazines or books. Anyway, I'd always liked the idea that poets were a kind
of secret society banded together against the world. Now it looks like it's
no longer a secret.

Maybe the poets will soon outnumber the world, and the world will have to band together against the poets.

DONALD JUSTICE: It sometimes seems that has already happened, though perhaps not really in the sense you mean. But I'm still missing part of your question.

Well, it's a very hard question. What kinds of things do you feel that a teacher in a writing class can really do for the students?

DONALD JUSTICE: Well, one obvious little thing, is to be a good copy editor. Another thing is to suggest directions the young writer can take in his or her own work. A teacher can recommend readings from the great poets of the past. I often found in the last years of my teaching that the young writers knew more about the contemporary scene than I did. My strength was to speak of the past.

It's impossible to comprehend what the present means unless you have some sense of the past.

DONALD JUSTICE: I certainly feel that way. Over the years, I would like to have been teaching, all that time, the meters and the forms as I see them, but the students weren't really interested, and if they don't want to learn, they're not going to learn. The whole tide of American poetry was set against that idea for at least a generation. Years went by when I was teaching the workshop at Iowa—and teaching very bright, talented people—when I got no poems at all in any recognizable meters or forms. There was simply no interest. Sometimes I look back now and I can't recall a single thing I taught any of my students except to try hard and have a conscience about writing.

Well, just the involvement can make a great difference. As you said earlier, maybe offering them some direction so they can explore it and see if it helps.

DONALD JUSTICE: But still, when I look at the work that's been published by some of my best students, I can see no evidence that those poets and I ever had any mutual interchange or influence. There are a few exceptions, of course, but on the whole that's the way it looks to me.

Well, your students certainly seem to think that you had a tremendous effect on their development, and their many grateful memoirs in the special issue of Verse *from a few years ago makes that clear.*

DONALD JUSTICE: Well, they were very kind.

Given what you've just said about meter and so forth, do you believe that young aspiring poets are really making an effort these days to learn their craft? In the sense of "The poet practicing his scales," as you put it in your "Homage to the Memory of Wallace Stevens"?

DONALD JUSTICE: Some are. More now, I think, than during any of my years of teaching.

In his short but excellent memoir in the Verse *issue, "Justice as Classmate," W. D. Snodgrass uses the word "perfectionist" to describe your approach to poetry. You yourself—and others—have also used the same word to describe your compulsion to work and re-work every line of your poetry, and it explains, to some extent, your generally slow writing process. Once you're under way in the writing of the poem, do you try to get through it roughly and then go back and re-work it, or do you tend to move through it slowly, line-by-line or section-by-section?*

DONALD JUSTICE: The first method would be the one I'd recommend, but it's one that I can very rarely manage myself. Usually I just keep going, piece-by-piece. Then, by the time I get a draft of the whole poem, it's a matter of fiddling with little details here or there or putting the pieces smoothly together. Usually, for me, it's small piece by small piece.

You've written and taught a great deal about revision, both small-scale and wholesale revisions. And you're a careful reviser of your own work. Yet often—like Ransom—you're not satisfied with your revisions, and you've admitted in the APR *interview, referring specifically to the two versions of "Incident in a Rose Garden," that "The awful truth is that the revisions just don't matter as much as I wish they did." Is there a danger in the revising impulse—especially given the fact that the poet generally can't publish different versions side-by-side as you did with "Incident in a Rose Garden"?*

DONALD JUSTICE: Actually, that was my editor's idea. I asked Harry Ford which version I should use because I couldn't make up my mind, and he suggested that I could use them both. So we did. But very few of my poems have two distinct versions like that. I've always liked revising, trying to get it right, although success is rare at best. Still, I keep fiddling when I can. As time goes by, you change your attitudes and beliefs—your aesthetic beliefs. At one time you might prefer this version, and the next time you might prefer another version because your ideas have changed at least somewhat—always taking seriously what is said in a poem and how it is done as well. Nevertheless, I think a lot of revision is a waste of time, a sort of solitaire.

And some poets—Ransom is an example—don't always improve their poems.

DONALD JUSTICE: That's right.

So there's a danger, even though it's necessary.

DONALD JUSTICE: Yes, and I don't know what one should do, really. For example, there's a poem in my latest book called "The Artist Orpheus." It's a small poem, fourteen lines, and I've worked on it a lot, off and on, for several years. I have innumerable versions of the last few lines, but I've never been satisfied with any of them—although some of them I happen to find quite interesting, even surprising. I hate to think that all those various endings are to be lost now. Probably I'll revise the poem at some point, totally changing the ending. I don't know.

How can I rationalize it? Maybe something like this: the text exists in a stage "A" somewhere, and it's published that way, so if you fool around with it and make it worse, it doesn't matter that much because there's always a superior version, whichever one that might turn out to be. Auden's posthumous publication demonstrates that nothing's ever lost. The Yeats variorum too.

In the tradition of Auden, you're one of a small handful of contemporary poets who can write with great effectiveness in a wide variety of forms—sonnets, ballads, villanelles, pantoums, sestinas, couplets, trimeter poems, dimeter poems, etc. I wonder if any particular form is a special favorite or if one might be especially difficult? And if there are ones that you've even avoided. Have you tried terza rima? I can't remember.

DONALD JUSTICE: I've never published any—mainly because it's such a difficult form. But I did try it once. It was in Lowell's class at Iowa, and it described a Southern scene from the Civil War, as I recall. I wrote one or two pages of it and then realized I wasn't doing a very good job of it. I think I put "etc." at the end of it—a surrender of sorts. I was influenced, at that time, by the terza rima poems that Tate was publishing at the end of his career—and very impressive poems they were. But that's a very hard form, and most of the so-called French forms seemed to me too frivolous to bother with, although the villanelle can be an exception.

Yes, writers have found various ways to make that form very effective—ever since Thomas, although you can go back to Robinson's beautiful little "House on the Hill."

DONALD JUSTICE: Yes, Robinson has that one very beautiful villanelle and several other passable ones, and there's the beauty of Joyce's villanelle in *Portrait of the Artist*, but the villanelles that influenced my generation were those by William Empson.

Although obscure in meaning, they're always amazing.

DONALD JUSTICE: Great refrain lines, that seems to be the key. But forms like the ballade I just can't take seriously, and the triolet I can't ever imagine writing—although Hardy wrote two or three very passable odd triolets.

And Wendy Cope has used it for humor.

DONALD JUSTICE: Oh yes, she's very funny. The Victorian poets also used the French forms for humor. That's always a possibility, but I'm not that funny myself, so I generally avoid those forms. I'm especially bored with the sestina—which has been so badly used. But the sonnet is always available, and blank verse is probably the greatest form in English, the iambic pentameter line. And there are still poets, like Tony Hecht, who have mastered that, who do it beautifully.

Yes, but tell me more about the sestina.

DONALD JUSTICE: How the sestina ever became a workshop form is beyond me. One reason, I suppose, is that it's awfully easy to write if you don't take it seriously. Originally, there was, of course, meter in the sestina, but in order to write the sestina easily you simply abandon meter, hit the end word and then stop, and then go on to the next end word. If the sestina were taken seriously as a form, it could remain a real possibility, but right now we need to declare a moratorium.

I couldn't agree more. Now I'd like to ask you about one of the primary themes in your poetry: a concern with loss and loneliness, which is often dealt with in very devastating ways. One of your early poems, "The Summer Anniversaries," concludes:

> Thirty today, I see
> The trees flare briefly like
> The candles upon a cake
> As the sun goes down the sky,
> A momentary flash,
> Yet there is time to wish
> Before the light can die,

If I knew what to wish,
As once I must have known,
Bending above the clean,
Candlelit tablecloth
To blow them out with a breath.

One of your much more recent poems, "Sadness," states that "It is as if life itself
were somehow bruised," and your well-known essay "Meters and Memory"
suggests that the control of poetic form can not only help to transform human
grief into art, but that the forms themselves can also help the individual poet
to deal with his own personal tragedies.

DONALD JUSTICE: Well, I do think that's true, true at any rate for the
serious, conscientious poet who respects the truth and the form both.

Douglas Dunn's tightest book, Elegies, *happens to be the one which deals*
with the death of his wife, and hopefully the writing of it allowed him, in
some way, to deal with the grief. Like Tennyson.

DONALD JUSTICE: Absolutely.

Edward Hirsch once described you in the New York Times Book Review *as*
"the resident genius of nostalgia" and "an elegiac poet of the first order."
I certainly think this praise is accurate and justified, but there's also a much
darker aspect of your work which deals not only with the sadness we all face
in life but with the terror that is somewhere lurking out there. The most
obvious example is your classic poem, "Counting the Mad," in which the
nursery rhyme about the five "little piggies" is transformed into a terrifying
vision of the occupants of a madhouse. The poem ends:

And this one thought himself a man,
An ordinary man,
And cried and cried No No No No
All day long.

Equally frightening are the callous seduction of Jane in "In Bertram's Garden"; the demonic vision of the narrator in "To Satan in Heaven"—who has "Seen thee in mirrors by morning, shaving, / Or head in loose curls on the next pillow"; the cemetery snake that slides near the narrator's mother in "My South"; and the creepy ballad you wrote with Robert Mezey about Charles Starkweather who went on a one-week murder spree in 1958. I guess my question, and maybe it's one that can't really be answered, is why a few, obviously blind critics have characterized your subject matter as too tame.

DONALD JUSTICE: I'm no doubt tamer than lots of poets. The aspect you've been talking about may be hidden from those who read quickly or those who may have an antipathy to the kind of thing I do. For instance, you mentioned "In Bertram's Garden." Well, it's in a neat little form, it sounds pretty, and hence it may be deceptive in this respect. I happen to like that kind of tension or friction between subject and attitude—and between the form and the language. I think that makes for an energetic mix of things, and I often seek it out. But it may be elusive because it's fairly well masked. That's a guess; I don't know.

Actually, that probably explains it, although it's sad to think that some critics are somehow unaware of the potential power that can be created by imposing formal structures on such harsh subjects—and that the restraint and the subject really can, if done properly, work hand-in-hand.

DONALD JUSTICE: Yes, but many poets and critics have an unconquerable prejudice against form and rhyming. Or against—let me put it this way—against poetry that sounds good.

Yes, unfortunately that's true. Now, I wonder if you could tell me how one of those poems, "The Ballad of Charles Starkweather," came to be written by you and Robert Mezey?

DONALD JUSTICE: Bob and I were fascinated by the crime story as it was breaking in the papers back in 1958. One day, we were sitting around in the coffee shop of the student union at Iowa, and we started making up stanzas dealing with the facts of the case and using for the refrain Charlie Starkweather's last words, as they were reported in the newspapers, "What's your hurry?"

So that's where the line came from?

DONALD JUSTICE: That's what Starkweather is supposed to have said—"What's your hurry?"—to the guards who came to lead him off to the death chamber. He was a tough little guy, I guess. So we used that as the refrain—although I worry that it gets rather boring before the poem is over. But we tried to make it fit each stanza.

I think it does fit. And of course that's the pleasure in reading a poem like that—when you know the refrain is coming, and you look forward to seeing what the writers will do next to lead you back to the refrain. I think it works wonderfully.

DONALD JUSTICE: Bob deserves most of the credit. He doesn't quite remember it that way, but I think he must have composed five-sixths of the poem. And every now and then, he came up with a real zinger, like the ending, as it refers to Charles' companion, Caril:

> His girl lay in her prison cell,
> Alone on her narrow bed,
> "Oh, Charlie, I wish I was down with you in hell!"
> "What's your hurry?" Charlie said.

Despite the tragedy of the real events, the poem was fun to do, and I'd like to try more with Bob one of these days.

That leads to my next question about ballads. Why do you think so few contemporary poets write ballads? Is it because they really are much harder than they seem? Because it's so difficult to tell a really good story? Or maybe it's just because the form's not considered fashionable.

DONALD JUSTICE: They're certainly not fashionable, but every now and then a poet tries them with great success. James Merrill wrote a very long story-telling poem in a ballad-like stanza about a town in New England, and it's excellent. And, of course, Auden did some wonderful ones, but he could turn his hand to practically anything. Still, ballads can be very hard to do, I think. They used to be a part of the folk culture, so it was easier then. Almost anybody could do it; not any more. Perhaps if more poets played guitar, there would be more ballads—but people who play guitar generally have no gift for writing, and I guess people who have a gift for writing don't play the guitar. Some kind of musical accompaniment would surely help in the composition of ballads.

I'd now like to turn to your wonderful love poem from New and Selected Poems *written for your wife Jean Ross. This perfectly-crafted, quatrain poem is entitled "On an Anniversary," and it concludes:*

> The estranging years that come
> Come and go, and we are home.
> Time joins us as a friend,
> And the evening has no end.

It seems to me a most optimistic poem—and thus not characteristic of much of your work?

DONALD JUSTICE: Well, it *is* "evening" in the poem.

Will there be more like it?

DONALD JUSTICE: I don't know. I can tell you that I had a heck of a time writing it. It took so long I had to change the first line, "Thirty years have come and gone." Now, it's actually forty-something, but when I first started the poem, it was twenty-something. Luckily, all those numbers keep the same meter—twenty, thirty, forty . . . .

Your poems are very much concerned with the phenomenon of memory, especially as a persistent, even relentless power in our lives. "Psalm and

Lament," for example, claims: "Nor does memory sleep; it goes on." Given your interest in both memory and perspective, and your special love of French literature and arts, I wonder if you have any special fondness for the films of Alain Resnais which, so often, deal with memory and its effect on our present lives?

DONALD JUSTICE: Resnais often seems too brittle and self-conscious to me. The French filmmaker I love most is Renoir. I don't know that his films have anything specifically to do with memory, but their powers of observation are marvelous and their human sympathy boundless. I especially like *La Chienne* and *Le Crime de Monsieur Lange*.

By coincidence, I just saw La Bête Humaine *again recently, though it's not as good—*

DONALD JUSTICE: It may be second-rate Renoir, but it's still a marvelous movie—I think that may have been the first Renoir I ever saw.

And we haven't even mentioned Grand Illusion, *which is spectacular.*

DONALD JUSTICE: It's a wonderful movie. Renoir is so relaxed as an artist that he lets the art happen without forcing it.

Well, that notion of the "relaxation" of the artist leads me to my next question. One of the consistent marks of your poetry is a wariness of the ego. This is expressed most wonderfully—and with humor—in your poem "A Local Storm" in which the narrator carefully watches the dark storm circle the house three times in "a sort of war dance" before the poem concludes:

> *The danger lies, after all,*
> *In being led to suppose—*
> *With Lear—that the wind dragons*
> *Have been let loose to settle*
> *Some private grudge of heaven's.*
> *Still, how nice for our egos.*

How do you explain to young poets the dangers of the self-conscious ego in writing poetry? Derek Walcott, for example, agrees with you on this subject, and he talks about it with his students.

DONALD JUSTICE: What does he do?

He actually discourages them from doing certain things when they write.

DONALD JUSTICE: I guess that I have been a more permissive teacher than that, but I do speak about such things—although I don't know if it's had any effect. I sometimes think about teaching—just as I did not quite get around to saying earlier—that if I'd done it differently, if I'd insisted on this or that, I might have been a less well-liked teacher, but probably a more effective one. I don't really know.

But in the end, students are going to go their own way anyway. All you really can do is make your points. Especially in the classroom, they're definitely not going to agree with everything you say, but at least you've said it—so it's out there, and maybe in time they'll come to see the usefulness of it.

DONALD JUSTICE: That's true. I hope so. Isn't it good to think so?

I wonder, as we approach the end of the interview, if you could comment on the current state of American poetry?

DONALD JUSTICE: It's very energetic and active. There're lots of poets trying to write as well as they possibly can, and lots of serious work going on. But the sad truth is, I don't like most of it. It often seems too surreal, too ill-organized, too self-indulgent. I guess I could invent a whole string of adjectives. I keep being disappointed. I feel, in my old-fashioned way, that more attention to the outward form would help the inner poem a good deal in many cases. There are, at least, some poets who've tried to bring this into their repertoire, but it can be difficult, and I don't know what the future will bring. One thing that might help would be a more intelligent, perceptive, responsible criticism. The criticism of the thirties in American literature was, I think, a great force for the good, and we simply don't have such a criticism going now. Present day criticism may support a handful of poets, but it doesn't, in my view, support poetry.

I know in the past you've spoken about the importance of anthologies to introduce poets to readers. Have there been, in your opinion, any particularly good recent anthologies that you would recommend to our readers?

DONALD JUSTICE: Most anthologies and anthologists now, I believe, are saddled with a great burden. Their publishers want them to represent diversity rather than excellence, and the two are not synonymous. That's a serious problem, and I don't know how Dana Gioia will have solved that dilemma in the anthology he's currently working on. It'll be interesting to see. But a good anthology could certainly be done. I'd love to do one myself, but nobody's asked me—and I wouldn't want to attempt it under the circumstances just mentioned. The situation is most unfortunate since anthologies are so important. As I was going through adolescence, the anthologists who principally guided my taste were Louis Untermeyer and then, later, Oscar Williams, and I'm grateful to them both.

Serious anthologists like Untermeyer and Williams never get the credit they deserve.

DONALD JUSTICE: In fact, they're often made fun of, especially if they included any of their own work in the anthologies. But I came across a number of important poets for the first time in Williams' yearly anthologies of the early forties. I first read Lowell there, for instance. And New Directions used to publish a small anthology—five young American poets each year or so—and one volume included Berryman and Jarrell together. Unfortunately, much more of that informed and taste-shaping sampling was being done in the forties than—as far as I can see—is being done now.

I'd like to finish up today with a few lines from one of your poems. Given your concerns about the appropriate role of the ego, it's quite natural that your poetry is filled with understatement—but it's understatement of a most marvelous and affecting kind. Reticence and aesthetic distance in your work never result in an indifference or an inability to clearly comment on the life around us. So I'd like to end today by citing the evocative, almost monosyllabic ending of your masterful dimeter poem "Bus Stop":

> *And lives go on.*
> *And lives go on*
> *Like sudden lights*
> *At street corners.*
>
> *Or like the lights*
> *In quiet rooms*
> *Left on for hours,*
> *Burning, burning.*

Thank you.

DONALD JUSTICE: Thank you, Bill.

DOUGLAS DUNN

The Cambridge Guide to Literature in English has described the Scotsman Douglas Dunn as "one of the most important of younger contemporary poets," and his 1985 reception of Great Britain's prestigious Whitbread Poetry Prize for his collection *Elegies* confirmed his position as one of Britain's foremost contemporary poets.

Douglas Dunn was born in Renfrewshire, Scotland. Trained as a librarian, he later studied English at the University of Hull in England where he also worked in the Brynmor Jones Library until 1971. Then, for a number of years, he worked as a free-lance writer, often writing for the BBC and various British journals, and occasionally taking writer-in-residence positions at universities such as the University of Hull, the University of New England (Australia), and the University of Dundee. In 1991, he became a professor in the School of English at the University of St. Andrews and Head of School in 1994. Since 1993, he has been the director of the St. Andrews Scottish Studies Institute.

His books of poetry include *Terry Street*, 1969; *Barbarians*, 1979; *St. Kilda's Parliament*, 1982; *Elegies*, 1985; *Selected Poems: 1964–1983*, 1986; *Northlight*, 1988; *New and Selected Poems*, 1989; and *Dante's Drum-kit*, 1993. He is also the editor of numerous books including *A Choice of Lord Byron's Verse*, 1974; *The Poetry of Scotland*, 1979; and *The Faber Book of Twentieth-Century Scottish Poetry*, 1992.

In addition to the Whitbread Prize, Douglas Dunn has also received the Somerset Maugham Award, the Geoffrey Faber Memorial Prize, the Hawthornden Prize, and several Scottish Arts Council Publication awards.

This interview was conducted at the School of English, St. Andrews University, in Fife, Scotland.

Since 1993, you've been the director of the Scottish Studies Institute at St. Andrews University where you're also the head of the English Department. What exactly is the Institute and does it offer a specific course of study?

DOUGLAS DUNN: We offer an interdisciplinary degree in Scottish studies focusing on Scottish history, Scottish art, and Scottish literature. Similar programs in other universities have a slightly different emphasis. In Edinburgh, for example, they're mainly interested in folklore, and so on.

So what's your emphasis at St. Andrews?

DOUGLAS DUNN: High culture, if you like, literature and art and history.

And how long does it take to complete the program?

DOUGLAS DUNN: Four years. It's a broad academic education. I should also mention that we publish a journal called *Scotlands* which is published by Edinburgh University Press.

Turning now to the Scottish poetry scene, I wonder how strong the influence of MacDiarmid remains on contemporary writers?

DOUGLAS DUNN: I'm not entirely sure, but I don't think MacDiarmid was ever a very specific influence on younger poets. He was certainly a very exceptional figure, and eccentric politically, but his real influence, I believe, was as a source of energy—as a general kind of example. But I don't think that the younger poets in Scotland—with one or two exceptions like W. N. Herbert—have been greatly affected by MacDiarmid's approach to poetry.

But didn't MacDiarmid encourage people to write in Scots and to think in certain nationalistic ways about being Scottish?

DOUGLAS DUNN: Oh, yes, he foregrounded his national identity in quite an original and most aggressive way. And that's part of this syndrome of energy which MacDiarmid generated for most of his life, and certainly he influenced several subsequent poets, like Sorley MacLean who writes in Gaelic. Interestingly enough, MacDiarmid himself, although he espoused the Gaelic cause, could neither write nor speak Gaelic. But most of the younger poets, even though they might have admired him as a major figure, found his politics extremely distasteful. This was a man who was a Bolshevik for ten years, then flirted, very briefly, with German Nazism, and then became a Stalinist Communist. Quite a difficult figure to swallow whole. In fact, it wasn't possible.

How about his contemporary Edwin Muir? Has he had much influence on contemporary poets?

DOUGLAS DUNN: Well, anyone interested in the poetry of Scotland would make a point of becoming familiar with the work of both MacDiarmid and Muir—who had their quite spectacular falling out in 1936 when Muir published his book *Scott and Scotland*. But I don't think Muir has been a very great influence either, except on the work of a number of poets worldwide who have a special interest in the religious and spiritual side of poetry. There's an old story related to Muir which I believe has a lot of truth in it. Sorley MacLean was digging his potato patch one day and a visitor was asking him lots of questions. And one of the questions was, "Sorley, what do you think of Edwin Muir?" And Sorley stopped digging and responded, "Ah, that was a wonderful poem that Edwin Muir wrote." And the interrogator said, "And which poem was that, Sorley?" And Sorley said, "Oh, just the same poem that he always wrote." And I think that's somewhat accurate. There definitely is a sameness about Edwin Muir's poetry, and I think that's what Seamus Heaney was attempting to describe in his essay on Muir.

Well, I can understand that notion of "sameness" in Muir's work, but I wonder how many good poems a poet has to write to deserve a certain stature. It seems to me that Muir has written a handful of exceptional poems.

DOUGLAS DUNN: I agree, and I think a poet really only has to write one.

Pound said, "Six lines can make you immortal."

DOUGLAS DUNN: Yes, but I'd go a bit farther than that. I'd say a whole poem. As for Muir, in summing up, I'd say that he's generally recognized as a major figure, and for many people he's a source of strength and energy. But overall I don't think his influence has been very widespread in Scotland, although he was very important to George Mackay Brown.

Turning to your own poetry now, I wonder if you could comment on the fact that you've never, as far as I know, chosen to write in Scots? And maybe you could also discuss the difference between Scots and Gaelic?

DOUGLAS DUNN: Gaelic is a separate language which the Scots call Gaelic, and the Irish, for political reasons, call Irish, which is a bit confusing. In Scotland we can't call it Scots because there's also an English-cognate language called Scots. This language is a form of English which developed in a different place, under different historical circumstances, and which reflects different linguistic influences. To make it even more confusing, Scots borrows a great deal from Gaelic, but true Scots is no longer a spoken language. What you hear in Scotland today is a very much diminished form of real Scots which has now become a literary language. I prefer to write in a living language.

In The Faber Book of Twentieth-Century Scottish Poetry, *an anthology you edited which Faber published in 1992, you included the work of a number of contemporary poets who still write in Scots. So you must think it's a worthwhile endeavor, even though you choose not to do it yourself?*

DOUGLAS DUNN: I think it's a worthwhile endeavor for people who've committed themselves to taking that chance—who have a belief in Scots as a working poetic idiom. But, I'm afraid, it doesn't work for me in poetry. In my fiction and my plays, however, I often have characters who speak in a contemporary form of Scots—which I speak as well. I grew up speaking that way, but I think a number of writers in Scotland who resisted that usage early on, later came to lament that fact and tried to go back to the language because they came to believe that it was somehow "truer" to them and their work. But I don't feel it's truer to me, so I exercise my right to make that decision. I'm very happy indeed to allow other people to go and do what they wish, as long as they don't bug me about it, but unfortunately some do. The Scots are a race of literary cannibals!

So there's still that pressure to be more "nationalistic"?

Douglas Dunn: That's right. It's as if a poem written in Scots somehow trumpets its nationality more clearly—or more significantly or vividly—than a poem written in English. But the cadences of my own language are already quite different from how speakers of English express themselves in England, or Wales, or Ireland. The Irish are much more relaxed about using English for their poetry than the Scots are, and I think the frustrated political scene in Scotland creates a pressure which, unfortunately, leads some Scottish writers, out of desperation, to become caricatures of themselves. But one of the heartening things of the last fifteen years or so is that this kind of cultural lack of confidence has been tremendously superseded by a number of successful, talented writers, such as the novelists Alasdair Gray, James Kelman, A. L. Kennedy and Janice Galloway—and a number of the poets as well.

Earlier, you were asking about the possible influence of MacDiarmid and Muir on younger Scottish poets, but I believe the greatest influences come from poets like the late Norman MacCaig, and Edwin Morgan, Iain Crichton Smith, and to a lesser extent, George Mackay Brown who also died earlier this year. These all remain extremely popular figures in Scotland, as are Liz Lochhead and Sorley MacLean. When a good poet in Scotland gets older—and many of them, thank God, have—they become rather popular figures. Someone was telling me just yesterday that Norman MacCaig gave a reading in Iberfeldy, and Iberfeldy is just about as big as its name suggests, and he had an audience of 200. So they must have come from all around to hear him read. Whenever Iain Crichton Smith or Sorley MacLean, for example, give poetry readings, they draw large audiences. So poetry is a very popular thing in Scotland, especially regarding the older poets.

You've already started to answer aspects of my next question about your opinion of the state of contemporary Scottish poetry. It sounds like a lively scene?

DOUGLAS DUNN: It's very lively, very lively indeed! I can remember what things were like in the early 1960's, and it was quite dismal, it really was. But now we have a whole group of interesting, productive young poets like Kathleen Jamie, Robert Crawford, W. N. Herbert, John Burnside, Don Paterson, and others. It's really a very encouraging situation, and, of course, it's very much the same in prose, both in the novel and the short story, with writers like Irvine Welsh, William McIlvanne, Allan Massie, Ronald Frame, and others. Sometimes, though, the map of literary reputations is distorted by politics and political frustration, but I'm sure that will knock itself out of the system in due course.

How do you feel that your earlier "exile" in Hull, England, and other places has affected your sense of Scottishness? Derek Walcott has remarked that the time he spends outside the Caribbean sharpens his perspective on his native land. Do you feel that this has happened to you as well?

DOUGLAS DUNN: Yes, I was based in Hull for seventeen years, a year of which I spent in France, and I came back to Dundee, Scotland, in 1981, after the death of my first wife. Since January 1984, I've been settled permanently in Fife. But for quite a long time before 1981, I'd wanted to come back to Scotland because I'd noticed that I was writing increasingly about Scottish things, and I thought that if one always does that from somewhere else, then it's possible for perspectives to become inaccurate and for perceptions to become out-of-date—and both of these pitfalls

I began to notice in my own work. So I found myself trying to get back to Scotland whenever I could just to get my proper bearings, and to hear the people actually speaking the language again. So my eventual return to Scotland was something I'd felt inclined to do by my work, but I was unable to do so earlier because my first wife had a career in Hull. She was the keeper of the art gallery there, and she liked her work very much. So it wasn't until several years after her death, when I had a girlfriend who really didn't care for Hull and wanted to live in Fife, that both factors—my work and my personal situation—encouraged my return to Scotland.

For just over a year, you lived in Akron, Ohio, working in the public library there. Did that experience affect your thinking or writing in any way?

DOUGLAS DUNN: Yes, at that time, I was working in the Akron Public Library, and I enjoyed myself very much indeed. It gave me an opportunity to read a great deal of literature which I might never have discovered otherwise. There were, I recall, two very significant anthologies published around that time that greatly affected me. One was Alvarez's *The New Poetry*, and even though I'd read some Lowell and Berryman before, it was really Alvarez's anthology that drew my attention to them. The other anthology was Donald Hall's *Contemporary American Poetry*, which was my first exposure to poets like Richard Wilbur, Louis Simpson, Anthony Hecht, Donald Justice, X. J. Kennedy, and a number of others. Also in Akron, I had a number of friends who were very interested in poetry, and that was my first real literary company. Earlier, I'd, of course, had writer-friends in Glasgow when I was in school there. One of them was Tom McGrath, and we organized various poetry readings and things like that, but the scene in Glasgow was too Beatniky, and there wasn't an awful lot of interesting work being done. But in Akron, I met quite a few people who were very serious about a wide range of writing, people like Liz O'Kane, Buck Cook, and his wife, Honorée Guilbeau. They all had remarkable collections of books, and they had many cultivated and interesting friends, many of whom were interested in literature. So that year in the States was very important to me in that I did a lot of reading and met a number of people who read books and liked discussing them.

DOUGLAS DUNN

Your first collection of poems, Terry Street, *was much praised for its "detailed observations of underprivileged lives" in a suburb of Hull. Many critics drew analogies between aspects of* Terry Street *and the work of Philip Larkin. And in your 1985 poem "December's Door," which was dedicated "in memoriam" to Larkin, you wrote "And now I can't repay the debt I owe." I wonder how well you knew Philip Larkin, and what, in particular, you feel your debt to him was?*

DOUGLAS DUNN: Well, it was a matter of friendship. I knew him quite well, and I liked him very much. He was very kind to me. It was Larkin who suggested that Faber and Faber should publish my first book, and he gave the book its title as well. So I owe him a lot. But now, if you look at his letters from around the time that my first book came out, you can see his remark on a reviewer's comment that I was "the best poet since Seamus Heaney." Larkin wrote that this was a bit like being described as the best Chancellor of the Exchequer since James Callaghan. So when I read that—along with many other things—I was quite upset.

Is it possible that he was just being clever—and that he might even have said it to you for a laugh?

DOUGLAS DUNN: I don't know. Anyone who knew Larkin and reads the letters—or Andrew Motion's biography for that matter—is obliged to draw the conclusion that Larkin was a different person with different friends and different correspondents. When I first read the letters, I was very shaken. First of all by revelations about his private life and opinions, some of which I knew a little bit about, but not much. Larkin was a very reticent individual, and people's private lives are people's private lives, and you just didn't pry. That's how I was brought up. I was raised to accept the fact that, okay, if you scratch hard enough, you'll find dirt. So don't scratch unless you really have to. I'd always held Larkin in very high esteem, and I was very fond of him as well, so when I read the letters I was greatly affected. When he referred to me as he did, I felt my sense of affection being undermined. But later, after I'd finished the book and had time to think it over, I realized that he was a different person to different friends, and that he really didn't think this was either insincere or dishonest. It was simply the nature of his personality. It took me a bit of time to accept that, but I think I'm right. I'd always enjoyed his company immensely, although we rarely spoke about poetry. He didn't like talking about poetry; at least, he didn't like talking about it to me.

But he must have liked your work, or he wouldn't have done what he did. That was quite a compliment.

DOUGLAS DUNN: Yes, it was. You know I still remember when my fourth book, *Barbarians,* was about to come out, and he asked me about it. He was a bit deaf, you know, so he'd crane over me, especially since I'm a bit of a mumbler—he once described me in one of the letters as that "short, bearded, mumbling Scotsman." So he asked, "What's it called?" And I said, *"Barbarians."* When he seemed concerned, I repeated the title louder, *"Barbarians. Barbarians."* "Oh, thank God," he finally said, "for a horrible moment I thought you said *Librarians.*" But that was pretty much the extent of our literary conversation. He did keep vaguely in touch with recent poetry through his involvement with the Poetry Book Society, and when I was working for him as the acquisitions librarian at the University of Hull, he gave me a special fund to fill any gaps we had in modern poetry and to make sure that we acquired all the interesting poetry coming out in English.

Nevertheless, Larkin's interest in contemporary poetry had begun to fade, and I now find this happening to myself. When you get to be about—I'm 53—when you get to this age, you're not quite as interested in new books as you once were. I used to be absolutely voracious. If I read a review and it seemed to suggest that this was an interesting poet, I'd hotfoot it down to the bookshop, but now I don't bother. If the book doesn't get sent to me, I probably won't read it. So I've tended to pull back a bit, which is one of the reasons I accepted the chair here at St. Andrews. I really do believe that poetry is an activity which young men and women take much more seriously than middle-aged men and women. But then, I've often noticed, the interest generally comes back in old age.

I remember Norman MacCaig saying much the same thing to me once. He really didn't hit his stride until his forties, and then for a period he didn't bother much about poetry at all. But later, in his seventies, his interest revived. I remember a few months before he died, when I told him about accepting the position here at St. Andrews, and he said, "Oh, that's a bad move, you'll never write another poem." And I told him that I'd noticed I'd begun repeating myself, and he understood. I always see a fair number of poets who are plugging away—determined to enhance their reputations—and then they start repeating themselves. There's no excitement in their work, and the poetry sometimes falls into unintentional self-parody. I once said to Larkin, "You haven't published a poem in ages. What's happening?" And he responded, "Well, you can't write a poem unless you have a poem to write. You get me a poem to write, and I'll write it." Now I know exactly what he meant. Something has to happen in your life. You have to see something, or something has to cross your mind that creates a compulsion to write. A lot of people fake it simply because they desire to see their names in the paper, but Larkin was right, you can only write a poem if you've got a poem to write.

J. M. Lyon has written of your own "Larkin-like strength as a poet" in which "the familiar and ordinary [is] realized and transmuted." This is high praise, and it applies not only to your early work, but to Elegies *and* Northlight *as well. One of countless examples from* Terry Street *is the end of "From the Night-Window" where the narrator is looking out his window at night watching the goings-on in the neighborhood:*

> *All windows open, this hot night,*
> *And the sleepless, smoking in the dark,*
> *Making small red lights at their mouths,*
> *Count the years of their marriages.*

Yet despite the success of Terry Street, *the poetic narrator of that collection— and the three books that followed it—is continually frustrated by the fact that he can't really "understand" the working class he worries about and pities. In "Young Women in Rollers," he claims, "I want to be touched by them, know their lives," but then he admits later that night, "I won't be there, I'll be reading books elsewhere." This theme is repeated in various poems in the first four collections, such as "The Hunched" of* The Happier Life, *"I Am a Cameraman" from* Love or Nothing, *and others. Given your own background, why is there this constant, frustrating alienation from the working class? Is it a result of education? Or the inadequacy of poetic expression? Or is it the result of the futility expressed in many of the poems like "Second-hand Clothes" from* St. Kilda's Parliament *which decides, "There's nothing to be done"?*

DOUGLAS DUNN: Well, I think it's a combination of things. Certainly the problem is something which someone from my kind of background is saddled with, simply because of the nature of British society—a society which imposes this kind of anxiety on you by encouraging you to feel guilty about your origins, about being who you are. British society is still relatively closed. It's definitely not as open as American society, for example. And so you can find yourself, as I have, worrying about trying to find the means for moving from one level to the next and also finding an accurate way of writing about it.

Your poem "Envoi," which you wrote for Terry Street *in 1981, concludes, "A curse on me I did not write with joy." It seems that you've decided that the collection is too pessimistic or, at least, unbalanced?*

DOUGLAS DUNN: That might have been a second thought. The retrospection that was bothering me at the time was about the two years that my first wife, Lesley, and I spent in Terry Street. They were two quite uncomfortable years endured for the sake of my getting an education. As it turned out, after a year in Terry Street, Lesley also went into higher education, to the College of Art in Hull. Earlier, when we'd come back from America, we looked at various apartments and couldn't find anything that suited us, so we bought a little house on Terry Street. But because we were students, and there weren't any other students living there, we often felt uncomfortable, and some of the people around us made us feel uncomfortable.

Your powerful 1985 collection, Elegies, *seems to mark a turn in your work in two ways that have been much discussed by critics: both a more formal poetry—accurately described by Blake Morrison as "sharp and measured," and a more intensely personal poetry, relating as it does to the 1981 death of your first wife, Lesley Balfour Dunn. Regarding the latter aspect of* Elegies, *critics have pointed out the reasonable analogies with Hardy and Tennyson. But I also feel that these are not just elegiac poems of grief, but lyric love poems as well, and I sense analogies with the Maud poems of Yeats, which were also about loss and love. So I wonder if Hardy, Tennyson, or Yeats occurred to you in your grief as you wrote those poems, or if you tried to remove yourself from thoughts of consciously writing in a specific tradition?*

DOUGLAS DUNN: Well, I certainly didn't set out to emulate either Hardy or Tennyson, but I knew all the classic poems of grief, such as Bishop King's tribute to his wife, and the poems by Donne and Milton and others. More recently, my friend Peter Porter had also been condemned to write a similar kind of poetry after the death of his first wife. So I made a point of rereading quite a lot of this kind of poetry after Lesley's death. When something like that happens to you, you do get a certain consolation from poems written by other people who've already experienced your own current difficulties. And I think it was that poetic consolation that made me less reticent about writing and publishing my own personal poems of loss because, perhaps someday, they might be of use to other people. I also believe that when something devastating like that happens to you, you'll eventually end up writing about it, and that if you suppress it or repress it, it's not going to do you any good. If a poet is what you are, and your work reflects your life, then it's inevitable. As I mentioned earlier, you can only write a poem if you've got a poem to write.

As for the poems themselves, my more recent collections had already included some fairly elaborate formal poems like "Green Breeks" and others. But in actually writing the poems in *Elegies*, I was always much more conscious of the melody than form. I usually discover the form of a poem, both the type and length of its stanza, simply by writing it. It's interesting that Larkin, who's generally considered a very traditional, formal poet, actually wrote very few sonnets. Only two or three, I believe.

And many of the stanzas he did use didn't come from the traditional stock. They were stanzas that he pretty well invented in the poems— discovering the stanzas as he wrote.

That's very common in the twentieth century.

DOUGLAS DUNN: I think it is. I've recently written a poem in one of Burns's well-known stanzas, but I find it generally goes against my grain to set out and say "I'm going to write this poem in this particular stanza. Or I'm going to write a sonnet, or I'm going to write a long poem in couplets."

So you let it happen on the page as you're writing?

DOUGLAS DUNN: Yes, I usually discover the form as I'm writing, and I usually move right along because I tend to be quick. One of the things that once crossed my mind—a critical insight perhaps—was that if you study the work of people like Chaucer, Shakespeare, Milton's *Paradise Lost*, Pope, Wordsworth, Shelley's long poems, Byron, Tennyson's long poems, and so on, you realize that these people must have written metrical verse just as quickly as you and I write memos.

Definitely.

DOUGLAS DUNN: I think this is one of the things which, in the twentieth century, has fallen into disuse: learning poetic technique so well that it becomes totally natural and, as a consequence, the poet will then compose rather quickly. So, these days, I generally set myself to writing poems as quickly as I can. This is very helpful since I have very little time, and there's always a strong possibility that I'm going to be interrupted before the poem is finished. So I think that I've developed an effective technique where I can write a poem, with both meter and rhyme, and it will happen quite quickly. And if it doesn't happen quickly, I stop and leave it alone—I walk away from it. Sometimes I might come back to the poem, but often I don't. So for the time being, I forget the false start, and maybe I'll give it another try in a week or so.

Or maybe abandon the idea entirely?

DOUGLAS DUNN: Yes, I've got a lot of unfinished poems that I don't think I'll ever finish. If a poem starts to disappoint me in the process of writing it, that disappointment is telling me something. And it's usually saying that the poem was a bad idea to begin with. This is something that young poets are very reluctant to believe. A young poet, almost by definition, is reluctant to believe or to accept the fact that the poem he's working on might be tosh.

Yes, and this idea, along with your earlier opinion about writing quickly— which was a common trait of the Renaissance courtier—certainly goes against the contemporary notion of the sweating, suffering writer/artist.

DOUGLAS DUNN: Well, I'm very suspicious of this idea of the young poet as a professional poet. Most of the best poets have been very busy people. Chaucer was a diplomat, Shakespeare was a man of the theater, Milton was a very productive civil servant, and Andrew Marvell was a member of parliament. It's in the nineteenth century, with Tennyson and Browning, where we start getting this notion of the professional poet. Do you know Edmund Wilson's essay from *The Triple Thinkers* called "Is Verse a Dying Technique?" He makes a very remarkable point, I think. He says that verse as a technique started to die in the nineteenth century with a poet like Matthew Arnold. Wilson claims that a lot of Arnold's poetry is just an organization of words used to set off a particularly poetic and beautiful phrase, and he claims that, in the modern period, this has become the diminished role of verse technique. A lot of it, he feels, isn't even poetry. After all, you can't be "poetic" all the time. I think it was Housman who said that. So I believe it's a very important essay, and if it's true, then it's also a bit worrying.

In the twentieth century, I believe it was Auden who understood this best and became the key figure in the effort to retrieve the traditional values of poetry. In the 1930's, under political pressure to make his poetry public, Auden revived stanzaic metrical poetry in a way that was vastly more modern than Thomas Hardy. Hardy was a wonderful poet, but even in the 1910's when he was writing his great poetry under the pressures of grief and guilt, he was, I think, creating melodies that were archaic. There's a kind of anachronism about Hardy's music, which is part of its beauty. But the language is not modern, and the cadences are not modern. They're very lovely, but when you read them, it's almost as if you're reading poems that were written in the 1860's. But Auden's poems, even though he revived meter and form, were very modern and very contemporary.

Yes, and it seems that Elegies *is very much in that tradition. Your previous collections, as you've already mentioned, had a number of poems in various forms, but* Elegies *contains an amazing variety of verse forms in regular metric—sonnets, blank verse, quatrains, couplets, and even terza rima in "Land Love." Was this just a natural development from the earlier formal work, or did the formality of rhyme and meter offer some kind of distance and/or control over the intensely personal subject of the poems?*

DOUGLAS DUNN: I think it was a way of trying to make sense of things, of trying to make sense of difficult experiences. Writing metrical poetry keeps us simultaneously aware of the technical aspects while also obliging us to examine and re-examine our sentiments and thoughts and feelings. And that's very important.

How about translation? In 1990, you published a version of Racine's Andromache. *Do you continue to do more translations, and has it had much effect on your own poetry?*

DOUGLAS DUNN: Actually, I translated Racine's *Andromache* mainly because I was asked to do it. At the time, I was still a freelance writer, and I was commissioned to do the play for Radio 3, so there was money involved. I've always loved Racine's classic French alexandrines, and I've always been interested in the contemporary verse plays of Christopher Fry, Archibald MacLeish, Tony Harrison, and others. For *Andromache,* I didn't translate the play into alexandrines. French verse isn't accentual; it's syllabic, and I think our iambic pentameter is the best equivalent. That's the classic English line, and the alexandrine is the classic French line, so I translated from the one classic line into the other, keeping the rhyming couplets. So it was a great technical challenge, and my intention was also to do a translation that was faithful—with no great departures from the original.

Another major problem was the diction. The entire vocabulary of Racine's play is something like 700 words, which is very small, especially when compared with English vocabularies. It seems Racine's overall vocabulary was about 1,000 words, whereas Shakespeare's is around 27,000, so the difference between the English language and the French language is huge. The French notions of clarity and lucidity don't really exist in English, which tends to metaphor. So the great challenge—not just technically in the sense of keeping the iambic line going for longer than I'd ever done before—was trying to avoid English metaphor and figurative language.

It was a bloody hard piece of work to finish, and it took me three months of doing nothing else, and I think it was universally agreed that I didn't fully succeed. I really do have, if I say so myself, pertinacity. I can persevere and stick to a job, working 10–15 hours a day, seven days a week. So I worked and I worked and I worked. Usually I got 10–20 lines in a day, and I can still remember the euphoria of once getting 50 lines done in a single day. Overall, it was a very hard task, and I think the element of slog probably comes across in the text. I feel there's a sense of the midnight oil being burned over the page. Nevertheless, I enjoyed it very much, even though I couldn't quite get the actors to perform it in the way I had in mind—in the classic French acting mode which is very majestic and courtly. But actors in Britain, of course, are trained in classic English drama, and that's the kind of acting they brought to it. Elizabethan and Jacobean theater produces a drama that moves outward. It's externalized, but French drama is very internalized, very psychological and very intense. But regardless of that, I truly enjoyed it. I've also translated *Tartuffe* by Molière, but it's never been published, and it's never been performed.

My school just did the Richard Wilbur version.

DOUGLAS DUNN: Oh, Wilbur's a wonderful translator.

Yes, he is. Now I'd like to move from translation to teaching and ask what kinds of things you believe can be done for aspiring writers in a classroom situation.

DOUGLAS DUNN: First I should mention that, being an ancient university, we don't have an undergraduate degree in creative writing at St. Andrews University. What we do have, though, is a one-year postgraduate program for the M. Litt. degree. In the poetry class, I introduce the students to the standard varieties of form and meter. They have to write a sonnet, for example. But I don't think that you can really teach the creative side of poetry. You either have that or you don't. But you can teach people meter, the technical side of poetry. At least, you can make them aware of it, so that they'll know what it is, and then encourage them to try to use it.

One characteristic of your own work, even in some of the lighter verse, is your use of the list, often composed of detailed descriptions or observations. How do you know when to stop such lists? Is it something you've consciously thought about?

DOUGLAS DUNN: I don't think so. I do like poems, as much as possible, to have concrete things in them, and I'd rather have a poem that was packed than one that was empty. Beyond that, I don't know. I'm sure that there must be some sort of intuitive discretion exercised in how long a list should be. In contemporary times, it's amazing the number of writers who do, in fact, make lists, and very often they associate like with unlike in the same list. I believe that a list could become quite tedious— well, any writing can—if it doesn't have a little element of surprise for the reader. That's the challenge.

Looking back over your first nine books, I wonder what kinds of changes you see in your own work? Would it be fair to say that your poetry is now, for example, more rural, more Scottish, less indignant, more personal, and maybe even more metaphysical? I realize that's quite a lot to ask in a single question.

DOUGLAS DUNN: Well, I'm quite heartened by what you're suggesting. It might mean, among other things, that I've mellowed a bit. It's certainly true that my poetry from *Elegies* onwards has been exercised by a more spiritual perception. I grew up in a part of Scotland that was still rural when I was a child, but because of the circumstances of my first book, there wasn't much of an opportunity to write about that life. I was no longer living in Scotland, and for some reason, that life was put to one side. But that's one of the things that's come back to me since I've come to live in Fife.

What projects are you currently working on?

DOUGLAS DUNN: I'm editing a selection of Robert Louis Stevenson's shorter fiction for Penguin Books, and that's just about finished. I'm also gathering together a collection of my essays and lectures. In the past, I've been very timid about publishing my criticism, but I've finally decided to publish the stuff. I'm also editing *The Oxford Book of Love Poetry*, but the book's seven years late. I've been doing it for a very long time!

English love poetry?

DOUGLAS DUNN: The whole world—as long as I can get good translations. The text will be in English. So perhaps I've bitten off more than I can chew, but I hope to get it finished next year. I'm also writing a book called *A Literary Guide to Scotland* that's in danger of being late as well. And I write a poem whenever I have a poem to write. I've also started writing a novel, which is one of the perverse things I do sometimes when I have so many other things to do and absolutely no time on my hands, so I start writing something new. It's a kind of mischievous behavior, I guess. So that's what I'm up to right now.

Well, I hope you'll have some more poems that need to be written. You've already—I hope you don't mind my saying so—written some of the most affecting lyrics of our contemporary times, and I'd like to end things up today by reading these beautiful last lines from "At Cruggleton Castle":

> *Good minutes make good days. Good days make years.*
> *A breeze dried on my lips; the Solway slapped*
> *Against the cliffs of Cruggleton.*
> *Wind in her hair, the wind composing her;*
> *The wind entangled in her summer dress*
> *Flew from her over the land, womanly.*
> *Doves in a kirkyard slumbered on the stones.*
> *That dusk was pure, pictorial, painterly,*
> *An innocence, a loss, a life away.*

Thank you.

Douglas Dunn: Thank you.

ROBERT CONQUEST

The distinguished poet and historian Robert Conquest was born in Great Malvern, Worcestershire, England. He studied at the University of Grenoble and later graduated from Magdalen College, Oxford. During World War II, he served in the Oxfordshire and Buckinghamshire Light Infantry, and, after the war, he was a member of H. M. Foreign Service, serving as a diplomat in Bulgaria and later as first secretary at the United Kingdom delegation to the United Nations. Since that time, he has worked at many universities including the London School of Economics, the University of Buffalo, and Columbia University. Since 1981, he has been a Research Fellow at the Hoover Institution at Stanford University.

In 1956, Robert Conquest was the editor of *New Lines*, an important and influential British anthology that included, along with his own work, poems by Philip Larkin, Elizabeth Jennings, Donald Davie, Thom Gunn, Kingsley Amis, and others. *New Lines* launched the literary movement later termed the "Movement," and *New Lines II* was published in 1963. His own collections of poetry include *Poems*, 1955; *Between Mars and Venus*, 1962; *Arias from a Love Opera*, 1969; *Casualty Ward*, 1974; *Forays*, 1979; and *New and Collected Poems*, 1986. He has also translated *Prussian Nights*, a long poem by Alexander Solzhenitsyn, 1977; served as Literary Editor at *The Spectator*; published a collection of literary essays, *The Abomination of Moab*, 1979; written two novels, the second in collaboration with Kingsley Amis entitled *The Egyptologists*, 1966; and edited numerous anthologies.

Aside from his literary work, Robert Conquest is also one of the world's most distinguished Soviet historians and the premier authority on Joseph Stalin. In addition to Conquest's two historical classics,

The Great Terror: Stalin's Purge of the Thirties, 1968, and *The Harvest of Sorrow: Soviet Collectivization and the Terror-Famine*, 1986, his other important histories include *Power and Policy in the U.S.S.R.: The Study of Soviet Dynastics*, 1961; *Kolyma: The Arctic Death Camps*, 1978; and *Stalin: Breaker of Nations*, 1991.

This interview was conducted at the Hoover Institution, Stanford University.

The literary critic John Press has described you as a "man of affairs who is also a man of letters." Given your two vocations as a poet and a professional historian, I wonder what course of study you pursued at the University of Grenoble and Oxford?

ROBERT CONQUEST: Well, actually, at Grenoble, I didn't study at all. I was there for about six months, and I don't think anybody who goes to a foreign university without needing to pass the exam does a stroke of work. I only went to the lectures to meet girls. Later at Oxford, I read "Modern Greats"—politics, philosophy, and economics—and eventually got a good second degree in them. But it's a typical mistaken set of studies because if you understand economics then you can't understand philosophy and vice versa! So getting any sort of degree in all three together isn't easy. Recently, I re-discovered the economics book I used for my exam at Oxford, and it wasn't really, as I seemed to remember it, called *Economics for the Half-witted Child*, it was actually called *Economics for the General Reader*. And I remember that, back then, we covered the book in five days of cramming because we thought the war was going to break out at any moment. But it came a bit later.

Did you come away from Oxford with a broad background?

ROBERT CONQUEST: I don't know. Well, I often get asked, "Did you do a lot of work at Oxford?" and I say, "Well, I did very little, just my two essays a week." "Then you must have played a lot of games?" "No, I didn't play any games." "Then you must have belonged to a lot of societies?" "No, I didn't do very much of that at all." "Well, why didn't you do anything?" "Because I was much too busy!" Undergraduate life was more than enough to cope with.

Then the war changed all that?

ROBERT CONQUEST: Yes, it did.

During World War II, you served in the Oxfordshire and Buckinghamshire Light Infantry, and then, after the war, you served in H. M. Foreign Service in Sofia. Is it true that you witnessed first-hand the Soviet takeover of Bulgaria by the Communists?

ROBERT CONQUEST: Yes, that's what it amounted to. And very unpleasant it was, too.

Was this the primary impetus for your later scholarly writings dealing with Soviet and Eastern-block history?

ROBERT CONQUEST: Well, before the war, in Paris, I'd known some Bulgarian students; then later in the army when I was serving as adjutant, a request came through saying they wanted officers to learn the following languages, "urgent." So I put my name in. Nobody wanted Bulgarian, so I put it down, and I was selected. Then, I remember, my Colonel shouted, "What's all this about your going on a four month course?" and I said, "You remember, sir, you signed the papers yourself." Soon I was learning Bulgarian, and I was flown into Bulgaria. At the time, I didn't know any Russian at all, no Slav language apart from Bulgarian. Then later, I was with the British legation in Sofia. Subsequently, back in the Foreign Office, where I was working in one of the research departments, I discovered that no one there was interested in the Russian side very much. So I got interested myself. It was rather indirect, and my Russian is still sometimes lousy. I mean I can manage it, but my grammar's still pretty poor.

Then in 1956, back in England, you edited the New Lines *poetry anthology which is still generally considered to be the most important British anthology in the second half of the twentieth century. Your introduction to the book, taken as a manifesto by some readers, expressed a revulsion from the loose, lush, overly-emotional and sometimes grandly rhetorical writings of the late forties and early fifties. Which writers did you have in mind? The New Apocalypse group? Or some of the more excessive work of Dylan Thomas?*

ROBERT CONQUEST: Yes, the New Apocalypse and some of Dylan Thomas' worst effects. Although I always admired Thomas at his best, which is more than Kingsley Amis did. But generally, *New Lines* challenged a sort of sloppy feeling and sloppy thinking in contemporary poetry. And it wasn't only the sloppiness of emotion, it was the whole thing. Of course, in the end, it does little good writing up a great manifesto and working against such things because they keep on coming back no matter what you do. Decade after decade. But regardless, as you say, the preface was taken as a manifesto. I remember that Philip Larkin thought it was too tough, and Kingsley Amis thought it wasn't tough enough. So in the balance, it seemed just about right. It certainly caused a lot of upsets back then, and it got a lot of abuse.

Which seems strange now because New Lines *called for a balanced approach to poetry—where both passion and the intellect were equally at work. "In the 1940s," you wrote in the preface, "the mistake was made of giving the Id . . . too much of a say in the doings of the orchestra as a whole." At the same time, you also warned against the equally dangerous excesses of an overly dry intellectual verse—as often produced by the neo-Empsonians—and you insisted that "an intellectual skeleton is not worth much unless it is given the flesh of humanity, irony, passion or sanity." Why was such a reasonable, balanced approach to poetry so controversial?*

ROBERT CONQUEST: Well, as always, people had a sort of investment in what was going on. In general, people get used to anything, and they were used to a rather low level of stuff, in my opinion. Curiously enough, the original draft of the preface to *New Lines* actually contained a paragraph attacking the Movement because the term "Movement" we then understood to be the Empsonians. The word "Movement" which was later applied to the *New Lines* poets was a complete import; it wasn't anything to do with us. As Thom Gunn said, there really never was a "Movement." We were just a group of serious writers who all had similar views in the broad sense. We were quite diverse really, and it's important to remember that *New Lines* had plenty of rhetoric and even some rather heavily romantic stuff, like Enright's. I think the term "Movement" was originally used in *The Spectator* referring to a large group of various people, some of whom were prose writers, playwrights, you name it. It was like the "Angry Young Men" idea. Something like that.

Yes, but despite the diversity of the New Lines *poets, the preface took some very definite stands. For example, you cited the group's refusal "to abandon a rational structure and comprehensible language," you took issue with the cavalier rejection of rhyme and meter, and you cited W. H. Auden as an influence. Yet, regarding Auden, you specified that his influence was "mainly a matter of technical influence," but looking back, it seems that Auden was a far greater influence on your own work—and that of Larkin and the earlier Davie—then you realized at the time?*

ROBERT CONQUEST: I think you're right. Perhaps less, in some ways, on Larkin, but yes, I think it was more powerful than we suggested there. But in the preface, I was stressing the formal side because, after all, it was really Auden who brought back the formality that had been destroyed by Pound and others. Although, of course, even *New Lines* was not all formalist since, as you know, Enright's verse is rather loose. But the contemporary abandonment of all techniques and structures had gone too far. Not that it hasn't gotten much worse of late.

In the wake of the New Lines *anthology, Larkin was wary of being associated with a literary "Movement," but Donald Davie's books on syntax and diction,* Articulate Energy *and* The Purity of Diction in English Verse, *seem to have been self-consciously written as "Movement" documents. Nevertheless, it was Davie who was eventually "Americanized," and Larkin who always seemed to maintain an allegiance to the general principles which you described in the introduction. Is that a fair assessment?*

ROBERT CONQUEST: Yes, I think it is. Donald was always very scholastically minded, as you know, and at that time his verse was almost all in rather strict, sort of, eighteenth century forms. Then he started experimenting, and he did bits of free verse. Eventually, I think he rather deplored Larkin's view of producing a "whole" poem since Donald had gone back to the bits and pieces theory.

Which is very curious because Davie came down very hard on Pound early, especially in Articulate Energy, *and then made some kind of pact with him later.*

ROBERT CONQUEST: Yes, he became a Poundian. Donald had a very curious mind, and I knew him quite well—I even lived with him here at Stanford for about a year—but I don't think he's comparable to Larkin for quality. Philip was an extraordinarily careful writer. Most poets, including most of the English poets, dashed off their odes or whatever very quickly—after all, half to three-quarters of Coleridge is a lot of nonsense. But Philip, although not every poem he ever wrote was first-rate, really worked at his craft with the greatest care. He was one of the most careful artists—artificers—I ever came across. Where does Yeats say, "A line will take us hours"?

"Adam's Curse."

ROBERT CONQUEST: Yes. And that was Philip. But he also had the ability to create a slightly overt awkwardness when he wanted to. Whenever he felt a line was too smooth, he could put in that awkwardness—a very artful awkwardness—for modulation.

Yes, and it's very effective throughout his work. In the larger sense, however, one of the most common charges against Larkin and the Movement poets in general was that their work was too restrained. Charles Tomlinson talked about an emotional "suffocation," and Donald Davie seemed to take the accusation quite seriously. But the work itself clearly proved the charge baseless, and, in your own poetry, for example, one of the primary themes is a love that's both romantic and sensuous. But how did you all feel about the charge at the time? It certainly affected Donald Davie quite a bit; he even wrote poems about his own restraint and the critics' charges.

ROBERT CONQUEST: Yes, I think Donald was extraordinarily self-conscious. He was always fearing that he wasn't getting enough intellect or enough emotion into his poems, but once you start doing that, once you start categorizing things, it hurts the work. I believe there was always a Donald Davie figure standing behind his back saying, "Not that, Donald, not that." But some of his poetry is really quite soft, and it gets ridiculous, as you say, to talk about the *New Lines* poetry being dry and restrained. Thom Gunn was extremely rhetorical.

Did the charge bother you at all?

ROBERT CONQUEST: No, not really. I didn't take it seriously.

One of the greatest influences on your own aesthetic thinking seems to have been George Orwell who was cited in the introduction for "his principle of real, rather than ideological, honesty." In a later poetic tribute titled "George Orwell," you wrote:

> *We die of words. For touchstones he restored*
> *The real person, real event or thing . . .*

Could you discuss this in terms of the Movement and your own poetry?

ROBERT CONQUEST: Well, it's rather hard to say more than just that. Orwell represented honesty more than anything else. That doesn't mean that he didn't sometimes make some rather foolish remarks, or that people, whatever their principles are, don't lapse sometimes. But I'm not really quite sure how this affects the poetry beyond the desire to be honest and true. In one of the essays in my book of criticism, *The Abomination of Moab*, I quote Gibbon, of all people, who said of the late silver age poet Claudian that he "does not satisfy or silence our reason." That seems a frightfully good account of what the poet should do, either satisfy or silence our reason. Or both, but that's a difficult combination and getting it right isn't easy. It's not much good writing a purely rational poem—if only because form and sound, as you know, are not working at the merely rational level. I think Housman says somewhere that these things appeal to something more primitive in our nature like the patches of swamp sometimes found in the neighborhood of Cambridge. So even though the Orwell virtues are great ones, they certainly don't cover the whole scale of poetic virtues.

In your own poetry, the power of love and the desire for love is a constant theme, and this preoccupation is portrayed in many different ways, but most often as a catalyst to this concept of truth and to the related creation of art. For example, in the poem "Susquehanna," the narrator observes two young women, one sunbathing and one running up the beach, and tries to absorb the powerful reality of the scene into the poem, concluding, "Come, / More passionate for accuracy, / And grip that vision, poem." And the ending of "Address to an Undergraduate Society" is even more sweeping:

> *Art in a crystal air, an essence of*
> *(Let's not be too complicated)—love.*

Could you discuss the idea that love is fundamental to so much art?

ROBERT CONQUEST: Well, certainly, we can all envision an art which doesn't involve sexual love, the Eros. The whole realm of satire, for example, which I've done a fair amount of, usually under pseudonyms. But my feeling's always been that Eros is a major force in the human being and intimately linked with the appreciation of "beauty." That's sort of hard to develop in poetry because even though you feel something very strongly, that doesn't mean you can write about it. I mean you can try, but it often doesn't come off. And I think there are quite a few bits that I should have cut from my own work. Maybe three-quarters of it.

For what reason?

ROBERT CONQUEST: Well, for not getting it right. It's very difficult to specify why something seems to have failed. I don't believe in any preconceived method of judging poetry really. Just put it in a drawer for ten years, and then see if it still works.

Beyond this difficult theme of love, your poems have a remarkable range, dealing with many topics such as special landscapes, music, painting, poets, war, and academia. The last is most devastatingly portrayed in "A Grouchy Good Night to the Academic Year," but it's also referred to in a number of other poems such as "Walk That Way" which comments:

> *While in their Departments, trying to explain,*
> *They deconstruct the love and the pain*
> *Into some sodding great thesis."*

Given that so much of academia has been taken over by "theorists," do you have much hope for the future, or will we be seeing more of "the buzz-sawed-up brains of the young"?

ROBERT CONQUEST: "Academic Year," curiously enough, was first published in the *Times* Higher Educational Supplement, though they did cut a verse or so. Nowadays, I don't have much to do with the academic side of literature. But a while back, I attended—with my wife who's an English teacher—an MLA Convention in San Francisco, and I saw all these academics and what they were doing. It was terrible. They looked like—well, they were scurrying around like beetles in some Sartrean Hell. And they looked as if they knew they were doing something perfectly useless and nasty. Maybe I should write a poem about it.

Do you think we'll be able to get back to more serious scholarship? Especially since so many of these people have now seized power, as you saw at the MLA Convention?

ROBERT CONQUEST: I don't know, but I do know it isn't just literature. It's true in history and politics and so on. I think what happens is that a group of these people forms in a department, and once they've got 20% or 25% of the vote, they can more or less manipulate things. It's certainly a blight on the landscape, and I think the only thing one can do is just say, as frequently as possible, "This is a lot of nonsense." There's no point in arguing. There's a wonderful description in Nadezhda Mandelshtam's book about how her husband, the poet, had a Marxist friend who could only argue at a Marxist level. So every time they argued, her husband's arguments and thought got lower and lower until they were *both* talking a lot of nonsense.

Do you expect to see some new literary trends that might somehow revive the current situation?

ROBERT CONQUEST: I'm not sure, but it's happening in other fields. There's a younger generation in both history and politics which is much better than the intermediate generation. Then you also find some people who have been on the bad extreme of things who still have, to some extent, elements of common sense and who eventually drift back to a more reasonable position. I've come across quite a lot of that, I'm glad to say. Even those people who'll tell you, "No, no, I favor the far out position," even they're pushed to a more moderate stance because the extremists get worse and worse, and it comes to a point where no one can stand it. Nevertheless, it does mean for the younger faculty that they'll be, unfortunately, fighting all the time. I know one guy, an Englishman, a professor of German at one of the worst universities, and his method is to always go to the newspapers. He never argues in the department; he just gives interviews. He'll call up the newspapers and say, "Do you know what's going on over here? Do you know what they're doing now?" This, of course, horrifies the university leadership, the faculty, the donors, and so on, much more than anything else he could do. And, of course, if he'd fought it out in his department, he wouldn't have accomplished anything. Maybe he'll start a trend.

Let's hope so. Now I'd like to get back to your own poetry, especially your interest in "light" verse. Over the years, you've written quite a bit of humorous verse, and you even published a number of limericks under the pseudonym Victor Gray in The New Oxford Book of Light Verse. *At one time, you were planning a collection of your humorous verse. Are you still working on it?*

ROBERT CONQUEST: Well, I've recently completed a collection on a single theme, almost entirely in common meter, which I'm thinking of publishing. I sent it to Vernon Scannell whom I saw in London the other day, and he said that his girlfriend thought it was sexist. And I said, "Well, my wife doesn't." Then I showed it to my wife again, and she said, "Hey, I think she's right!" So I have to do some of it over. But it's not really very sexist; it's more "blokeish," if you know what I mean.

Is it a long poem?

ROBERT CONQUEST: It's about thirty short poems.

Each titled separately?

ROBERT CONQUEST: Yes. They all have "Fred" in the title: "Fred and Fifi," "Fred Fails," "Good for Fred," "Fred Faraday, Philosopher," titles like that. So far, as with all my other work, I've only had time to publish a few.

Well, aside from your poetry—both light and serious, you're also a renowned historian and the world's foremost authority on Soviet history. Your classic study The Great Terror *(Macmillan 1968, revised Penguin 1990) exposed the Stalinist purges to a complacent West, and, in the words of* The New York Times, *is still "the definitive compilation of the horrors of Stalin's purges of 1936–38." Your more recent book* The Harvest of Sorrow *(Oxford 1986) revealed the murderous extent of Soviet collectivization, the "liquidation" of the Kulaks, and the state-created famine that led to over ten million deaths. John Gross of* The New York Times *wrote that this meticulously researched book is "indispensable reading for anyone who wants to understand the shaping—and misshaping—of the modern world." How much resistance did you encounter in the West from an academia and media that was often sympathetic to the Soviet version of their sordid history?*

ROBERT CONQUEST: Surprisingly, not as much as you'd expect, at least not when I wrote *The Great Terror*, which was back in the 1960's. It was well reviewed by both the left and the right, in the *Tribune* and everywhere else. But by the time of *The Harvest of Sorrow* in 1985, a new lot of semi-pro-Stalinists had emerged. The book was generally well reviewed, but there were two or three hostile reviews from academia, arguing, well, not really arguing very much, but saying that I was relying on émigré material. Well, as there wasn't anything else at that time, I was naturally using émigré material. As it turned out, within three years, identical stories were being published in the Russian press by people who'd stayed behind. So much for that criticism. Unfortunately, there were still a handful of people in Russian historical departments in the West who maintained that Stalin only killed a few thousand people. Later, they had to up the number to 30,000. Now they're up around 600,000. But 600,000, even though the real number is much higher—in the millions—is quite a lot of people. It's the kind of academic thing that happens everywhere including English departments. Some guy makes a "career" by saying something absolutely contrary to the facts and common sense. And they still get jobs and tenure, and often they pervade the professional journals. But you don't see them very much in, say, *The New York Review of Books*. The big journals—*The Times Literary Supplement* too, for example—these sorts of journals are in many ways far better than the so-called professional journals.

Now that the Soviet Union no longer exists and complete vindication has come for those two books and your many other scholarly works on Soviet history, I understand that you have a wide readership in contemporary Russia, Ukraine, and the other parts of the former Soviet Union and the Eastern Block?

ROBERT CONQUEST: Well, of course I originally wrote *The Great Terror* for a western audience, and it never occurred to me that it would ever be published in Russia. But they did a Russian émigré edition, and I've never met a Russian who hasn't read it. And I'm talking about 10 years ago, before the fall. After that, it was published in a million copies in 1990 in a serialization for a Soviet magazine.

A million copies! How many issues did it take?

ROBERT CONQUEST: About ten, something like that. And this happened to the other books as well—sections of all of them were printed in the main journals. Before its fall, I knew, like Orwell, that the Soviet Union couldn't last. Orwell said that it will either democratize or perish. Now I didn't know *how* it would happen, but I was certain that it would. It couldn't have gone on any longer. It just wasn't viable.

Despite your lifetime interest in historical matters, your poetry only occasionally deals with such subjects. Is that due to a concern about "political" poetry in general, or is it personal taste, or is it something else?

ROBERT CONQUEST: Well, I think there's very little good political poetry in English, apart from "An Horatian Ode." Most English poets have written political poetry, and most of it is forgotten. Look at all the people who wrote poetry about slavery in the 1800's. As a leading historian of slavery points out, most of it was "drivel." It wasn't something they could really engage themselves in. The only political poetry I've attempted has been satire, and not much of it was about Russia. Maybe two. It's very difficult to do. I can think of very little good non-satirical, political poetry these days, and, of course, there's very little good satire these days, period. Like the lyric as well. Lyric and satire seemed to have faded away.

One project that managed to combine your two vocations was your 1977 translation of Alexander Solzhenitsyn's Prussian Nights *for Farrar Straus. How did it come about?*

ROBERT CONQUEST: Well, it happened when I first met Solzhenitsyn in Zurich soon after he came out.

Did he know your work before he got out?

ROBERT CONQUEST: Yes, he did, and when I inscribed one of my books to him, he said, "I wonder if you could translate a little poem of mine?" So I said, "Sure." And the next thing I knew I was stuck with 1200 lines, or whatever it was. It was hard going. But it began moving pretty well once I got into it. It had many lyrical passages, but it was in a sort of thrusting ballad meter, and it pulled itself along.

That comes through in the translation, and you used a lot of trochaic openings on the lines to give it that forward movement. Did you get much feedback from Solzhenitsyn?

ROBERT CONQUEST: Well, naturally I sent drafts to him and to his friend Alexis Klimoff. Solzhenitsyn checked through it, helped me with some things I didn't understand, and it all worked out well.

You've received many honors for your poetry in England, and, just last week, the American Academy of Arts and Letters awarded you the Michael Braude Prize for Light Verse. Nevertheless, do you feel that John Press is correct when he suggests that your "reputation as a historian of the Soviet Union has overshadowed [your] poetic achievement"?

ROBERT CONQUEST: Yes, that's true, but there's not much I can do about it. It's also true that I wish I had more time to write more poetry, but it's hard to find enough time. I'm currently writing a large, general book on what went wrong with the twentieth century, as I see it, and it takes up a great deal of my time. What I'd like to do when it's done is to work on a sort of autobiography and finish some light verse projects and some "heavy" verse projects. One light verse one is a sort of a neo-Hudibras. In fact, the main character's called Hugh D. Brass, and he's a rather trendy American academic.

Do you make an effort to set aside a specific time for your poetry?

ROBERT CONQUEST: Not on a regular basis. I often find myself composing verse on airplanes, and I'm usually working on bits of drafts of about four or so poems. It takes years sometimes.

How do you come to determine the specific forms of your poems? While you're writing them? Or are they formulated beforehand?

ROBERT CONQUEST: Well, this is an important question which applies to everybody who writes poetry, and I've done both. For example, most of my light verse is in strict meter, so I know what I'm going to do.

But ordinarily, with more serious verse, I'll get a line, or a couple of lines, or a notion, and then it'll generate another line, and so on. So I don't necessarily know what's going to happen until I've got five or six inchoate lines in mind. Then it suddenly seems to determine itself. So I continue to work on it, and if it doesn't work out, I junk it.

Do you ever write whole poems in your head, like some poets do?

ROBERT CONQUEST: Not really. Only a few lines at a time. I prefer to work on the page, although it often gets out of hand in about half an hour, and the page is covered with illegible scrawl.

In 1979, in your controversial Memorial Lecture to the Annual General Meeting of the Royal Society of Literature, "But What Good Came of It at Last: An Inquest on Modernism," you suggested that a fundamental aspect of Modernism was that "the artist took the decision to abandon the laity" and to insist on an "almost total independence from an audience." Even now, this situation continues. Do you see any way that poetry can retrieve some of its lost general audience, or are poets to be left continually writing for themselves?

ROBERT CONQUEST: Actually, I think the old problem when the poets ignored the laity has given way to a situation where they now bash the laity on the head. The public has been sort of buffaloed, and, of course, as you know, we now have arts establishments which encourage ridiculous excesses. I imagine one could create a book of modern verse with condoms attached to the pages and called "poems."

It's probably been done. You'd probably be accused of plagiarism.

ROBERT CONQUEST: I'm afraid so. But, on the other hand, I don't think bad poetry in this century ever really sold enormous numbers of copies.

But in the first half of the century, the general public knew about Robert Frost and Edward Arlington Robinson, and many had read Edna St. Vincent Millay's poems as well, but it's not really like that anymore.

ROBERT CONQUEST: That's right. Unfortunately, the good poets here in America are not known by the general public, and they get very little publicity, unlike, say, Ginsberg, who had very little going for him, or Ferlinghetti, who has nothing going for him. Did you know they're trying to name a street after him in San Francisco?

No, I didn't.

ROBERT CONQUEST: Yes, sadly enough. The public's been cut off from the talented poets who are really doing the quality work, and this is true in the other arts as well. And then there's the problem of proliferation. I recently saw a review in the *San Francisco Chronicle*, and it said of the reviewer, "Mr. So-and-so is one of the leading Bolinas Bay poets." Bolinas Bay—how big can that be? Ten thousand people?

Probably all ten thousand are poets.

ROBERT CONQUEST: I wouldn't be surprised. Can you imagine the number of poets there must be in this country!

A century ago, Yeats thought there were too many poets at the Rhymers' Club.

ROBERT CONQUEST: Yes, a dozen or so.

Let's take a moment to talk about Yeats, whom you recognized in the New Lines *preface "as the great poet of the century." In your opinion, how did Yeats—and maybe Frost as well—resist the traps of modernism represented by Pound and others?*

ROBERT CONQUEST: Well, Yeats, in his own way, sort of out-flanked them, didn't he?

Well, he was already established by 1909.

ROBERT CONQUEST: Yes, but even later, he sort of preempted modernism on his own. He sounded even more modern than Pound, in fact. Pound was full of "thous" and "wouldsts," even though he had that air of, "Don't trifle with me, I know more than you do."

Speaking of Pound, during the Royal Society lecture, you said "that one of the notoriously bad effects of 'free' verse is that large numbers of people educated during the last half century no longer understand the structure of real verse." Do you feel that any progress has been made on this front?

ROBERT CONQUEST: Well, I don't really know how much they're instructed in the schools these days, but judging by some of the leading magazines, it can't be much. Someone once said that American poets no longer see the need for meter and rhyme. Geoffrey Grigson commented that if that's the case, then American poets aren't poets in any sense known to civilization for the past three thousand years. They come and go, all these non-structured poets. They disappear. But it's not only free verse; it's the lack of anything interesting in so much of the poetry. Nevertheless, there are still some good poets around, both in America and England. I like Vernon Scannell's poetry, for example, and I gave his recent book a boost in the *TLS* Christmas number.

Any other signs of hope?

ROBERT CONQUEST: Well, I see that children still love and sing rhymed songs, so the essence of the thing always manages to survive at the folk level. So there's always hope.

That's right. And your hope for the possibilities of poetry is beautifully expressed in the last stanza of your poem "So"—which is the final poem in your New and Collected Poems *(1988):*

> *The poem, firm,*
> *Sees with the eye of the storm,*
> *Up and out and through the starlit*
> *Perspective of infinities.*

Thank you.

ROBERT CONQUEST: Thank you.

JOHN FREDERICK NIMS

In 1993, John Frederick Nims received the O. B. Hardison Poetry Prize from the Folger Shakespeare Library. From his first poetry publications to the present, John Frederick Nims's work has been praised for its "craftsmanship and wit and educated sensibility," and his formidable translations from several languages are internationally recognized. As Philip Murray comments, "Rarely in the translator's art have such knowledge, skill, sensitivity and breadth of interest coincided so felicitously in a single hand."

John Frederick Nims was born in Muskegon, Michigan, and he received his undergraduate and masters degrees from the University of Notre Dame. After completing his Ph.D. in comparative literature at the University of Chicago, he has taught at many universities including the University of Notre Dame, the University of Toronto, Bocconi University in Milan, the University of Florence, the University of Madrid, Harvard University, and the University of Chicago. From 1978 to 1984, he was the Editor-in-Chief of *Poetry* magazine.

His various books include: *The Iron Pastoral*, 1947; *A Fountain in Kentucky and Other Poems*, 1950; *Of Flesh and Bone*, 1967; *Selected Poems*, 1982; *Western Wind: An Introduction to Poetry*, 1974, 1983, 1991; *A Local Habitation: Essays on Poetry*, 1985; *The Poems of St. John of the Cross*, 1959, 1968, 1979; and *Sappho to Valéry: Poems in Translation*, 1971, 1980, 1990.

This interview was conducted in Mr. Nims's home, an apartment above Lake Michigan in Chicago, Illinois.

In the introduction to your Selected Poems, *you wrote that "From the time I was five or six, I thought poems were a part of the natural world, as real certainly as the rabbits and collies we kept." Was this the result of a natural infatuation with nursery rhymes or was there a special love of poetry in your childhood home?*

JOHN FREDERICK NIMS: There was. My father liked poetry very much, and I must have been about four years old when I first heard him recite, "Break, break, break, / On thy cold grey stones, O Sea!" and the rest of the Tennyson poem. And there were also many books of poetry around the house. I can still remember reading, a few years later, the Longfellow poem called "Killed at the Ford"—"He is dead, the beautiful youth, / The heart of honor, the tongue of truth" or something like that—about a Union soldier killed in the Civil War. A sniper's bullet goes through his heart, and then, in a vision, it heads northward and kills a loved one several hundred miles away. It seemed a wonderful poem at the time. So, yes, I did grow up hearing and reading poems, and, of course, they all had rhythm and rhyme in those days.

Eventually, you studied at Notre Dame and received your Ph.D. in comparative literature at the University of Chicago. What languages and literatures did you specialize in?

JOHN FREDERICK NIMS: My Ph.D. program was in the history and theory of tragedy in the Greek, Latin, French, and English. The thesis itself was an edition of a play by James Shirley which was published about ten years ago. It was a kind of pedantic thesis, and I deliberately chose to do it because I knew so many friends who'd spent ten or twelve years on their Ph.D. theses, and the Shirley play was something I knew I could do in a couple of years. I always feel that I was terribly lucky in graduate school. I read most of the Greek tragedies, and I also had excellent courses in French tragedy.

What about the Spanish and the Italian?

JOHN FREDERICK NIMS: I began studying Spanish in high school because all of the kids took it. It was supposed to be easier than French, which was also available. I didn't get to the Italian until much later.

Eventually, we lived in Italy for a couple of years, and I knew some Italian before we went because I'd taught courses in Dante at Notre Dame.

Were any of these foreign languages, the modern ones, spoken in your home?

JOHN FREDERICK NIMS: No. I suppose my earliest experience with foreign languages was when I was an altar boy and got to know some Latin and realized that there were other ways of saying things. Actually, I knew the meaning of very few of the words. Almost none. *Dominus vobiscum*, maybe, and that was about it.

What about literary influences? In a number of your essays, Paul Valéry seems to have made a marked impression on your thinking about poetry. When did you first encounter his work?

JOHN FREDERICK NIMS: Quite a few years after my Ph.D. Maybe fifteen years later. I remember being especially struck by one line he wrote. I was walking down the street reading "The Graveyard by the Sea" and came across the line, *"L'argile rouge a bu la blanche espèce"*—"The red clay drank the white clay," representing human burial. I thought that was remarkably striking, and I later translated the whole poem. I also read quite a few of his essays, usually in English. So I read the poems in French, but the essays in English. It seemed to me that Valéry made a lot of sense about poetry and also about translation, especially when he said that the translator of poetry should strive for an "equivalent effect" and not a word for word translation, which he felt almost everyone did. For Valéry, "equivalent effect" meant that the translator should take into consideration the form, the sound, the rhythm, and the level of language—all the things that dictionaries can't tell you.

What about Yeats and the contemporary poets?

JOHN FREDERICK NIMS: I think I was quite a bit behind there. I never had anyone, either in high school or early college, who called my attention to contemporary poetry. I still remember one professor I had in college who said, "Well, I like some modern poetry. I like Walt Whitman." And that's about as far as he got. When I was younger, I liked Millay for a while, as everybody did in those days, especially her sonnets. Yeats came later. He was and probably still is my favorite poet, and I've spent more time on his work than on anyone else in English. But when I began writing poetry seriously, which was early in college, I was reading Catullus and Sappho. I still have the edition of Catullus I used back then, and I see that I translated some of his poems during my first year in college—two or three are written in the margin of the book, all in Catullus's meters. So my interest in foreign languages was always connected with the various rhythms that the poets wrote in.

Your first volume, The Iron Pastoral, *was highly praised for its intelligence, wit, and craftsmanship, but, as you've discussed in the preface to the* Selected Poems, *your subsequent volumes were more personal and less intellectually complex. Did you decide that the first volume was too "difficult"?*

JOHN FREDERICK NIMS: I don't believe that I ever thought it was too difficult, but the second volume was definitely more relaxed. I moved away from writing the "thing" poem, the *Dinggedicht,* which is about something very specific. In the first book, for example, there were poems called "Movie," and "Seashore," and "Poolroom," and "Magazine Stand," and "Penny Arcade." In the second book, there was less of that kind of poem and more relating to personal experience. I'm not sure that the change was ever a deliberate choice though. One just goes along with the flow, and that's the way the flow seemed to move.

Maybe it was a very natural evolution because, despite this question about The Iron Pastoral's *complexity, one of your most admired and anthologized poems, "Love Poem," comes from your first book, and it employs all of the virtues associated with the first volume along with a very real and personal portrayal of the poet's love. She's affectionately described as "my clumsiest dear," who's clearly a bit of klutz with the objects of the world, yet "With words and people and love you move at ease." The poems ends:*

> For should your hands drop white and empty
> All the toys of the world would break.

Despite its wit, it's hardly a poem devoid of emotion. So maybe there wasn't such a tremendous transformation between the first book and the second book.

JOHN FREDERICK NIMS: That's right. That poem was written to my wife before I married her, and she married me anyway, in spite of the poem! And the poem's still around.

And she's been immortalized in a beautiful poem.

JOHN FREDERICK NIMS: Well, it's just as things really happened, and it's really just like her. It still is, in fact. It surprises me.

In your second volume, A Fountain in Kentucky, *one of the most affecting poems is "First Date" which describes a young bather gradually moving into the water of an ocean or a lake. It's quite a creepy poem, and it ends:*

> *The mottled sand. Two heelprints*
> *Pooling in moonlight there.*
> *A gleam, in the dark we stare on*
> *—Swimming arms? or a star?*
> *Colored lanterns blink on the dune.*
> *Undertow by the shore.*

It's a poem, it seems, about the tragic loss of innocence?

JOHN FREDERICK NIMS: Yes, my wife and I were staying with friends up on Lake Michigan somewhere, and there was a young girl about sixteen or seventeen who was going on her first date, and there was a lot of excitement in the house. And, yes, I did feel that she was now wading into something which might change her whole life. Her first date. Recently, I've revised the poem and added a reference to Tristram and Isolde.

Is it still as ominous?

JOHN FREDERICK NIMS: I think so. There's still the gradual immersion into the water of the lake—where things grow more out of control the deeper one gets. But the young girl did have a happy life, and a nice marriage too.

You've written two remarkable elegies about the loss of a child. Commenting on the first poem, "Masque of Blackness," James Dickey wrote that it was, "for my money, one of the most memorable, moving, and believable elegies in English." This particular elegy is mostly narrative with many moving and telling details: like the mother bringing the child's toy to the hospital to show the doctors that the little boy can still "play," or the grieving parents buying a dog, "a collie pup," "Because someone was gone." The "Masque of Blackness" is also a sonnet sequence consisting of ten poems. Did the title come from Ben Jonson?

JOHN FREDERICK NIMS: Yes. At the time I wrote it, I knew the Jonson masque very well because that was my main Ph.D. field of study, Elizabethan and Jacobean drama. But I think I took that title primarily for the sake of the title itself, and also because there's a good deal of dramatic imagery that runs through the sequence.

The second elegy, "The Evergreen," is totally different in structure and tone. It consists of eleven octaves consisting of questions and answers beginning with, "Under this stone, what lies?" The language is simple, almost childlike, and very powerful. Did the rhetorical structure of the sequence have a model? Maybe the old English ballads where questions are often asked back and forth?

JOHN FREDERICK NIMS: Actually, it had a rather complicated model, and I'm always pleased when I do something like that and nobody quite recognizes what it is. It's the classical elegiac couplet with each line broken in half. Auden wrote a number of elegiac couplets in some of his later epigrams. It's a hexameter followed by what looks like a five-beat line, and I broke each of those lines in half, connecting two of them with half rhyme, and the other two with full rhyme.

And the "question" format? Did that come from anywhere in particular?

JOHN FREDERICK NIMS: Maybe the *Greek Anthology*, I'm not sure. But there are a number of little Greek poems, only two or maybe four lines long, in which someone will say to a tombstone, "Who lies here?" and the tombstone will say, "I was a sailor," and then describe the storm that killed him or something like that. And that also, I think, had something to do with my choosing the elegiac couplet because it sounds like an elegy. I must say, I'm glad you didn't recognize it. It was disguised, and I think pretty well.

Yes, it was. In attempting to characterize your work, Dudley Fitts once said of your poems that "in their moral passion lies their peculiar strength," and M. L. Rosenthal felt that your work, from the beginning, was marked by a "social and moral integrity." Some of your most powerful poems, like "The Lover" and "Last Judgment," deal with divine retribution. "The Lover," despite its wit, is a frightening vision of a vain, promiscuous man newly-arrived in hell. At first, hell seems like Eden, especially when he sees what he believes to be a beautiful woman beckoning him from the shrubbery. The "lover" then falls to his knees and kisses the figure's body from her ankles to her throat only to discover that she has no human facial features—she's a blank—and when he reaches out for her hair, "a viper of lightning hissed the air."

JOHN FREDERICK NIMS: Well, I don't tend to think of myself as being primarily a moral writer, but I did have someone in particular in mind when I wrote that poem. His attitude toward women annoyed me quite a bit because there were many women in his life, and he didn't seem to care about any of them. It wasn't a loving kind of love, and the imaginary girl in the poem has no facial features because, to him, there was no mind at all—or anything else except her body.

Now the other, lighter side of your work is marked by delightful wit, irony, and humor. This is most clearly seen in your many excellent epigrams contained in Of Flesh and Bone *and* Zany in Denim. *For example, there's the couplet poem, "Philosopher":*

He scowled at the barometer: "Will it rain?"
None heard, with all that pattering on the pane.

Or the "Visiting Poet," also a couplet poem:

> *"The famous bard, he comes! The vision nears!"*
> *Now heaven protect your booze. Your wife. Your ears.*

I wonder if you were affected by the epigrammatic verse of J. V. Cunningham which also has a telling, classical tautness? And whether you knew him personally?

JOHN FREDERICK NIMS: Yes, I did know him. Not well, but he was at the University of Chicago during part of the time that I was there. He was an instructor, I think. And I saw him several times, and yes, I did know his poems and admired them very much. Incidentally, an odd thing happened concerning that little rain poem. About ten years after I first published it, *The New Yorker* printed a cartoon of a man walking under an umbrella and saying to himself, "Is it raining?" and, as I remember it, the title of the cartoon was "The Philosopher." So I've always liked to think that my little poem was made a bit grander by inspiring a cartoon in *The New Yorker.* But maybe it was just a coincidence.

Have you been writing more epigrams?

JOHN FREDERICK NIMS: Yes, and I think I have enough for a third book, but I don't have any immediate publishing plans.

My favorite of the earlier epigrams is the devastating, "Avant-Guard":

> *"A dead tradition! Hollow shell!*
> *Outworn, outmoded—time it fell.*
> *Let's make it new. Rebel! Rebel!"*
> *Said cancer-cell to cancer-cell.*

JOHN FREDERICK NIMS: I still remember how that little poem annoyed my doctor at the time. He was a reader of contemporary poetry, and he thought the poem was, I guess, excessively conservative. But I thought it was as much about cancer as about literary movements.

But titling the poem "Avant-Guard" surely draws attention to the artistic reference?

JOHN FREDERICK NIMS: Yes, it does. There's an old quotation, again from Paul Valéry, that goes something like this: "Everything changes except the avant-guard." I've always wanted to find *exactly* where he said that, if indeed, it was Valéry, but I've never been able to track it down. He wrote so much. It's really such a mean remark, even though, in a way, it's certainly true.

Over the years, you've been one of the most eloquent defenders of poetic form since Frost. In the preface to Selected Poems, *you wrote that in your youth, "All the poems I had ever known throbbed with a physical rhythm, had what is called* form. *Form is what I thought poems came into the world with, as plants and animals do. Poets, I might have said if given to such talk, have to be careful about how many feet they put into their lines, just as nature has to be careful about how many feet she puts on her own creatures: six for insects, four for animals, two for the likes of us." Why do you believe that so many twentieth-century writers have abandoned the metrical foundations of English verse?*

JOHN FREDERICK NIMS: One reason, I suppose, is that there's been so much bad metrical verse. When I was editor of *Poetry* magazine and I'd open up an envelope and find a pile of weak sonnets, my heart would sink because bad sonnets are just a little bit worse than any other kind of bad poem. There's a philosophical saying from the Middle Ages, *Corruptio optimi pessima*, meaning that the corruption of the best thing is the worst kind of corruption. So I suppose many modern poets became fed up with fuddy-duddy sonnets, and old-fashioned diction, and so on, and they wanted to get away from it all and do something different. Even the meter itself, when used by unskilled writers, can be boring and monotonous, and I suppose there are still some people who think an iambic pentameter line is always da dum da dum da dum da dum da dum. But it practically never is exactly that. Not if the poet's any good.

*You've also been a great defender of rhyme, which you discuss at length in
your* Western Wind: An Introduction to Poetry. *In that book, you write that
"the necessity of finding a rhyme may jolt the mind out of its ruts . . . [and]
Force it out of the world of reason into the world of mystery, magic, and
imagination." Yet many writers and critics are vitriolic in their condemnation of rhyme. Is it the same reason, in your opinion?*

JOHN FREDERICK NIMS: I think so. It's clear that many people have
used rhyme badly. They think if a word rhymes, then it's okay, but that's
not the case. It has to be right in *every* way. Sometimes Frost would focus
on just the rhymes in a poem, and if he found a single rhyme word that
would not have been there in normal English, he would say, "The rhyme
scheme won; the poet lost." Rhymes have to be right in every way, and
that can be very hard to do. In translating, of course, it can be extremely
hard. So I think a lot of people just gave up rhyming because it's so often
abused and because it's so hard to do right.

From 1978 to 1984, you served as the Editor-in-Chief of Poetry *magazine,
but you'd worked there earlier.*

JOHN FREDERICK NIMS: Yes, I was the Visiting Editor in 1960, and
before that, back in the forties and fifties, I was on the editorial staff.

*Were you ever accused of having some kind of blind spot or bias or some-
thing like that?*

JOHN FREDERICK NIMS: Not very much. There were a few articles
about *Poetry* that claimed I was too conservative, but I didn't get many
angry letters that I can recall.

Did you enjoy the experience?

JOHN FREDERICK NIMS: Yes. It was great fun to see that stack of manuscripts. And *Poetry* got a great many. I used to know the precise figures,
but I can't remember exactly. I think we used to accept one poem out of

every three hundred or so, something like that. Maybe not even that many. But it was always fun to hope that you'd come across something good in the pile, and, often, I thought we did.

The odds at Poetry *are, of course, much greater now. 300 to 1 almost sounds good.*

JOHN FREDERICK NIMS: Yes, that's true.

Aside from your own work and editing Poetry, *you're also one of America's foremost translators, as the quality of* Sappho to Valéry: Poems in Translation *makes clear. Philip Murray, echoing widespread praise for the book, describes your translations as "absolute miracles."* Sappho to Valéry *was dedicated to Dudley Fitts and Robert Fitzgerald, and I wonder how well you knew both men and how much they influenced your work?*

JOHN FREDERICK NIMS: I knew them well, and I think of them as among my best friends over those years. My wife and I first met Robert Fitzgerald in Italy, and we saw a good deal of him there for at least a year, and then, later, back in this country, we saw him rather often. Dudley Fitts I knew through Bread Loaf, and we got along very well because both of us not only liked Greek poetry but the *same* Greek poetry, and I thought he was a wonderful translator of the little poems from the *Greek Anthology*.

And Fitzgerald was extraordinary as well.

JOHN FREDERICK NIMS: Yes, and they were great together.

Your classic essay, "Poetry: Lost in the Translation?" serves as the introduction to Sappho to Valéry. *Allen Tate wrote that your "essay on translation is the best by anybody," and he insisted that "All future translators must study it." Not surprisingly, in the essay, you emphasize the translator's obligation to sound and tone as well as meaning. You remind your readers that "For Frost, the sound is 'the gold in the ore,'" and you concluded that "Surely among the commonest faults of translation are faults of tone." Could you discuss this a little?*

JOHN FREDERICK NIMS: Well, since there are so many things that a translator has to keep in mind, I feel the most helpful thing I can suggest is working with a native speaker. With most of the modern languages I've translated, I've had help in this way. When we lived in Florence, I went through most of the *Divine Comedy* with a young Florentine who was a college instructor, and he would read a line of Dante, and then I'd read it after him to get the feel of the Florentine lilt. Then I would ask him about individual words, and he would tell me the kind of things that no dictionary could ever tell me. For example, he'd say, "Well, that's a very old-fashioned word," or "Parents wouldn't like their children using that word," or "That's a word you might use in Sienna, but not anywhere else," or "That's a very learned word." Unless translators have that kind of advice from a native speaker, it's extremely difficult to comprehend the tone of a foreign language poem. Unfortunately, there isn't always a helpful native speaker available, but I've been very lucky in being at universities where there were always speakers of many foreign languages. And we also, as I've mentioned, lived in Italy for a couple of years, and in Spain as well. Without such help, all kinds of problems can happen. A famous example is the Spaniard who translated Emily Dickinson's poem beginning "I never saw a moor" without knowing what Emily meant by the word "moor." It can lead to some funny mistakes.

Yes, and it's not surprising given the many difficulties, and the fact that very few people are truly bilingual.

JOHN FREDERICK NIMS: Yes, very few. I've know a couple of people who were trilingual, but they're *extremely* rare.

Curiously enough, your own translation of Canto I of the Inferno *is written, uniquely I believe, in tetrameters. Could you discuss this? I think it had to do with the fact that, in the Italian, the words generally have more syllables than in the English?*

JOHN FREDERICK NIMS: That's right. I realized that fact when I was reading Dante many years ago in Florence. Words that in Italian have two or three syllables are often monosyllabic in English. English is actually a very monosyllabic language. Words such as night, day, love, death, boy, and girl, are all polysyllabic words in their Italian counterparts. So I began to wonder if a typical Italian line shouldn't have more syllables than an equivalent English line, and I tried it in one canto from Dante.

Have you considered finishing the Inferno?

JOHN FREDERICK NIMS: Yes, I worked very hard on Dante, and I once started an edition of my own, but the chief reason I didn't complete it was that my friend John Ciardi was doing it at the same time, and I felt that I might be poaching on someone else's territory.

But many people translate Dante.

JOHN FREDERICK NIMS: I know, and I probably should have done it since I knew Dante better than I've ever known any other foreign poet. But I must admit, by the way, that the eight-syllable lines might not be the best idea. The tetrameters don't have the dignity that Dante's poetry ought to have. I think he needs the pentameter like Shakespeare. The tetrameter just isn't the great line of English poetry, and since Dante was using the standard line of great poetry in his language, it seems to me now that, in English, his work should be translated into iambic pentameter.

I wonder if you could also discuss the challenge of translating "The Dark Night" by St. John of the Cross? How does one approach a poem that has so much underlying religious belief behind it—not to mention mystical commentary by the author himself?

JOHN FREDERICK NIMS: Well, I think one reason that St. John is such a good poet is that even when he's writing about the loftiest and most spiritual things, it's always rendered in a simple, worldly language. They're really love poems to God, and God is always called with affection, "my beloved" or "my dear." One authority on St. John of the Cross says that he never breaks with the laws of this world when he's dealing with another, higher world. He always puts things in terms of the senses, as a poet has to do. So the translator has to translate that as honestly as he can and then hope that the sensual imagery will carry over into the English with the same spiritual suggestions that it has in Spanish. The translator can't be overly concerned with all of the religious meanings in St. John's poems, but he must do his best to clearly translate the quite simple words that the poet used.

So the mystical commentary and the love poems, despite their connection, need to be seen as two separate things?

JOHN FREDERICK NIMS: Yes. In the introduction to my translation of St. John of the Cross, I give an example of that. I cite a stanza from St. John and then his explication of it, which is over five times as long and very complicated indeed. But the marvelous thing is that St. John didn't let the commentary confuse the poetry, which always remains very simple.

So it's almost two ways of the saint trying to say the same thing.

JOHN FREDERICK NIMS: That's right. And the poems are very straightforward and colloquial. St. John was very fond of the popular love songs of his time—which he always heard with religious overtones.

Over the years, it seems that you've translated from at least six major languages. Is there one that's a particular favorite?

JOHN FREDERICK NIMS: Well, I was very pleased that some of my Goethe translations ended up in the new, complete edition that Princeton's now publishing. I think I have about eight Goethe poems in there, and German is the language I know least well. I've never actually spoken German, but for two or three years I read it intensively, reading only Goethe and Rilke, with the help of a German professor. Until then, I'd always thought of Goethe as being boring, you know, like a marble bust in the library or something. But when I really got into his poems, they were wonderful.

And passionate.

JOHN FREDERICK NIMS: Yes. I loved them. So for three or four years, I read a lot of Goethe and Rilke, but I've hardly looked at it since. I once meant to do more extensive translations of Goethe, and I probably should have.

So, in the end, you've gotten the most satisfaction out of your translations from the language you know the least?

JOHN FREDERICK NIMS: That's right. I guess I've always been kind of lucky with languages. When we were in Spain, I met a Ph.D. student who'd just had a class in old Spanish, and I couldn't resist the opportunity to read some old Spanish, and that's what we did. And a similar thing happened with a language called Galician, which is spoken in northwestern Spain and is said to be like medieval Portuguese. Galician had a wonderful poet called Rosalía de Castro whom I'd read about in Gerald Brenan's history. Then I ran into someone who was a native Galician and who knew the poet's work very well. So we did the same thing, reading her work together. These were the kinds of lucky things that happened to me with languages. The trouble is, they were things I did for a year, or two years, maybe three years, and then went on to something else. Maybe I should have stayed with one foreign language over all of those years.

Recently, you've been translating the sonnets of Michelangelo. Are you almost finished?

JOHN FREDERICK NIMS: Yes, I've just finished. And I've not only translated his sonnets, but all of Michelangelo's poems. He wrote 301, and the sonnets are, of course, the best known, and I think they're the best.

Do you feel he's a significant poet for his time?

JOHN FREDERICK NIMS: I do. He gets about ten pages in a history of Italian literature that I've been reading, and Montale wrote in an essay that "For a combination of tough technique and ineffable thought, he is alone in literature." There's nobody else like him. Maybe you noticed the recent article on Florence in *The New Yorker*? It referred to the "opaque magnificence" of Michelangelo's poems as described by George Steiner. But it's not always opaque, although it's often magnificent. Yes, Michelangelo's very good, and if he'd never painted that ceiling or done those statues, he'd still be known as an important Italian poet.

What else have you been working on?

JOHN FREDERICK NIMS: The other thing I've done lately was a translation of one of the Greek plays. One of the first translations I ever did, not long after I got my Ph.D., was Euripides' *Andromache* which is in the University of Chicago series. Not long ago, when I heard that the University of Pennsylvania was doing a new series of the Greek plays, I offered to do one, and they gave me Euripides' *Phoenician Women* which I finished about a year ago. I just got the proofs yesterday, and when I finish with it and the Michelangelo, maybe I'll get back to what we call "my own" work.

Well, I'd like to finish up today by reading from your own work—it's one of the beautiful quatrain poems from Of Flesh and Bone, *and it's called "Love":*

> *"For when we have blamed the wind, we can blame love."*
> *Who'd blame the mindless wind? Sleepers that start*
> *In fear when the ceilings heave like seas above?*
> *Girls with their shattered dresden in the heart?*

JOHN FREDERICK NIMS: Yes. The first line is from Yeats' "Old Memory," and the rest of the poem comments on it.

It's a wonderful last line.

JOHN FREDERICK NIMS: Thank you, Bill.

Thank you.

WENDY COPE

Aptly described as "a scintillating satirist," "a gifted parodist," and "a sensitive poet," Wendy Cope is also one of Britain's most popular living poets.

Born in Kent, England, Wendy Cope read History at St. Hilda's College, Oxford, and then worked as a primary school teacher in London for fifteen years. She was also a free-lance writer, and a regular columnist for the *Spectator*. Both of her collections of poetry, *Making Cocoa for Kingsley Amis* (Faber, 1986) and *Serious Concerns* (Faber, 1992), were best-sellers in Britain. She has also written or edited a number of books for children including *Does She Like Word-games?* (Anvil, 1988), *The River Girl* (Faber, 1991), and *The Orchard Book of Funny Poems* (Orchard, 1993).

In 1987, Wendy Cope received the Cholmondeley Award for Poetry, and in 1992, she became a fellow of the Royal Society of Literature.

This interview was conducted during the Exploring Form and Narrative Poetry Conference at West Chester University in Pennsylvania.

James Fenton once described you as a "protest poet" and others have used the word "subversive." Are you comfortable with those descriptions?

WENDY COPE: Yes, I like them very much. The word "subversive" was first used by a British reviewer, and since I liked it so much, my editor, Craig Raine, used it in the book blurb. Later, of course, people copied it, and I didn't mind at all. On the other hand, that phrase "the most accomplished parodist since Beerbohm" was something that Craig made up, and he put it in the blurb as well, and now it plays all over the place. But I never really cared for it, and it didn't actually come from a genuine review, so I've told my publishers never to use it again. I'm quite fed up with it, but it keeps popping up.

One aspect of this subversiveness is that you began writing formal verse when it was quite unfashionable.

WENDY COPE: That's right. I was writing free verse at the time, and then I took an Arvon course and things changed.

What's an Arvon course?

WENDY COPE: The Arvon Foundation started in the 1970's. We don't have much of a history of creative writing workshops in England, and, even though there's a few more of them these days, they're generally not approved of. But back in the 1970's, the Arvon Foundation got going with a lot of support from Ted Hughes. The courses themselves last five days, and admission is completely open—first come, first serve. American writers who've come over to tutor these workshops are often rather shocked to find out that they're completely unselective. So you can get some very good students along with some complete beginners.

When I was getting very interested in writing poetry, I went to my first Arvon course with great fear and trepidation. I'd read about them in the newspaper, and it sounded like what I needed. At the time, I was writing and reading poetry on my own, but I didn't have anyone I could talk to about it. Some of my friends were teachers who'd done English at University, which I hadn't done, so I tried to talk to them about it. But they didn't know very much about twentieth century poetry, and they seemed a bit embarrassed about it. I was an elementary school teacher at the time, and, despite all my fears, going on an Arvon course seemed like a real holiday. They're all in very nice places, and it was very pleasant to get away from the city and be with other people who shared my interests. Most of the people who participated worked quite hard on those courses, and I found them very stimulating.

Then one time, I was on a course with D. M. Thomas. I'd actually signed up for the course because of the other tutor who was female.

I thought that she was someone I could learn from, but Don turned out to be much more helpful. So one night, the subject of clerihews came up over dinner—or after dinner—and he said, "Everyone write a clerihew." So I wrote about six, and we read them out loud, and he said, "You're good at this kind of thing." Then he said, rather jokingly, "You should drop all that other stuff you're trying to write." It was really a joke, but it made me realize that I had an aptitude for that kind of writing. So I wrote some more and people laughed, and it made me think that I should try other avenues of expression.

Wasn't that excellent villanelle, "Lonely Hearts," one of your first formal poems? Or one of your first published?

WENDY COPE: Yes, it was both. It seemed as though something came together when I wrote that poem. I'd just been on a course where Gavin Ewart was one of the tutors. He's such a lovely man, and, although in one-to-one teaching situations, he's not really a great teacher, it was always stimulating to be around him. There'd been a lot of talk about form on that course, and I'd been reading Gavin's work, and I eventually managed to write that villanelle, and it seemed okay. It wasn't my very first poetry publication, but it appeared in the *TLS*, and obviously it was an important breakthrough.

One critic has said that your poetry has a "subversive vision, particularly of male sexual behavior," and your second book, Serious Concerns, *is primarily about men and male-female relationships. Among my personal favorites are "Men and Their Boring Arguments," which wittily examines the male compulsion "to show off and compete," and the clever quatrain poem "Bloody Men":*

> Bloody men are like bloody buses—
> You wait for about a year
> And as soon as one approaches your stop
> Two or three others appear.

Harsher still is the sonnet "Faint Praise" which begins "Size isn't every-thing," and ends: "You're almost human. You could make it yet." Yet despite some very acerbic comments, there never seems to be a stridency about these poems—there's never an ideological dismissal of men in general, and the narrator of the poems always keeps trying to make something work.

WENDY COPE: That's right. There's nothing at all ideological about the poems. When my first book was published, one feminist reviewer said she didn't like the way I wrote about men because it was too self-deprecating. But all I'm doing is telling it like it is, or telling it like it was for me, and ideology doesn't come into it. The poems just reflect something about me and my relationships, not some ideological point of view.

And not all the poems are so negative. "Giving up Smoking" is really full of a kind of humorous praise, and "On a Country Bus" is a very gentle and hopeful love poem that ends with the narrator deciding to sit back in her seat:

> *And think about the things you say and do*
> *And nothing else. The journey takes almost an hour.*

WENDY COPE: And there's others too, like "Flowers." There's clearly a lot of love and affection for men in the poems, but there's also a lot of ambivalence. That's what I think a very large proportion of grown-up women feel about men, and the poems reflect it. It's definitely not the same thing as being a "man-hater," and I find it quite irritating when people who've only superficially glanced at my books make assumptions that the poems are "anti-men." They certainly do say some very negative things about men, and I don't apologize for that one bit. But what they really reflect is an honest ambivalence. The poems are about the ups and downs of somebody's love life, and since I happen to be a heterosexual woman, it's about men. "Two Cures for Love" goes:

1 Don't see him. Don't phone or write a letter.
2 The easy way: get to know him better.

Now the poem says "him" because I'm a woman getting over being in love with a man, but it's equally true from the other point of view—from the male perspective. The same's true of "Bloody Men." It could've just as easily been titled "Bloody Women." For example, that idea of the buses all showing up at once isn't limited to one sex. We all know that feeling. When someone fancies you, you feel more attractive, and you draw more attention. Since I'm female, my poems are about men. I do realize, however, that it would be a lot more difficult at the present time for a man to write with the same freedom and honesty about his ambivalence towards women.

That's definitely true.

WENDY COPE: And it's a great pity that contemporary fashion prevents some people from saying what they really feel. I'm fully aware that it's my good fortune to be writing at this particular time—when a woman can write honestly about how she feels about men. And maybe this gets back to that notion of "subversiveness" because I don't give a toss about political correctness. Even if some of my views do coincide with contemporary points of view, I'm not going to tow anyone's political line, and I'm not at all concerned that people discuss my "complete disregard for literary fashion." I'm comfortable with that.

Like writing in forms?

WENDY COPE: Yes. There was definitely a pressure to write in freer forms in the seventies. Formal poetry never completely vanished in England—it wasn't as bad as America—and I wasn't the only one who made the choice to be different. I believe that part of our desire to write in forms was "bloodymindedness" because we *knew* it wasn't the fashionable thing to do. In every period, there are always unwritten rules of literary fashion. The general public doesn't fully comprehend them, but poets learn them in creative writing courses and by reading poetry reviews and so on. And it's a very good idea for a writer to be aware of them, but, eventually, anyone who's any good will get fed up with them and decide to completely ignore them. So at one point, I said to myself, "To hell with it. I'm going to write what I want to write." But it took me a while to get there. It wasn't easy, but eventually I worked through it—and was able to dare to write the way I wanted.

You often have fun debunking contemporary fads, for instance, the Green movement's adulation of animals at the expense of human beings. The narrator in "Kindness to Animals" admits to liking a bit of lamb, but is quick to point out:

> *I have never, ever eaten a barn owl,*
> *So perhaps I am OK.*

My favorite of these poems is "Goldfish Nation" where the pretentious narrator exalts the virtues of goldfish, a fish that eats its young, and finally concludes:

> *It's obvious that goldfish are better than people.*
> *Goldfish are better than you.*

How have these poems been received?

WENDY COPE: Do you know about the poem "Whale Nation" by Heathcote Williams?

No.

WENDY COPE: Well, it's a long poem that came out, if I remember correctly, in the late 1980's. They brought it out in a rather beautifully-illustrated book full of very nice photographs, and it was promoted with a great blast of publicity. People like Ted Hughes and Blake Morrison, who's usually pretty sensible, went on record saying how wonderful the poem was. So when I read it, I couldn't believe all the commotion because it was absolute garbage. I usually try not to make negative remarks about other poets' writings in public, but "Whale Nation" is just dreadful. And one of the things that people kept praising about it was all the "information" it contains about whales. So I went to the library and got lots of information about goldfish and then used it like Williams' poem—bits of boring prose information chopped up into short lines of poetry. Parts of "Goldfish Nation" are probably a breach of copyright because it's the exact information I got from the library. So it's full of real facts about goldfish, if you care. And then, just like "Whale Nation," it's interspersed with bits of zenish, mystic stuff about how wonderful goldfish are. In Williams' poem, there's the definite implication that whales are much nicer than people. So that was my response, and I'm very glad that it works for you, and other people, who haven't read "Whale Nation." But we all, I guess, recognize that sort of thing: that we're not as good or as important as the animals.

Have animal rights groups protested?

WENDY COPE: No, they only do that to people cutting up cats for medical research. People don't take much notice of poetry, but one of my friends decided that he didn't dare include it in an anthology he was putting together.

Maybe the group most deflated in your poetry is the poets themselves. For starters, you've created a self-important philistine poet from the South London suburbs called Jason Strugnell. How did he come into being?

WENDY COPE: When I first started to get seriously interested in poetry, it became like a religion, and I thought of poets as saints and angels. Obviously, any young woman with that attitude is heading for trouble. Then I began to meet a few poets, and inevitably there was a certain amount of disillusionment. So Strugnell grew out of that clash between the idealization and the reality. But there's also bits of me in Strugnell. I was pretty much unpublished when I started writing the Strugnell poems, so he was the neglected genius, always moaning about his situation. I was, of course, laughing at myself, but there's also bits of other poets too, like the womanizing poet and the drinking poet. So there's bits of many different people I've bumped into over the years, and things I've observed going on—like the mysterious process by which poets, especially male poets, however revolting they might be, seem to be surrounded by flocks of admiring young women.

You've also written about "tumps," described as "a typically useless male poet," and your devastating "Triolet" is about the disappointment that the narrator has when she discovers that poets are hardly the Byronic types she had assumed, but rather:

> *They're mostly wicked as a ginless tonic*
> *And wild as pension plans. . . .*

What's your relationship with the contemporary poetry scene in England?

WENDY COPE: These days I have very little to do with the poetry scene in England. I have some poet friends that I see individually, but I seldom go to the kinds of functions I used to. I also don't live in London any more, and I hate going to London anyway.

How far are you from London?

WENDY COPE: About seventy miles, but it's not far enough, in my opinion. Back in the seventies, when I first got interested in poetry, nothing was more exciting than spending an evening at the Poetry Society and meeting other poets, but that's not what I want to do now. There's a certain amount of awkwardness and even bad feelings among certain poets who resent the attention I've received. When my first book made the best-seller list, there was all this fuss, and then it kind of quieted down, and I tried to keep a very low profile. Then, when the second book came out and went right to the top of the best-seller list, it was too much for some people.

I can take criticism, and I'm learning to deal with envy, but what I really find hard to deal with is that I *know* there are people who haven't even read my books who have dismissed them out of hand. One such person, who fell in love with me for a while, actually repented and admitted it. Then he read the poems, and he kept saying, "You're a good poet, you know."

But when my first book came out, he'd decided, without reading it, that it was a bad thing—that English poetry had to be saved from the dreadful Wendy Cope. And there were many like him. One woman admitted, "I didn't read your book when it first came out because I don't like that kind of thing." But then her husband encouraged her to read it, and she told me, "So I did, and I really enjoyed it." Can you imagine being told that somebody didn't read your book because "I don't like that kind of thing"? I find it very hard to be condemned by people that haven't even read my books, so I've become quite paranoid about the poetry scene right now. That's why it's so nice to be visiting here in America.

But, nevertheless, it's a fact of life that, even among like-minded poets, if one suddenly becomes a best-seller and gets a lot of attention, it's hard for everybody else. And I'm perfectly aware that there are other poets at least as good as me who get a lot less attention, but it's not really my fault. I'm not some great self-publicist, and my publishers are just efficient people who do their jobs. I certainly didn't set out to write popular commercial poetry, but, I must admit, I'm very pleased that a lot of people seem to enjoy my work.

You also seem to be losing patience with critics, most notably in the title poem of the second collection which cites a quote from The Spectator: *"She is witty and unpretentious, which is both her strength and her limitation." So, in the poem, the narrator announces her determination to "overcome her limitation," and then asks:*

> *"Now should I work at being less witty? Or more pretentious?*
> *Or both?"*

WENDY COPE: Actually, that guy wasn't even a critic. He was just someone who'd been sent to write about the Cheltenham Festival for the *Spectator*. So it wasn't a very serious piece of criticism; it was just an article about the festival. He's a school master somewhere, and I'm told he's quite proud that his name popped up in my book. As for critics in general, I do think there have been a few intelligent reviews of my work, and I appreciate that.

One thing you don't appreciate is the term "light verse."

WENDY COPE: That's true. Unfortunately, it's often used as a negative term to categorize and demean. When I was growing up in England, I had the impression that Betjeman wasn't really a proper poet. He was on my mother's bookshelf! There was an understanding that Betjeman didn't really count because he was so popular—because he was read by "ordinary people"—and I feel that's been done to me. I've been categorized as a writer of "light verse" and that often implies that I'm something different from a "real" poet, and, naturally, I find that very hard to take. I hope I'm not coming off as completely paranoid!

Maybe you are getting a little paranoid. Most of the people I know value humorous, witty verse. And they value it highly.

WENDY COPE: But the very term "light verse" isn't a very helpful category because so much funny poetry isn't really "light." There are, of course, some poems that could sensibly be described as "light" poems—even some of mine, especially when I'm playing and having fun. But a lot of so-called "light verse" poems are really not. How can we read Dorothy Parker's "Résumé"—you know, "Gas smells awful; / You might as well live"—and call it "light"? The sad thing about Dorothy Parker is that she eventually tried most of those things. So how can we use the term "light verse" to describe a joke about suicide, about different methods of killing oneself, written by someone who actually tried them? It may be funny, but it's definitely not "light" in any reasonable sense of the word. It's really very "heavy" indeed. So it's not just a question of the term sometimes being used as a put-down, but it's also that the word "light," in my opinion, has all the wrong associations.

What do you prefer?

WENDY COPE: I have no problem with "humorous verse" or "comic verse."

But the kind of poem you were just discussing goes far beyond the comic.

WENDY COPE: Yes, so nothing will fully satisfy, but at least it indicates the humor. I think one of the things that gives light verse such a bad name is the kind of stuff, which often appears in anthologies, that's neither funny nor serious.

You've remarked a number of times that your couplet poem "Some More Light Verse" is the key poem in your second collection, Serious Concerns, *because it deals with a desperate narrator who tries everything to improve her life and nothing works, but she keeps trying. You've described the poem as suicidal, but there's definitely a determination to survive. Could you discuss the poem?*

WENDY COPE: In the first draft of the poem, I wrote the lines, "And when there's nothing left to try, / I guess you just give up and die." That's exactly how I was feeling when I started writing the poem. I'd tried everything, and life seemed quite terrible and unbearable. But, eventually, while writing the poem, I worked through my suicidal feelings, and the poem began to veer away from it. In the end, the word "die" didn't appear in the final version of the poem, even though it rhymes with the key rhyme words—"cry," "sigh," and "try"—and I guess I had hopes that some readers and critics would recognize what the missing word was. But I was hoping for too much, and it's nice to have a chance to explain it.

I'd like to go back to the time before you began writing poetry, when you went to Oxford for history. What kind of history did you study there?

WENDY COPE: It was English history from the beginning to 1939, and the period that you concentrated on usually depended on which tutors you worked with. I did the Anglo-Saxon period and the Middle Ages, but we also managed to go right through English history and focus on a period of European history.

After graduation, when you were teaching elementary school, weren't you teaching music?

WENDY COPE: Not in the beginning. I started teaching a regular primary school class—where you teach everything. But I got very interested in primary school music, and I went on lots of development courses. I could already play the piano and sing, and I taught myself guitar. Such people are in great demand in the primary schools, and I got very keen on it. Eventually, I had a year or two where I didn't have a regular class, and I taught just music, which was great. So I became something of a specialist.

And then you became a free-lance writer?

WENDY COPE: At first, I was still teaching, so I free-lanced part-time. Then, when my first book came out, it sold very well, and people were asking me to do so many things that I finally had to give notice at school.

Is it true that you began writing poetry to deal with the loneliness you felt after the death of your father?

WENDY COPE: It's mostly true. My father died in 1971, and I was already quite a depressed person. After his death, things got so bad that I just felt I couldn't manage. I wanted to find some help, but I didn't know where to go. That was the era of *One Flew Over the Cuckoo's Nest* and all the other scary films and books about mental hospitals, so I definitely didn't want to get involved in the state system. Eventually, even though I didn't have much money, I went into analysis, and I started writing poetry within my first six months.

Did the therapist encourage you to do this, or did you do it on your own?

WENDY COPE: I started doing it myself—trying to comprehend my own feelings, and trying to find a way of dealing with them somehow. But there was another motivation as well. When I was a primary school teacher, it was the era of "creativity in the classroom," and I did lots of poetry with the kids, and it stimulated my interest. I started to think, "I can do this myself." So both of those things played an important role in my desire to write poetry.

Did writing the poetry help you deal with your father's death?

WENDY COPE: It did. I know some people sneer at the idea of poetry as therapy, and I know it's produced lots of bad poetry, but when a poet is writing as a way of dealing with some great grief or loneliness or pain, something can happen in the course of the writing that makes it work both as a poem and as a factor to mitigate the suffering. It obviously won't cure anyone of his grief for a dead relation, but it might help matters, and it might also give the writer some useful insight. I know there's always the fear of self-indulgence, but I don't worry about that. Whenever I hear an English poet worrying that he's been too self-indulgent, I always suspect that he might have written something rather interesting. I'm terribly self-indulgent, and I know it. What I think is the real danger is self-pity. When Dick Davis reviewed my first book, he mentioned in passing that he felt I'd struggled with self-pity, and, in a sense, won, and I was very pleased with that. There's lots of self-pity in my notebooks, but those poems don't make it into print.

Do the forms help?

WENDY COPE: Very much. When you're dealing with a very powerful emotion, expressing it in a very strict form helps both the poem and the attempt to deal with the problem.

Like Douglas Dunn's poems about the death of his wife?

WENDY COPE: Yes, or Tony Harrison's poems about the death of his parents. This is one thing that I've definitely learned from all my reading and writing: that the combination of powerful emotion contained in a strict form works very effectively.

I know that you admire the work of such contemporary poets as Gavin Ewart, James Fenton, Fleur Adcock, and others, and that you've grown especially fond of A. E. Housman. What appeals to you in Housman?

WENDY COPE: Well, he makes me cry, and, on the other hand, he can also be very funny. The Christopher Ricks edition, *Collected Poems and Selected Prose*, contains quite a lot of what I prefer not to call Housman's light verse—his funny poems. And reading through the book, I thought, "Oh, I'm just in love with him. He's so wonderful." And then I immediately thought, "Well, he certainly wouldn't have appreciated that coming from me." And that's when I wrote the poem that begins, "I think I am in love with A. E. Housman." I suppose my feelings also related to my personal circumstances at the time. I was very lonely back then, but even now, when my life is so much better, I *still* like Housman. I even did a selection of Housman's poems for a book that was published in England last year called *Poets on Poets*. Various contemporary poets were asked to make their own personal selection from the work of a poet they admired, and then write a short introduction. It's a very interesting book, and I was glad to do Housman.

I'd also like to mention your "Variation on Belloc's 'Fatigue.'" Belloc's original poem goes:

> I'm tired of Love: I'm still more tired of Rhyme.
> But Money gives me pleasure all the time.

WENDY COPE: Good, isn't it?

Yes, and you respond in your poem:

> I hardly ever tire of love or rhyme—
> That's why I'm poor and have a rotten time.

WENDY COPE: Unfortunately, some English poets found that hard to take because they think I'm not quite as poor as they are. They feel

I didn't have the right to say that because I make more money from my books than most other poets. But compared with people in other fields of endeavor, I really don't make very much money.

And how about Belloc? He's a very underrated poet.

WENDY COPE: Yes, he is. I've just reread his work for an anthology I'm doing, and I enjoy him very much. Especially those little epigrammatic poems, although I'm not terrible keen on the *Cautionary Tales*— the animal poems.

How about Betjeman?

WENDY COPE: People have always expected me to be especially keen on Betjeman, but I've only come to him quite recently. When I was younger, he did lots of television, and he was perfectly adorable. And I always felt that he was sneered at for being so popular, and now I feel a definite affinity with him. But my problem with his well-known poetry is that I grew up in the English suburbs, and all this stuff about tennis club dances and everything was exactly what I've spent my life trying to get away from. To a certain extent, Betjeman is celebrating a kind of suburban life that's a horror to me. So he always put me off when I was younger.

But recently I went through Betjeman's collected work looking for some funny poems for an anthology, and what I found most interesting were his religious poems. He's a wonderful religious poet. None of us think of Betjeman as primarily a religious poet, but it seems to me that's exactly what he is. And I can't imagine anything less fashionable than Betjeman writing those poems about going to country churches at the time when he was doing it. It was certainly subversive. Entirely. And terribly unfashionable! And I can appreciate this even more right now because I'm back at church and very into being an Anglican. So this is exactly the right moment for me to be reading Betjeman's poetry. Another impressive thing about Betjeman is that he dealt with this huge area of English life that was being completely ignored by all the other poets. That's quite a poetic accomplishment in itself—and very rare.

All writers have blind spots, and I'm now very interested in locating my own. I'm trying to see if there are other huge areas of subject matter that we're all ignoring.

A few years ago in an interview with Gerry Cambridge of The Dark Horse, *you said that you were very fearful of putting out a third collection.*

WENDY COPE: That's right, but I'm still not finished with it anyway. It's about three-quarters done.

Is it fear of all the hullabaloo?

WENDY COPE: Yes. It's partly that paranoia I discussed earlier. The feeling that there are people out to get me who haven't even read my work. And I also have concerns about how well the book will sell and about dealing with the press again. The British press is so intrusive! They think that if you're seeking publicity for any reason, even a book, then you've completely sacrificed your right to privacy. One of the nice things about doing this interview with you is that I know I won't get a bunch of stupid questions about my love life and other personal stuff. In England, even if you do an interview with a journalist from a national paper, even a respectable national paper, they're very intrusive. And they also get things wrong all the time. And then there's television. I hate television because you have to worry about what you look like, so mostly I don't do it any more. Pre-recorded radio is okay, but, in general, there's just too much running around doing things you don't get paid for—and doing things that are very upsetting. I know I shouldn't grumble because it would be far worse to be a poet who published a book that was completely ignored. So I know that I'm very lucky, but it's certainly a mixed blessing.

Years ago, when your program about Jason Strugnell was first broadcast on the BBC, you clearly enjoyed the experience.

WENDY COPE: Yes. That was great. Absolutely great, but I wasn't in it—I wasn't on the screen. All I had to do was sit by the producer and watch.

It was great fun, especially meeting all those actors I'd seen before on television. At the time, I was quite new as a writer. I hadn't even published a book yet, and it was very exciting to see my work performed on the BBC. But that's completely different from having to go on the air and promote your book. But I mustn't complain! It's awful if they don't promote your book, and it's awful if they do! So I shouldn't moan about it, but I know you want an honest answer, and I simply don't enjoy it. It's actually quite scary. All authors worry that their books will be failures, so I'm just scared like everyone else. Maybe I'm not tough enough to be who I've become.

You also told Gerry Cambridge that you had new interests that might lead to new poetic avenues.

WENDY COPE: Yes. My life had changed a lot around the time when I talked to Gerry. It was all much more "new" than it is now, and I was completely open-minded about what might happen—even about the possibility of not writing at all. And I certainly don't write as much as I used to. Years ago, a lot of my poems were written out of a kind of misery and desperation, but my life is much better now. These days, I write poems in other ways, with different motivations. I'm just not as compelled to write poems as before—as say Douglas Dunn was compelled to write his poems after his wife's death. Since my life is less difficult now, my poems come less frequently—and from less dramatic sources, like gardening and going to church, for example. This past year, I've actually been too busy with other things to write any poems, and that's why I thought this visit to America would be good for me. I need to set aside some time to get back to the poetry.

When you write, how do you go about it? Do you start with a line or an idea or a rhythm? Or something else?

WENDY COPE: For me, things often start with a line I'd like to use as a refrain. Right now, I'm working on a line I want to use, but I'd better not tell you! You know how superstitious poets can be. Which is very interesting because playwrights, for example, will tell you the whole plot of their play before they've written a single word. But poets have this odd superstition that if we tell someone our idea for a poem, they'll take it and use it themselves. At any rate, I love refrains and often begin there, although, of course, not all my poems have refrains.

So let's say that you have a refrain line you like, then how do you decide whether to use it in a villanelle or a triolet or whatever?

WENDY COPE: Trial and error. Often I'll start out with a short form like a triolet because it's easy and uncomplicated. But then I might realize that I want to say more on the subject, and it'll expand into another form. For example, if the refrain began as a couplet, it might end up in an English sonnet or a villanelle or something else. So, in the beginning, one form often transmutes into another until I'm finally satisfied that I've got the appropriate structure.

You've written very effectively in a wide range of poetic forms—sonnets, quatrains, triolets, villanelles, etc.—do you have any favorites?

WENDY COPE: I love villanelles. When I'm reading a book, and I come across a villanelle, I always think, "Oh good!" I always enjoy them. When I first discovered that the form existed, I was very intrigued, and it's become a special favorite of mine.

In the past you've discussed the desire to invent new poetic forms as Kipling often did. Have you had any success with this?

WENDY COPE: Somewhere along the line, I realized that we don't always have to stick to the set forms. That we can do a lot of inventive things by allowing ourselves to alter the rules a bit—or making up our own rhyme schemes. So I do it more often now.

In your poem "An Argument with Wordsworth," you question his notion that poetry is "emotion recollected in tranquillity," and claim that "Sometimes poetry is emotion recollected in a highly emotional state." Is that generally true for you?

WENDY COPE: Tranquillity is not something I often experience. These days, there's definitely more tranquillity in my life than there used to be, and it's certainly something I long for, but, as you can see, I'm basically a very tense, anxious person. There's just not a lot of tranquillity in my life.

As a final question, I wonder what advice you'd give to aspiring writers?

WENDY COPE: That's easy. They have to read. There's nothing more important, is there?

No, but I guess I'd mention reading across the scale. Sometimes, kids read only contemporary poetry.

WENDY COPE: That's right. They need to read the poetry of the past as well as the poetry of the present. On the other hand, sometimes you get older people, older beginners, who haven't read anything since Tennyson.

That's true. Well, I'd like to finish up today by reading your short poem "Favourite," which is one of your most tender poems, yet it still encapsulates your unique ability to say serious things with wit and clarity:

> *When they ask me, "Who's your favourite poet?"*
> *I'd better not mention you,*
> *Though you certainly are my favourite poet*
> *And I like your poems too.*

Thank you.

WENDY COPE: Thank you, Bill.

FREDERICK MORGAN

For fifty years, Frederick Morgan has been the guiding force behind the prestigious literary quarterly, *The Hudson Review*. He is also a distinguished writer and translator, and, as Daniel Hoffman has written in *The Southern Review*, he is "one of our most original and accomplished poets."

Born and raised in New York City, Frederick Morgan studied under Allen Tate and R. P. Blackmur at Princeton University. During World War II, he served in the U.S. Army's Tank Destroyer Corps; and after the war, in 1947, he co-founded *The Hudson Review* which quickly became one of America's foremost literary periodicals, publishing, among others, Pound, Eliot, Mann, Williams, and Stevens.

In 1972, his first collection of poems, *A Book of Change*, was published by Scribner and nominated for the National Book Award. His subsequent books include *Poems of the Two Worlds*, 1977; *Death Mother and Other Poems*, 1979; *Northbook*, 1982; *Poems: New and Selected*, 1987; and *Poems for Paula*, 1995.

This interview was conducted during the Exploring Form and Narrative Poetry Conference at West Chester University in Pennsylvania.

One of the most recurring images in your poetry is that of someone, often a young boy, looking out a window and reflecting on—or fantasizing about—the world outside. Is that an image of childhood in general or does it refer to a specific autobiographical sense of loneliness?

FREDERICK MORGAN: I think I've generalized from an actual, pervasive feeling of loneliness which I had as a young boy. I was an only child, and I grew up surrounded by adults in my parents' house on West

Eleventh Street in New York City. Aside from my parents, there were two or three servants in the house, and my father's mother would join us for a couple of months each summer when we moved out to vacation in the "country"—what is now suburbia. So I was a solitary child surrounded by older people; and although I had some opportunities to play with other children in both the city and the country, I still spent a great deal of time alone. As a result, I did a lot of reading. I was able to read at a very early age, and I read a tremendous amount of children's literature, especially fairy tales and fantasies of various kinds. So I had this highly developed interior life along with an undeveloped social life, which seems to have worked both ways. On the one hand, I could be very lonely, and I was even subject to depression from time to time, but on the other hand, I greatly enjoyed the reading, and it created a valuable resource which I've always been able to draw on. So I think that's the source of that particular image in my poetry—which no one has ever commented on before except my friend Emily Grosholz who once said, "You know, you're always looking out the window."

It's a very powerful image, not just in poetry, but also in film—with its sense of separation, and maybe longing or imagining, all kinds of things.

FREDERICK MORGAN: Yes, exactly.

As an undergraduate at Princeton University, you studied under Allen Tate who was a new instructor at the time. Did you get to know him well? And in what ways do you think he might have influenced you?

FREDERICK MORGAN: Allen Tate arrived at Princeton in the fall of 1939 as the university's first teacher of creative writing, and it was the same semester that I arrived there for my freshman year. The university didn't call him a "professor" at the time because the traditional departments, displeased with the idea of creative writing classes, looked down on Tate as an intruder. So I was a member of the very first creative writing class at Princeton which was one of the earliest in the United States.

Back then, it was an experiment which, of course, would later mushroom out of control. There were about twelve of us in the program including Joseph Bennett, and we felt that we were a special group, which, in truth, we were, because Tate had chosen us from a large pool of applicants. As it turned out, he was a marvelous teacher. I found him opening doors with every session because he introduced us to modern writing—to James and Joyce and Eliot and Stevens. These were all writers who, in 1939, were only on the fringes of recognition in typical university English departments. When I was at Princeton, for example, the English Department didn't go beyond the end of the nineteenth century, and that was one of the reasons I became a French major, because there were French courses that covered Valéry, Gide and Proust. At the time, we felt the English Department was hopelessly retrograde. It taught according to the old-fashioned methods of biography and literary influences, and we had a youthful contempt for that outlook. I now feel that that contempt was unwarranted and not entirely fair because I can see a great deal of merit in that approach. Personally, I think we should have another look at those methods now. But at the time we were very excited by Tate and the New Critics. He introduced us to the critical writings of Eliot, Empson, I. A. Richards, Winters, John Crowe Ransom, R. P. Blackmur, and the whole New Critical gang. Through Tate, and through these readings, I first seriously studied the Metaphysical poets. Up until then, they always seemed like some odd people in the anthologies, but now they suddenly came alive. I also studied the French Symbolists, and got a great deal out of reading Baudelaire and Rimbaud. So I owe a lot to Tate since he helped form my intellectual outlook. He explained, for example, how Flaubert was different from Dickens, and we learned to put tremendous value on *le mot juste*—and on writing with a very careful, self-conscious point of view. Unfortunately, that was, I must admit, accompanied by an undue feeling that Dickens wasn't really a first-rate writer because he wasn't as meticulous; but, of course, as I've gotten older, I've developed enormous admiration for Dickens, without losing my admiration for Flaubert. So our approach to literature was definitely one-sided, as I think many new and exciting literary ideas are. As we became focused on certain aspects of literature that had not been fully appreciated in the past, we tended to overlook the merits of what was being displaced, but historically, of course, they both performed a crucial service. So I was taught to see things from a new and exciting point of view by a marvelous teacher.

What was Tate like personally?

FREDERICK MORGAN: He was a man with marked opinions, with a very strong and individual personality. He was warm-hearted and generous but, at the same time, quick-tempered and slow to forgive. He was quite easy to offend, and, if you did so, he tended to stay mad at you for a long time. But Bennett and I responded to him very favorably, although not all members of our group did. The following year, 1940, R. P. Blackmur joined Tate at Princeton and eventually took over the program. Blackmur was a very different kind of man: extremely secretive. He liked to draw the students out and have them confide in him, but he never revealed very much of himself. Of course, many students were quite willing to confide in Blackmur—not only their academic problems, but their personal ones as well. But I always shied away from that kind of involvement because I felt that he was getting vicariously involved in the lives of his students. Tate was never that way; he was totally professional. If somebody had a domestic problem, he'd be very sympathetic, but he never encouraged his students to talk about the details of their personal lives. He kept things focused on the literature, and I preferred it that way. In those days, of course, the relationship between teacher and pupil was much more defined than it is now. Yet despite that natural separation, he was very generous. Later, after the war, he greatly encouraged us when we started up *The Hudson Review*. So looking back, I feel that I owe more to Allen Tate than to any other teacher I ever had, although I had other very good teachers in both high school and college.

What writers from the past do you feel have most affected your writing and critical thinking? Some critics have suggested Catullus, Lucretius, Blake, and Mallarmé.

FREDERICK MORGAN: All those writers have definitely influenced me. I've read Blake with great admiration and attention, and I've similarly read Lucretius at various intervals in my life. But I would have to add Yeats to the list. Yeats means an enormous amount to me.

Were you reading him as an undergraduate?

FREDERICK MORGAN: I first read him as an undergraduate, but the real impact of Yeats's poetry didn't hit me until the early sixties. He means a great deal to me now, as does Byron. I particularly admire the verve, passion, and elegant jauntiness that Byron achieved in his later work.

While you were at Princeton, World War II broke out, and you served as a Staff Sergeant in the U.S. Army Tank Destroyer Corps. Where were you located and what were your responsibilities?

FREDERICK MORGAN: I was sent to Texas for basic training, to Camp Hood, as it was called back then. My assignment was decided by a lottery, by chance. I could have been sent to artillery school or an infantry post or whatever, and Camp Hood just happened to be the tank destroyer center, a special branch of the service which has not survived as such. It was the brain child of some high Army officer who believed that a special weapon was needed to counteract Rommel's Afrika Korps in North Africa. I had no particular expertise or aptitude for being assigned to that particular group, but I was, along with some of my Princeton classmates who were called to active duty at the same time. Like a number of other students at Princeton, I'd enlisted in the army about a year earlier, nine months before my scheduled graduation, on a plan that allowed us to continue our studies and get our degrees on an accelerated schedule, with the understanding that we'd be called into the army at any moment thereafter. And that's what happened. I was called about three weeks after graduating, in January of 1943, and I did my basic training in Texas—including artillery training and training for armored vehicle combat. But when it was over, instead of being shipped to active duty in one of the combat regiments overseas, I was kept at the tank destroyer center to train other soldiers. Part of the reason for that, I suspect, was my vision. I wore glasses then, as I do now, and I remember that my service record was stamped with some kind of limitation. I can't remember the exact initials, but it meant that I shouldn't be considered immediately qualified for combat duty because of my eyesight. So I remained at Camp Hood throughout the time of my service and ended up in charge of the files of the entire organization.

One of the few poems that you've written about your wartime experiences is "I Call It Back . . ." from your recent book Poems for Paula *(1995) in which you write of "the war":*

> *with all its cruel rituals of loss—*
> *the horror that had overhung my youth*
> *full-blown at last and ready to devour.*

FREDERICK MORGAN: Yes. That poem actually refers to my time at Princeton immediately before being called into service, and I wrote the poem to convey the exact experience. Years later, Paula Deitz and I were having dinner in a New York restaurant—it was candlelit, with a pleasant atmosphere—and they played "Blues in the Night" over their sound system, and it all came back to me.

A popular song of the time?

FREDERICK MORGAN: Yes, "Blues in the Night" by Johnny Mercer. I think it's a masterpiece—a pop masterpiece—and it was out in late '41 or '42. So the song tied the present to the past in the poem, one that was revised many times and took a long time to complete. As for my army experiences, I once wrote a sequence of poems about life at Camp Hood, but I'm not fully satisfied with them yet. They're on my agenda of projects to work on.

After the war ended, what inspired you to create The Hudson Review?

FREDERICK MORGAN: When we were still undergraduates, I remember Allen Tate saying, "Now, some day you boys ought to start a literary magazine of your own." "You boys" was the way he referred to us collectively, but in this particular instance he was addressing Joe Bennett and me. Tate knew that we'd been working on the *Nassau Literary Magazine* which was a very important experience for Bennett and me. We'd met in creative writing class, but it was while working together on the *Nassau Literary Magazine* that we became close friends and first had the actual experience of editing a literary magazine. It was an invaluable experience.

After you founded The Hudson Review *in 1948 with Joseph Bennett, it quickly became one of the most important and influential literary journals in America. Looking back, as you celebrate the journal's fiftieth anniversary, have your objectives changed very much from those early days in 1948?*

FREDERICK MORGAN: Not very much at all; they remain pretty much the same. The chief difference is that in 1948 we only had a vision—one that lacked substance. We didn't have the writers yet—I only knew one or two personally—and our aims were all directed towards what we hoped to accomplish in the future: discovering new writers and so on. So now, fifty years later, I feel that we've accomplished some, at least, of our objectives, and that we've accomplished them reasonably well.

What was William Arrowsmith's role in the beginning?

FREDERICK MORGAN: Bill joined us before we actually published the first issue, but he wasn't really there at the very beginning, during the long formation of our plans. Bill joined us in '46 or '47, at Joe's suggestion, so I don't think of him when I remember the actual beginnings of the magazine when we were still envisioning the future.

The Hudson Review *established itself very quickly.*

FREDERICK MORGAN: Yes, and I suppose by the 25th anniversary I could have said that we'd already done what we'd set out to do; but it was still very exciting to continue, especially since more and more interesting younger writers kept popping up all the time. That's what makes editing the magazine such a rewarding job, and that's why Paula is so excited about carrying on. Just this morning, she's already read a couple of new manuscripts, and we were discussing some new writers before you arrived.

Unlike most journals, The Hudson Review *has been justly praised for its various endeavors: its poetry, its fiction, and its commentary. Looking back, what were some of the more gratifying publications?*

FREDERICK MORGAN: Joe and I were very excited in the early years to get our first piece from T. S. Eliot, and we felt the same way when Thomas Mann sent us an excerpt from his latest novel for our third issue.

Which novel was that?

FREDERICK MORGAN: *Doctor Faustus.* I had this very lucky and special relationship with Thomas Mann, and he told Knopf that I could have any chapter of *Doktor Faustus* I wanted for *The Hudson Review.* They didn't like the idea, and, now that I'm older, I don't blame them at all. We were certainly stealing a bit of their thunder, but Thomas Mann wrote his own ticket and got whatever he wanted. He had a soft spot for Princeton, and I'd written him when I was an undergraduate, and he remembered that when we started the magazine. He was very generous, and it was a real thrill.

How about Pound?

FREDERICK MORGAN: That started, amazingly enough, when I went down to visit him at St. Elizabeth's, and he handed me something for the magazine. It was quite overwhelming.

Didn't he start writing you every day for a while?

FREDERICK MORGAN: Yes, and he got to be a real pain in the ass.

I'm sure he wanted to take over the journal.

FREDERICK MORGAN: At first, I was very flattered. I thought, "Wow, here's this great man writing me all the time!" and I worked hard to decipher all the arcane references in his letters. But I couldn't make heads or tails out of a lot of them. He was mostly talking about monetary theorists and that sort of thing. Eventually, he started telling me to "do this" or "don't do that," and I found him rather tiresome.

You also published William Carlos Williams.

FREDERICK MORGAN: Yes, that was also very exciting. Williams had been avoiding *The Hudson Review* at first because he felt that we represented people who didn't like his work. So in the fifties some time, I wrote him a letter, and he responded very generously. We published a number of his late poems and a wonderful story called "The Farmers' Daughters." After he died, his widow, writing in response to my letter of sympathy, said that *The Hudson Review* was Bill's favorite magazine in his last years—the one he most relied on. So we were very fortunate over the years. I still remember the excitement of discovering Anne Sexton's first poems—and Louis Simpson's. I believe that we were the very first magazine to publish Louis Simpson, and we published both Anthony Hecht and James Merrill early in their careers. We also published Malraux. In the late fifties, while I was on a flight to Rio de Janeiro, I read his excellent piece about T. E. Lawrence in a French literary magazine. So I wrote him, and said, "If we have it translated, may we publish it?" and he agreed. I ended up doing the translation myself. That was great fun. And so was publishing Mark Twain. About twenty-five years ago, I read in the *Times* that a critic named Charles Neider was collecting various works of Twain, and that a selection from these writings about religion had been accepted by the *Atlantic Monthly*. But the *Atlantic* reneged on the agreement because they had decided the material would be too offensive. I thought, "Well, let's have a shot at this," and I managed to reach Charles Neider by phone. He was down in Florida at the time, and he sent the piece to me, and we published it. It had something in it to offend everyone!

You were always regarded as an editor who would tolerate a wide range of strong opinions from your contributors. Did that cause problems?

FREDERICK MORGAN: In the early years of the magazine, Bennett tended to be conservative in his views, and Arrowsmith tended to be anti-establishment. This was intriguing—because Bennett was conservative but not part of the literary establishment, whereas Arrowsmith was very anti-establishment, yet constantly receiving prestigious academic positions. It seemed the more he kicked the academy, the more they offered him special professorships of this and that! At any rate, the two sometimes had major disagreements—which was very interesting, too, since it was originally Bennett's idea that we involve Arrowsmith in *The Hudson Review*. At the time, I thought it was a good idea, but then the two of them began fighting occasionally, and it was generally right-wing versus left-wing. So I found myself in the mediating position, which also gave me the swing vote on a lot of decisions, which was fine with me. I could always appreciate their different points of view, but I've never been a very ideological person, and I've never been able to get worked up about political programs. There are certain matters, of course, that I can get angry about, but they have to be pretty gross and extreme. So I guess there are some limits to my editorial tolerance. But within a certain spectrum, I feel that all opinions should be expressed, and I've enjoyed letting that happen. In the early days, we got a lot of heat when we published Ezra Pound. There was a barrage of hate mail from people who'd decided that since Pound was anti-Semitic and Fascist, that made us anti-Semitic and Fascist as well. Then, around the same time, we published a piece by Eisenstein on film, translated by Jay Leyda, which ends with a brief paean to the Communist party and "our great leader" Joseph Stalin. Leyda said, "You can cut that if you want," but I felt, "No, he wrote it that way, so why cut it?" But it certainly didn't make us Communists! So we did what we thought was best. Most of those kinds of difficulties took place in the early years when I was younger and less experienced and less thick-skinned about it. Nowadays, in all honesty, I just don't care. Someone's always accusing you of being this, that, or the other thing. You just can't worry about it.

From 1948 to 1968, you published occasional poems, but your first collection of poetry, A Book of Change *(1972), wasn't published until you were fifty years old. Is it true that during those two decades, you abandoned your own poetry for your editorial responsibilities at* The Hudson Review? *And is it true that the shock of your son John's death in 1968 rekindled your interest in writing poetry?*

FREDERICK MORGAN: Yes, both are true. Inescapably true. At the time of my son's death, I went through such an emotional crisis and upheaval that it resulted in breaking up my marriage. Not long after that, I became very close to Paula, so a great deal was happening in my life during that period. It was, without doubt, the greatest personal crisis of my life—the crucial watershed—and I was very grateful in those years to have *The Hudson Review,* because I could always stick to that when everything else seemed to be falling apart.

Up until that time, was it always a plan in the back of your mind to eventually give more time to your own writing?

FREDERICK MORGAN: Yes, but I kept postponing it. I would always say to myself that "next year" I'll arrange my schedule in such a way that I'll have more time to write, but it never happened. I was enmeshed in so many different things at the same time. Besides *The Hudson Review,* I also had children to raise and, after my father's death in 1964, I had family business responsibilities to manage. There were a number of important financial obligations involving other family members that I had to deal with, so I kept putting off the poetry until after John's death. Then my life fell into chaos, and I somehow began writing, and that resulted in the publication of my first book.

As a number of literary critics have remarked, your poems are clearly unafraid of the grand themes that we traditionally relate to poetry: love, death, sorrow, redemption, and eternity. One of your most important poems, which seems to touch upon all of those themes, is "February 11, 1977" in which the narrator, nine years after the death of his son, reflects on his own mutability versus the permanence of his son. The poem ends, powerfully:

and so I age from self to self
while you await me, always young.

In this poem, as in many of your poems, there's a "message" or truth that the narrator can't quite grasp, yet it still doesn't seem totally unattainable.

FREDERICK MORGAN: Well, I think that's the ambiguous, ultimate question which all religions try to cope with—and many non-religious people as well. I've had a few experiences in my life which I could call—which, in fact, I *do* call—timeless moments: moments in which one reaches a certain kind of awareness of a state of being of which one is a part. It's unclear whether this state of being is an aspect of one's self, or outside one's self—whether it's the transcendent self or the transcendent power behind the universe, or both somehow merged together. Those are wonderful moments, but they're also, in a way, always beyond one's grasp. They can only be apprehended briefly, at least in my own case, but they're profoundly affecting. One sense that you have is that there's really no great hurry about anything in life, and another is that there's an aspect of one's self that's permanent, that's there all the time. And these ideas, as you've pointed out, have clearly influenced a number of my poems like "February 11, 1977," "The Breathing Space," "The Summit," and others.

Why do you think that so many contemporary poets avoid subjects like spirituality, prayer, and the notion of redemption?

FREDERICK MORGAN: That's a difficult question to answer because I can't speak for other people, but maybe most of them haven't felt the urge or the need for these things. Maybe many poets, like many other people, feel that they're beyond discussion right now, or that there's something pretentious and self-regarding about even attempting to understand them. Or maybe, for some people, they imply an unhealthy need for some kind of bogus emotional reassurance.

That such an interest might indicate a personality weakness?

FREDERICK MORGAN: Yes, and I can understand that point of view. Maybe my own sensibility along these lines is something that's becoming obsolete in human life.

In human life?

FREDERICK MORGAN: Well, not really in human life. Just in poetry. And if it's still part of the human frame of possibilities, then it *should* be perfectly acceptable as subject matter for poetry. My own belief on this subject was best expressed by something that Lorenzo de' Medici once said. I got it from Goethe who quoted Lorenzo. Lorenzo said that the person who hasn't contemplated eternal life and immortality hasn't really lived, but one mustn't put on airs about it because death is certain. And that's how I feel. I think he got it exactly right. It's part of being a human being to have such aspirations.

And sense of wonder?

FREDERICK MORGAN: Exactly. There's a great mystery there. A few years ago, I read a marvelous collection of essays by Martin Gardner, the masterly popularizer of science. Have you ever read him?

Yes, the mathematician and skeptic. I've been reading him since I was a kid, and I was astonished to learn that he wasn't a complete materialist—that he had religious views.

FREDERICK MORGAN: Yes, he's very open about things, and I think that's the most honest way you can be.

One of your most famous poems is "Hideyoshi." It's about a brutal Asian warrior, who, after a battle in which his enemies have been "cut to pieces," tries to clear his mind before deciding the fates of the vanquished by making a flower arrangement. Where did the idea come from?

FREDERICK MORGAN: I read the story in a book about Japanese history which I borrowed from someone years ago. The anecdote explained that Hideyoshi was just as brutal as the other warlords, but had, in addition, a great political talent, and actually began the process of unifying feudal Japan. One of his principles of action was that after battle he didn't automatically humiliate or kill his vanquished enemies. He would try to judge the situation calmly and make efforts to arrange for a lasting peace. This statesmanlike aspect of his personality was implemented by the Japanese ritual of flower arrangement, and that practice—like the tea ceremony and the arts of archery and swordsmanship—was a traditional Japanese ceremony ultimately related to the Zen discipline.

So it's something he really did after battle?

FREDERICK MORGAN: It's a story about him, at any rate. Maybe it's like George Washington and the cherry tree, but I think it has more substance. I found it fascinating, and I tried to tell it in as concise a form as I could manage.

It's a wonderful poem. I'd also like to ask you about the source of your narrative poem, "The Trader," in which a Western trader, who has "married" a native in a bogus wedding ceremony, comes to appreciate her love after she nurses him through an illness. Where did that idea come from?

FREDERICK MORGAN: From a story by Robert Louis Stevenson called "The Beach of Falesá." Actually, there's a section of the poem that's a direct quote from Stevenson about seeing the natives in their colorful garb. But, if I remember correctly, I made up the parts about the fake wedding ceremony and the woman nursing him back to health. I'd have to reread the short story to see exactly where the story ends and my invention begins.

It seems appropriate that Daniel Hoffman once praised you as an excellent translator of some of Baudelaire's more horrific poems since you've written so many creepy poems yourself: like "1904" where the children did something unmentionable many years ago, "The Body" where a corpse floats up in a lake, or "The Skulls" who rattle on about what they seem to know. Is Poe a possible influence here? I know that as a child you read Weird Tales, *and even attempted to write one.*

FREDERICK MORGAN: I'm sure Poe influenced me. It might be very submerged, but it's there. When I was young, I read Poe with horror and fascination, and, off and on, I still take a look at him. Some of his best work still connects with me. "The Body," however, came directly from a trashy piece of pulp detective fiction that I read in paperback years ago.

So you were reading pulp novels at some point.

FREDERICK MORGAN: Oh, I've read more trash than you could load into twenty-five huge trucks. I've read all kinds of junk, especially when I was younger. Science fiction, thrillers, stuff like that.

In 1995 you published something very different—a collection of love poems, Poems for Paula, *dedicated to your wife and co-editor, Paula Deitz. It's a wonderful book, of a kind not often attempted any more—direct, unabashed, and sincere. I wonder if you found it hard to celebrate, so publicly, your personal feelings for your wife? It's something that people tend not to do anymore, or at least, not while both parties are still alive.*

FREDERICK MORGAN: I was aware that I was putting myself on the spot, and I weighed each poem in the book very carefully. I'd had the idea for the book in the back of my mind for at least twenty years, and, when it was done, it was rejected by a number of publishers. This was while I had an agent who thought she could market the collection as a sort of beside-the-cash-register book. She worked hard at it but eventually gave up, and I told Robert McDowell about the book. When he read the manuscript, he offered to publish it at Story Line Press, and I was delighted. So I'd given the book a great deal of thought over many years. I wanted it to be a combination of outspoken, direct poems—more or less intimate stuff, without going over the edge—with other more abstract, thoughtful poems in which the connection to Paula might only be apparent to her and to me—poems that had a particular meaning for her. For example, "The Summit," which I repeated from an earlier book, has always been one of her favorites because of a shared philosophy. From my point of view, it has always been associated with her. Then to give the book structure, there's a seasonal progression, ending up with an Easter poem, followed by a final section which goes off into that timeless region that we were discussing earlier—and which climaxes with "The Summit."

So you felt confident about your individual choices?

FREDERICK MORGAN: By the time the book was published I did. I'd lived with those poems for many years, and I'd eliminated some that were, in my opinion, too outspoken—that might have been considered in poor taste. I also circulated the manuscript among a few close friends who gave me good advice and helped me see certain weaknesses in earlier versions of the manuscript.

The overall structure is very tight and helpful.

FREDERICK MORGAN: I hope so. Tightness was something that I was very concerned about because I feel that my earlier collections suffered from being so diverse. That diversity made it hard for readers and critics to grasp an overall direction in those books, which I think suffered as a consequence. They were so diverse that they were hard to describe as a whole, and I didn't want that to happen with *Poems for Paula*.

Aside from your own poems, you've also done a wide range of excellent translations from Catullus, Dante, Baudelaire, and many others. You said earlier that you were a French major at Princeton. Did you begin translating poetry at that time?

FREDERICK MORGAN: Not at Princeton. After the war, I taught myself to read Spanish, which was a pretty simple matter since I already knew French and Latin. I got hold of a Spanish grammar, subscribed to a Spanish newspaper for three or four years, and at one point started reading a little anthology of Spanish poetry which a friend of mine had used as a textbook at Princeton. Just as an experiment, I started to translate some of the poems into English. It was simply an exercise to help me learn the language, but I enjoyed it very much. Then, around the same time, my friend Francis Mason, the dance critic who was then ghost writing a book for George Balanchine called *101 Stories of the Great Ballets*, asked me to do a translation of Mallarmé's "L'Après-midi d'un faune." What a challenge! I said, "But Francis, that'll take me years. Have you looked at that poem? Do you know what you're asking me to do?" And he said, "Yes, I do, Fred, and Doubleday will pay you quite well for it." I can't remember the exact fee, but it was quite substantial for the time. So after a lot of hesitation and more reservations, I decided to give it a try, and I became absolutely fascinated and engrossed in the work. There was no rush, and I took two years to do it, and Francis was very pleased with the result. Ironically, although I got my fee, the poem was never published in the book because his manuscript came in at 1500 pages, and Doubleday insisted that he cut out a third or so. Naturally, Francis was very embarrassed, but I assured him it was okay, and I stuck the poem into *The Hudson Review* with Joe Bennett's approval. I've revised it over the years, and it's something that I feel very good and confident about even though it doesn't follow Mallarmé's line exactly. I did something unusual with that poem, something I've never done since. I translated the French alexandrine line of 12 syllables into English tetrameters. So, roughly, that comes to 3 lines of my translation to every 2 lines from Mallarmé, and I'm very pleased with the result. That was the project that started me translating from the French and re-reading all the Symbolist poets, notably Baudelaire and Verlaine and Mallarmé. I became especially fascinated by Baudelaire's "Un Voyage à Cythère" which Angel Flores used, along with a few other of my translations, in his Anchor book of modern French poetry.

He used quite a few of your translations in that anthology. It's a wonderful book.

FREDERICK MORGAN: Yes, but it's out of print now, unfortunately. I owe him a lot because of his encouragement, and I loved doing those translations.

Your New and Selected Poems has a wide variety of your translations. Do you have enough for a book of selected translations?

FREDERICK MORGAN: I do, if I could persuade a publisher to do a book of scattered translations—a handful from French, a handful from Latin, and a handful from classical Greek, etc. But publishers, understandably, don't have much use for that kind of a book because it can't be marketed the way a more focused book can—like Charles Martin's translations of Catullus, for example. Over the years, I've been asked a number of times to do such projects, but I've always had to decline. Years back, it was suggested that I translate all of Paul Valéry's poems. This offer came from Jackson Mathews, the great editor of *The Collected Works of Paul Valéry*, published by the Bollingen Series. More recently, I was tempted by an offer to translate the poems of du Bellay, but I was just too busy at the time to attempt those projects. In recent years, I have had to reserve my limited writing time for my own poems and not for translation.

Hayden Carruth once wrote of your own poems that they're "musical, rhythmic, inventive. In short they are well-written, in the sense once common among people who knew something about prosody—literate people—but now often ignored." You also write in a wide range of forms: quatrains, cinquains, blank verse, villanelles, even triolets. But you've written very few, if any, sonnets. Have you never felt the impulse? Or are you avoiding them for some reason?

FREDERICK MORGAN: I published some fourteen-line, unrhymed poems in *A Book of Change*, but I don't really think of them as sonnets. In recent years, I've only written one real sonnet, "May Night," which appeared in *The New Criterion* and should be in my next collection. I believe it's the only sonnet that I've done since those early pseudo-sonnets. "Winter Poem" is a thirteen-liner which I thought might turn out as a sonnet, but I didn't want to pad it, and it ended up at thirteen lines. Your observation is correct, and I'm surprised myself when I think about it. Sonnets are something I should write more often. Now that I expect to have more time for my own writing, I intend to follow up on more "formal" projects. That's my plan, and I'm looking forward to carrying it out.

You once said that, "different poems come with different rhythms. It's like the color of their eyes." Could you describe how you find those rhythms?

FREDERICK MORGAN: Almost inevitably, a poem starts for me in one of three ways. The first is with actual phrases and lines that appear in my head, touched off by idle thoughts, reflections, something I'm reading, or something I've heard somebody say. Since these are actual phrases, or lines, or fragments of lines, they already have a certain rhythm that I can work from. This is true even if they're fragmentary—the beginning or the end of some statement—something with dot dot dot in front of it or dot dot dot at the end. The second way a poem can begin for me is more ambiguous and somewhat formless. It's a kind of a rhythmic agitation. I don't know quite how to describe it. The words aren't clear yet, but some kind of emotion has been stirred up, an emotion associated with a certain rhythmic but wordless feeling. The third way is a kind of "forced labor." You say to yourself, "I've got this form, and I'm going to fit something in to it and make a real poem." That can be very risky because you may grind out something trite and uninspired. But it can also be very successful. So that's how they start with me. Usually after I've worked on a poem for four or five days, I pretty well know whether it's working and where it's going—and whether it'll be a tightly formal poem like "Washington Square," or a sort of relaxed pentameter like

"The Trader"—which seemed appropriate given its prose derivation from the story by Stevenson.

But "The Trader" has a definite rhythm.

FREDERICK MORGAN: Yes, and there's a lot of rhythm in Stevenson's original prose. That's one of the things that attracted me to it. I said right from the start, "It's going to be a narrative, and he's going to talk in a prosy blank verse."

You also mentioned "Washington Square." How did that come about?

FREDERICK MORGAN: It's the most ambitious poem, and certainly the longest poem, that I've published since *New and Selected Poems* over ten years ago. It has a very elaborate and formal stanza pattern with rhyme and meter, and I set about it quite deliberately. It took me over a year to write the poem, concentrating on nothing else, and I discovered, as I wrote it, the truth of James Fenton's words which Wendy Cope quoted last night: that the discipline of following the demands of the form will help the writer zero in on exactly what he wants to say. I certainly found that to be true in the case of this poem which began in a casual sort of way as I began searching for an appropriate content for this pre-determined format—something I seldom do. When I recalled a child-hood event in a park where I used to play when I was a little boy, several lines arose in that format, and I said to myself, "All right, you're really on the hook now because you've started this poem in this difficult form, and now you've got to finish it"—which wasn't easy. After many halts and wrestling matches with myself, I managed to break through various blockades and press on. There would be long periods that lasted weeks and weeks when I couldn't move on to the next stanza, but I'd finally get it going again and move forward. Then I revised, and revised, and revised, and, eventually, the poem came out to my satisfaction. Later, having done such a long and intricate poem, I wrote the sonnet "May Night." There I wanted to capture a certain flavor of what downtown New York was like, specifically Greenwich Village, years ago, immediately after World War II.

I also wanted to paint a vivid yet somehow ambiguous scene involving two lovers, so I tried it in the sonnet form, and I enjoyed it very much.

I'd like to finish up today with the last few lines of your excellent "Winter Poem," which also begins with two lovers in the city, but after they awaken from their rest, they discover that their room has been magically transported to a "dark woods frosted in snow." In amazement, they stare out through the windowpanes:

> *No men there—some small animals all fur*
> *stared gently at us with soft-shining eyes*
> *as we stared back through the chill frosty panes.*
> *Absolute cold gave us our warmth that night,*
> *we held hands in the pure throes of delight,*
> *the air we breathed was washed clean by the snow.*

Thank you very much for your time today and for your poetry.

FREDERICK MORGAN: Thank you.

W. D. SNODGRASS

W. D. Snodgrass has been described by Peter Porter in *London Magazine* as "a virtuoso, not just of versification but of his feelings," and *The New York Times* has called the Pulitzer Prize-winning poet, "One of the six best poets now writing in English."

W. D. Snodgrass was born and raised in Wilkinsburg, Pennsylvania, and he attended Geneva College before serving in the U.S. Navy during World War II. After military service, he attended the Writers' Workshop at the University of Iowa where he received his bachelor's degree in 1949 and a Master of Fine Arts degree in 1953. He subsequently taught at a number of universities including Cornell University, Wayne State University, Syracuse University, and, from 1980 until his retirement in 1994, the University of Delaware.

His books of poetry include *Heart's Needle*, 1959, for which he was awarded the Pulitzer Prize; *After Experience*, 1967; *Remains*, 1970; *The Fuehrer Bunker*, 1977; *Selected Poems: 1957–1987*, 1987; and *The Death of Cock Robin*, 1989. His other books include *In Radical Pursuit: Critical Essays and Lectures*, 1975; *Selected Translations*, 1998; and *After Images: Autobiographical Sketches*, 1999.

This interview was conducted at the University of Evansville in Indiana.

After your service in the U.S. Navy during World War II, you enrolled at the University of Iowa and planned to be a playwright, but you were never satisfied with your plays. Why was that?

W. D. SNODGRASS: They just weren't any good, and I had terrible teachers. In fact, the only way I could have made my plays worse was to do what my teachers were telling me to do. I had no respect for any of them, but one was particularly bad. She was a woman who'd kept Tennessee Williams in booze and food while he was a student there. We assumed that they were lovers, not realizing that he was homosexual. She was known around the whole campus as "The Bitch," and, in those days, you didn't talk about teachers that way on campuses. I still remember how she carried my first scenario, which was about the Fuehrer Bunker, through the classroom, pinched between her fingers and holding her nose with the other hand.

Yet your interest in monologues and performance indicates a natural dramatic impulse.

W. D. SNODGRASS: Yes, I love the theater, but I still feel that my plays were never very good. Eventually, *The Fuehrer Bunker* was done in a number of different dramatic formats, the best of which was directed by Annette Martin. But it isn't really a play; it's more of a theater piece. It's not realized as a play because there's no real conflict between Hitler and the other characters. Hitler's still in charge, and he'll squash anybody who questions him in any way. So the conflicts are all *within* the individual speakers, and that, no doubt, has something to do with my own nature. I'm not particularly good at portraying conflicts in the outside world—most of mine are internal. That doesn't mean that I don't get messed up now and then and get into trouble with people and things beyond myself, but I don't seem to be able to dramatize that very well, and I've focused more on interior conflict.

You once said that your earliest and most powerful poetic influence was William Empson. What attracted you to Empson's very careful, dense, and highly intellectual poetry?

W. D. SNODGRASS: It probably had a lot to do with the intellectuality, and also with the fact that I was very young at the time. Young people, when they discover ideas for the first time, think, "Oh, how wonderful! *This* is what will make the world manageable." And, of course, that's not how it works at all. But I still admire quite a number of those Empson poems. Admittedly, some are too intellectual and *too* removed, but for what they do, some do it very well indeed, and I still appreciate them.

They're very bold.

W. D. SNODGRASS: They certainly are. And they have a lot of character. They're different. They're definitely *his*. You know that right away when you read them. They're like a fireworks display.

Eventually, however, you began to write a very different kind of poetry, and after some of your very personal poems were published in Heart's Needle, *you were considered, by many critics, to be a "confessional" poet. But you've never liked the term, first coined by M. L. Rosenthal, and you've always felt that it didn't apply to your work. Why was that?*

W. D. SNODGRASS: No, I don't like the term. It seems to suggest that you're either a religious poet, which I'm not, or that you're writing some kind of bedroom memoir, which I'm *definitely* not. Please! That's the last thing—well, that's *one* of the last things—I want to be doing. I'm not seriously attracted to lurid sensationalism. At least, I hope not.

Often the confessional label seems to include not just sensationalism, but self-conscious exhibitionism—showing off your failings.

W. D. SNODGRASS: Absolutely. And showing off how the poet can break all the rules of propriety. I have no interest in that. So the term "confessional" seems to me a kind of journalist's term. Maybe I shouldn't accuse M. L. Rosenthal of being a journalist, but I think he just threw that term out there, and to my horror, it stuck.

Now when you began writing these more personal poems—which, from a historical perspective, were very unique at that time—you actually felt that you were returning to a poetic tradition that had essentially been abandoned. Could you discuss that?

W. D. SNODGRASS: That's right. At the time, it was considered highly improper to write poems about having a divorce or losing a child through divorce, or whatever—or even worse, writing a poem that used your own name. You just didn't do that because Pound and Eliot were "in," and Eliot was saying things like, "Poetry . . . is not the expression of personality, but an escape from personality." Of course, most people didn't bother to read the very next sentence where Eliot explained that you have to have a personality in order to want "to escape" from it. Now the reason that Eliot was saying these things, of course, was that he was disguising his own work, which was, in a certain sense, very confessional. At the time, we didn't fully understand "Prufrock"; we had no idea what it was really about. It wasn't until I heard Randall Jarrell discussing the poem that I realized that there was a lady in "Prufrock" whom he was planning to proposition. It was an absolute revelation! We also didn't understand *The Waste Land*, but, eventually, biographical matters were revealed, and we saw that, yes, these were poems about his own life. We must have been out of our minds! *Why* should anyone believe what a poet says about his own work? But we did, and, as a result, everybody was trying to write poems about "the loss of myth in our time" and stuff like that.

But for me, at that time, my personal life had begun to impact on my ability to write at all. Eventually, I was at a point where I hadn't been able to write for about two years. My first marriage was breaking up, and I was devastated, particularly by the imminent loss of my child. So I went into a shallow-level therapy at the university's hospital, and finally decided, partly in therapy, that I was going to write about all these things that were affecting me so greatly. I didn't care about the loss of myth in our time. I'd had plenty of myths in my own life; I'd grown up with them. In my family, there was nothing but lies, and myths, and more myths— myths about my mother's cooking, about my parents' intentions, about religion, about everything. And I didn't want any more of it, so I decided, okay, I'll write about what I really care about—about what I was interested in, and not what everyone else said I should be interested in. So that's how it happened. And my teachers were horrified. Well, at least, Lowell was. I think Paul Engle was more sympathetic, but Lowell was very opposed and very upset. At the time, I appreciated his concern, but I naturally hoped he was wrong.

How did your classmates at Iowa respond?

W. D. SNODGRASS: It varied. Some of them were very comfortable with it, some of them were kind of baffled, and some of them just backed away.

Even aside from the personal aspects of those poems, their clear and direct style was also quite a departure for those times.

W. D. SNODGRASS: Yes, and I think I was influenced by one of my classmates, Robert Shelley, and probably by the work of Richard Wilbur. But even Wilbur's language was far from barroom conversation, being obviously elevated and very elegant.

Wasn't Jarrell critical of your earlier, more elaborate, rhetorical style?

W. D. SNODGRASS: That's right. He said, "What are you trying to do, turn yourself into a fireworks factory?" He had no use for all the fancy language I'd been using.

And didn't he say something like, "You're striving to be a second-rate Lowell"?

W. D. SNODGRASS: He said, "You're writing the very best second-rate Lowell in the country."

Did it shake you up?

W. D. SNODGRASS: Yeah. A hell of a lot.

But isn't it natural that young writers will imitate the poets they most admire?

W. D. SNODGRASS: Of course. Jarrell would say, "Young poets are like little dogs who have a mistress who sings, and they love her voice so much that when she practices they sit under the piano and howl." He was very witty. His normal conversation could make a cat laugh—one of *his* phrases. He was an amazing man, but he could also be terribly brutal, and in public. He'd sit out on the plaza at the student union, surrounded by students, and he'd pick up one of your poems, and read it out loud, and howl with laughter, banging his thigh, and saying, "Snodgrass! Snodgrass! You wrote this!" And I wanted to kill him.

Had anything at Iowa prepared you for that?

W. D. SNODGRASS: Good heavens, no. I mean we were all very serious and kind to each other. But Jarrell could be awful. Maybe he was kinder to people whose work he didn't think showed much promise.

So if he saw some talent, he'd push harder?

W. D. SNODGRASS: Maybe. It's a possibility. I never got to know him well enough to be certain about what he was doing. But I've known other teachers like that, who'll ride hard on somebody they think has talent. I do know that Jarrell recognized some ability in my work, especially the translations.

You were translating back then?

W. D. SNODGRASS: Yes, I remember that there was a Rilke translation that he liked a lot. He said, "Look, I can understand this!" and I thought to myself, "Oh, *that* makes a difference. You're *supposed* to be able to understand the poem." Whereas the way we were generally taught, if you could understand the poem, it was somehow deficient. Then Jarrell said, "Look, I know who the characters are, I know what's happening, and I have a sense of development." And I thought, "Oh, all that matters too." So it was a whole new angle on things for me and very important.

It sounds like people were writing poems to be "studied," rather than to be read and enjoyed.

W. D. SNODGRASS: Absolutely! That's exactly what was going on. And, even today, there are plenty of people still doing it, and plenty of critics still making a living off of it.

Another very important influence for you was music.

W. D. SNODGRASS: Yes. I think the thing that moved me more toward a personal, passionate, clearer style was music, particularly two things that had a great influence on me. One was Mahler's "Kindertotenlieder," settings of poems by Rückert, which I discovered at Iowa. I then realized that many German poets in that earlier period had written poems about the death of a child, even some who'd never had any children. It was a standard situation that poets used to express a general sense of loss—of having dear things ripped away. The other major musical influence was the recordings of Hugues Cuénod, a Swiss tenor. He was an absolutely remarkable singer, a student of Nadia Boulanger, who sang right through the nose. Pang, pang, pang, on the notes. He'd put out a recording of Italian and Spanish songs of the sixteenth and seventeenth centuries, and I still remember the first time I heard them. My hair just leaped on end. They were incredible—immediate, and full of straight-forward passion. So I said to myself, "Okay, my poems are very intelligent and moral, but they don't have any passion." And I decided, "*That's* what I've got to go for!" But then of course, you start to realize how many other poets in the past not only wrote about their personal lives but did so with passion and clarity. Hardy, for example. As a matter of fact, if I'd known Hardy's poems about his dead wife— those poems of 1912 or so—I'm not sure I would have dared to write any personal poems of my own. So I came to realize, gradually, that poets had always done this, except during my own time, when Eliot kept saying, "Oh, you can't do that. You can't write about your love life."

Even though Eliot's writing about his own love life.

W. D. SNODGRASS: That's right! Of course, he was! That's why he was saying you couldn't do it! To keep us all in the dark.

One of the truly amazing things about your early personal poems—which you were writing as a student in the Iowa workshops—is that they had such a great effect on your teachers, particularly Robert Lowell and John Berryman. As Lowell later admitted, your early poems were the source of what eventually became the confessional movement. This must have been a very odd experience: influencing, so dramatically, the work of your famous teacher—and one whom you admired so much.

W. D. SNODGRASS: Yes, it was very traumatic for me.

Traumatic?

W. D. SNODGRASS: Heavens, yes.

Didn't you feel you were helping his work? Giving him something back?

W. D. SNODGRASS: I didn't think he needed any help. I thought he could have "trounced me" easily, any time—without any help from me or anyone else. It was very difficult to have somebody who'd been my idol, whom I'd admired *too* much, suddenly saying that he was imitating my work—or taking some of my poems as a model. He said it quite literally once, and it really shook me up. The poems had been brought back to his attention by Gertrude Buckman, the former wife of Delmore Schwartz, who was also at Iowa at the time. I'd been complaining that nobody would publish my poems, and that I couldn't get my first book accepted, so she showed them to Lowell, and he suddenly changed his mind about them.

In his Paris Review *interview, Lowell said of you: "He did these things before I did, though he is younger than I am and had been my student. He may have influenced me, though people have suggested the opposite." But didn't Lowell acknowledge this influence even more forcefully in a letter he wrote to you back then?*

W. D. SNODGRASS: Yes, but I can't remember the date. The letter's now somewhere in the archive.

At the University of Delaware?

W. D. SNODGRASS: Yes.

Robert Lowell also once referred to you as "the American Philip Larkin," and John Hollander, in reviewing Heart's Needle, *also compared you to the English poet.*

W. D. SNODGRASS: Well, I was just glad to have my name mentioned in *any* way—you know, "Call me names, but spell my name right!" Poets are as bad as politicians. You'd rather be blackened than ignored. But I certainly felt honored by those comparisons with Larkin.

Were you reading the contemporary British poets at Iowa?

W. D. SNODGRASS: I can't remember, but I knew who Larkin was, and I certainly knew some of his poems, like "Church Going," which is very impressive. But I don't think we knew a great deal about our British contemporaries, except that Donald Hall did—he'd been over there and knew them all personally. My reading has always been spotty—even more so in recent years. I don't read very many poets, but the ones that I like, I read again and again and again. But it's pretty selective, or haphazardly selective.

You once told William Packard in a New York Quarterly *interview that "It seems to me you're getting much closer to the poem when you get away from ideas and into emotions." Later, you added: "I think that for a poem you've got to have one of three things: either a new idea, which is awfully unlikely, or a new set of details, or a new style." Could you briefly discuss these ideas, which are covered in depth in your essay "Tact and the Poet's Force"?*

W. D. SNODGRASS: Well, in my opinion, the poet should offer readers something they can't get anywhere else. Why else should potential readers take time away from the business of earning a living, or their sexual and romantic pursuits, or any of the other ways they'd normally spend their time? I think this is crucial for the writer, and the problem is that a new idea doesn't turn up more than once every three hundred years, and once it's stated, it's not very interesting to simply restate it. We've all experienced the enthusiastic young poet who comes up and says, "I have this burning idea!" And you say, "Quick, what is it?" And he says, "Don't kill your fellow man," or something equally new and sparkling. So it seems to me, that the best way to make an "old" idea useful and "new" and interesting is for the writer to find a new set of details—an idiosyncratic and personalizing set of details—that reaffirm the concept, and that create a new way to arrive at the familiar conclusion. The only other possibility is to create a new style, and, since I believe that style equals personality, this will also individualize the idea in the same way that a unique set of details will. This is also where questions of meter and form come in, because it's in the unique application of those stylistic choices and their arrangements into language that personality and emotion can express themselves. And it's also how the writer can offer readers something that's different—something that's worth their while.

Yet people still claim that poetry needs to carry new ideas.

W. D. SNODGRASS: Yes, and political correctness above all. But we've heard all those ideas, and there's nothing valuable in being told them again in the same terms. In my poem about Spinoza and the combat instructor, both figures are expressing the same fundamental idea, but it certainly means something different when it comes from the mind of Spinoza than when it comes from the mind of a hired gorilla. It just isn't the same thing at all—it becomes something different and unique.

Discussing your long poem, "Heart's Needle," Louis Simpson wrote: "Divorce may be to this century what the frontier was to the last; Mr. Snodgrass's poem is a sort of American epic." Well, the poem's not really an epic, but it is dealing with this huge subject that probably hadn't been dealt with so intensely before, at least to my knowledge, in an extensive poem. Did you originally conceive the poem in such a broad context?

W. D. SNODGRASS: Well, that's a long time ago now, but I don't believe that I did. I just thought to myself, "I'm going to write about what I'm feeling regarding this situation—and what the facts really are." What I do remember is that I tried to write the poem in such a way that it would be a successful poem even if none of this had historically happened to me. Like those German poets I'd heard about who'd never really lost a child at all, except in their imaginations. I can also remember having the sense, while writing the poem, that it should be possible for a poet to take the events of his life and treat them as a kind of myth, turning one's life into one's own mythology, which was something Rilke and Lorca had done.

And Yeats.

W. D. SNODGRASS: Yes, certainly. Although I'm not sure that I was thinking about Yeats. But maybe I was at some level. I knew his work and admired him a lot. At any rate, I don't remember having a specific sense of the epic nature of the subject; I just knew that divorce was one of those things that you weren't supposed to write about, and later on, when the poem was done, I thought, "Well, maybe that's what made it worth doing," *if* it was worth doing, which we won't know for about 150 years anyway! But the loss of my child—having her ripped away from me by a person who didn't really want her, and who was only using the child for revenge, and, perhaps, a well-deserved revenge—that was terribly hard. And it was awfully hard on the child as well.

Your second book, Remains, *contains poems about your family that are so sensitive you decided to publish them under the pseudonym, "S. S. Gardons." The poems dealing with your parents are especially brutal and honest, and I wonder if you had doubts about publishing them at all—especially the ones that expose your mother's failings.*

W. D. SNODGRASS: Yes, I did. But I was trying to be honest—trying to deal with what I really felt at the time. I'd had great difficulty breaking away from my family, an experience which had exposed my own failings as much as theirs, although my personal failings had been formed, at least partly, by theirs. Then, after the break, my sister's death was extremely upsetting. I felt that she'd simply been devoured by my mother, and I was very angry and shocked and horrified by the whole situation, and I thought, "Okay, nobody's written about this recently, except for Tennessee Williams in *The Glass Menagerie*." I remember when my first wife and I saw a performance of that play at the University of Iowa not long after my sister had died, and we both came out weeping, crushed with grief. When she died, I was emotionally overwhelmed, and I felt that I needed to write about it. On the other hand, I didn't want to damage my parents. It was clear that they were doing what they felt they had to do, maybe the *only* things they were able to do, and being blamed for that would only make them worse, so I put the poems under a pseudonym, figuring that, in that way, my mother wouldn't walk into Kaufmann's in Pittsburgh and see a book with my name on it and buy it. I knew she'd never recognize that the name is, pretty much, Snodgrass spelled sideways. But at the same time, I felt my friends would know and understand.

Many of the most powerful poems in Remains *are informed by the tragedy of your sister's death at the age of twenty-five. One of these, "Disposal," ends:*

> *We sent back to its maker*
> *A life somehow gone out of fashion*
> *But still too good to use.*

Were you very close to your sister? And were you home when she died?

W. D. SNODGRASS: No, I wasn't there. She'd had asthma for many years, and she became ill while she was away at college, and my parents went and fetched her home. I can still remember my wife and I saying at the time, "Well, that's the end of her." But, of course, we had no idea just how accurate that statement would be. Then one morning, on the fourth of July, she simply got out of her bed and dropped dead. My brother was in the room next door, and he rushed to her bedroom, and she died in his arms. But the family doctor wouldn't say very much about it, just that the machine had "run down" at the age of twenty-five. She'd had no social life of any kind, and she'd only had one date in her life, which the family dismissed because he was Jewish. Yet she was quite a charming young woman. She had a marvelous sense of humor, but she was terribly, terribly shy and terribly tied to the family. Also, no doubt, there were some personal feelings of guilt on my part. I was the first child, and she was the second, and I'm sure that I resented her from early on. I later realized that I'd intentionally done a number of things while playing games that had endangered her life, but fortunately she was never hurt. I later came to understand just how much I must have resented her—that some part of me was trying to get rid of her. So then, when somebody else really did get rid of her, it was extremely upsetting, a terrible thing.

Weren't they ordinary kids' games?

W. D. SNODGRASS: Not really. There were games where I would get her to hold something, and I'd run a bayonet through it—where she could have easily been cut. Or worse, there were games where I would get her to lean out of a window, telling her that I was holding something she wanted to see, getting her to lean out farther and farther. It's sometimes called original sin.

Many of these poems about your family illustrate one of your most striking assets as a poet: the ability to bring your poems to a powerful, effective closure—often with an understated but unforgettable, declarative final line or lines. This trait has remained consistent throughout all your work, for example: "And you are still my daughter" ("Heart's Needle"); "Nothing is different here" ("The Survivors"); "I tell you love is possible, / We have to try" ("To a Child"); "Next morning you had gone" ("Partial Eclipse"); "We go about our business; / I have turned my back" ("The First Leaf"); and "We would no doubt have other rooms then, / Or other names" ("Leaving the Motel"). When you're writing and rewriting your poems, do you concentrate on closure? Is it something that you begin with, or is it something that just happens as you're creating the poem?

W. D. SNODGRASS: Well, I never begin there. I was just re-reading that Robert Frost line where he says, it's "but a trick poem and no poem at all if the best of it was thought of first and saved for the last." If there's no surprise for the writer, then there'll be no surprise for the reader. So when I'm writing, I simply press on—revising a great deal—until I find what seems like the right ending.

Well, that makes sense given that these final lines, written in a very straight-forward declarative manner, have accumulated a tremendous amount of weight given what has come before them in their respective poems.

W. D. SNODGRASS: That to me is almost the essence of a poem. The parts of a poem have to feed off each other, and if they don't, to me it isn't poetry. Well, maybe that overstates the case a bit since I've read some good poems that don't do that exactly, but *most* of the poems that I admire do manage to achieve that—they feed toward a climatic expression of some kind, a "knock-out" blow.

Your long poem, The Fuehrer Bunker, *is a series of dramatic monologues which begins with a powerful citation from Mother Teresa who explains that she began her ministry of care for the poor, "On the day I discovered I had a Hitler inside me." In the past, you've admitted that the poems in* The Fuehrer Bunker *"aren't really about the Nazis, they're about me," and you've claimed that they're "more confessional than the other poems I've written." Could you discuss this a bit?*

W. D. SNODGRASS: Well, first, I'd still have to stress that the poems are about the Nazis. I read all the memoirs and histories and documents until I was absolutely sick of them. So, it's definitely about them, but, on the other hand, everything I write comes out of my own mind—and my personal recognition of those characters and their thoughts.

And when you try to comprehend the darker aspects of those historical figures, you have to look inside yourself?

W. D. SNODGRASS: Yes. Which was very hard sometimes, especially with Hitler. It's hard to admit to yourself that you hate other human beings that much, but there's a part of you that does. With Hitler, you also have to explore the fact that you hate being human, that you hate the limitations of being exactly what you are. So it was very difficult to try and understand him. Whereas somebody like Himmler has certain aspects of caricature about him, much more than Hitler did. Himmler was actually a fuddy-duddy in many ways, but he was also the horrible man who killed all those innocent people. Once when he attended an execution that he'd ordered, he got sick to his stomach and almost fainted. Yet he actually said all those incredible things he says in the poem, like, "To have been through the things that we have had to go through [to kill six million Jews], and still to have remained basically decent, upright, and honorable men, that's remarkable." It sure is remarkable! It's blood-curdling! You can hardly believe it, but it's there in his speeches. And many different people recorded those speeches, so we know that he really said these things.

Shifting now to your wide-ranging translations, many of which are included in your recent Selected Translations *published by BOA, I'd like to ask about your practical methods of translation. I know you often use collaborators to help you with your translations, and I wonder if you could describe the procedures you use?*

W. D. SNODGRASS: Well, very often, we have to work by mail. That's what I did with Lore Segal when we did many, many—perhaps 150 or 170—poems of Morgenstern. We began working at Yaddo, where we were both guests one year, but, after that, we usually worked by mail. She'd send me a prose version of the poem, with lots of footnotes, and I'd compose a poetic version and mail it to her. Then she'd tell me why I had to do it over again, and then I'd do it again, and so on. I have also had a lot of fun, along with my wife Kathy, working with Szaruga, a Polish poet that we met at a conference in Bad Ems. He's a former member of Solidarity, and his father was a very famous poet in Poland. We got to talking at the conference—through interpreters—about

Herbert, the great Polish poet whom I admire enormously, and I got interested in reading some of Szaruga's own poems, and we decided that we would translate a few. But he knew only a few words of English, and I knew only a few words of Polish. Fortunately, there was a Hungarian at the conference who knew both Polish and English somewhat. So the four of us got together and started working on these translations, and Kathy and I greatly enjoyed it. That's when she first got interested in doing poetry translations, and she's done a lot since—some from the Polish, but mostly from the Spanish. Later, I took the Szaruga translations to a Polish woman who also speaks excellent English, and we checked things over. Naturally, I'd prefer to work directly with my collaborators, especially to get them to read the originals out loud, but, in the end, you have to work any way you can. Recently, I've done a lot of Romanian translations, and Kathy has done some as well.

Are you working individually or collaborating with Kathy?

W. D. SNODGRASS: It varies. But even when we work separately, we always end up showing what we've done to the other, and being told to do it again. You get weary working at your desk by yourself all the time, and it's very nice to be able to work with other people. I especially love working with musicologists on early music folk songs. For some reason, everybody assumes that those songs are dry as dust, but they're not, and nobody knows that better than the musicologists. So it's a great joy to work with them.

Aren't those songs particularly challenging since they place so many restrictions on the conscientious translator?

W. D. SNODGRASS: Yes! Again and again a line that will seem terrific on the page will simply refuse to sing well. And nobody, at least as far as I've been able to discover, fully understands what makes a line "singable." Often, in trying to translate those songs, I've written lines that I thought were brilliant, but I had to take them out when they wouldn't sing to the melody. Auden, who translated *The Magic Flute*, says a few things about this problem, and so did Bainbridge Crist, who wrote a little booklet about setting words to music, but there's not much to go on, so you just have to keep trying things, and singing them, until you get something that works.

Aside from translating a number of the Romanian folk songs, you've also translated epitaphs from the Sapintza Cemetery in Transylvania. Does your family have Romanian roots?

W. D. SNODGRASS: No, I have no Romanian background. But shortly after I got the Pulitzer, the State Department called me up and wanted to send me on a reading tour in Europe. So they sent me to a couple of places, and they were going to send me to Russia, but it was canceled. The Russians were pretending that they were mad at us for being in Vietnam, when actually nothing could have pleased them more. At any rate, in pretending to be angry, they canceled their U.S. cultural exchange for that year, which meant that they canceled me and *Hello Dolly!* So I was very disappointed, but, two weeks later, the State Department called up and said, "How'd you like to go to a bunch of little Iron Curtain countries instead?" And they gave me a list of the countries, and said, "We're not sure you can get into all of these places. Some of them haven't had visitors for ten years, but we'll try." At the time, I didn't even know the capital cities of these countries, I didn't know what the money was, I didn't even know what the language was, but it was very hard to say no, and I decided to go.

When I arrived in Romania, it was during Christmas time, and unfortunately—well, fortunately—all the poets were away on vacation someplace, and the U.S. officials were very apologetic, but I said, "That's fine." Poets are sometimes very nice people, and sometimes they're rotten people, but since I didn't speak Romanian, we weren't going to be able to talk about poetry anyway. So they said, "Well, who would you like to see?" And I said, "Early music people, folk music people," and they said, "Oh, that's a shame because there's a wonderful folklore institute right here in Bucharest, but if we apply for permission, it'll take six weeks." But the cultural attaché said, "Look, just walk over there, completely naive, knock on the door, and tell them what you want." So I tried it, and to my astonishment, I was taken to the head of the institute, a wonderful man named Dr. Mihai Pop, who was also a great ethno-musicologist and spoke perfect English. We talked for a long time, and he generously gave me armloads of books and records and other things when I left. So it was through Dr. Pop that I discovered some of the great Romanian ballads, in particular the one called "Miorita," which is the most highly-regarded of all, and known in some version by everyone in the country. Eventually, I was able to get a recording of that song and others, and I fell in love with them completely. In time, I began to translate the songs, working with a great number of people over the years. It's very, very hard to do, but I've managed to finish five of those ballads, which I think are absolute masterpieces in the original, although they're quite unknown here. "Miorita" is known only in Romania, whereas the second great one, called "Mesterul Manole"—meaning "The Master Builder Emmanuel"—is known throughout Europe.

You sent that one to us, and we published it in The Formalist.

W. D. SNODGRASS: Yes, of course! Unlike "Miorita," there are many versions of that song all over Europe, known by type as the "The Walled-up Wife." There's a wonderful Greek version, for example, and a marvelous Hungarian version as well.

You generally spend a great deal of time revising your work, often with the result of lengthening the original composition. Do you worry about prolixity? Or lack of compression?

W. D. SNODGRASS: Yes, I do worry about it, but it still happens. When you try to say something that you think hasn't been said before—at least in your own particular way—then it's worth the risk. The problem arises in my prose as well. My piece on Walt Whitman for *The Southern Review* expanded quite a bit before publication, and the piece I'm doing for them now about metrics started out around thirty pages and it's now up to sixty or seventy pages. It's damn near a book! And, of course, it's exactly what no one wants to read anyway! It's full of all kinds of technical things, and it involves being able to read music, but I think I've got a few interesting things to say about meter that nobody has ever discussed before.

Although you write in both formal and non-metrical formats, you once said that form facilitates your ability to "define" emotion. Could you discuss that?

W. D. SNODGRASS: Well, first of all, it seems to me that formal matters, which are related to spatial matters, are much more associated with the right side of the brain where the emotional things are happening. But there are even more important reasons than that, and they have to do with music and stress. The crucial thing in English poetry is always stress. And when you set up a pattern that's going unstressed, stress, unstressed, stress, soft, loud, soft, loud, weak, strong, weak, strong, you're also setting up an alternating pattern of a function-syllable and a meaning-syllable—form, fact, form, fact, etc. Take the simple example, "I saw a man who kissed his wife good-bye." In that iambic pentameter line, the key words are "saw," "man," "kissed," "wife," and "bye." That's where the meaning is—the information about the outside world. The other syllables are about syntax, how the sentence is constructed. Now, of course, this gets more complicated with polysyllables, but let's just stick to monosyllables. Once the writer sets up the pattern—form, fact, form, fact, form, fact—it can get very dull and put the reader to sleep. This is probably enhanced by the fact that the meaning-syllables, the stressed syllables, are, on the average, twice as long as the short ones: short, long, short, long. So even this alternating duration of syllables can get monotonous. The remedy, of course, is stress variations. Not varying the number of syllables, but the number and position of stresses. Then you create basic syncopations, and these musical syncopations will coincide with clusters of meaning-syllables—along with many other interesting ramifications that I discuss at length in *The Southern Review* essay. But the fundamental point is that these syncopations carry a great deal of personality with them, along with individual character and emotion. So it's all in the variance, and above all, in the stress variance, where these things occur.

So variant stresses can create more poetic power.

W. D. SNODGRASS: Absolutely. Enormously more power. Take the line, "Snow falling, and night falling fast, oh fast," which I cite in the essay. You can rewrite that line in pure iambics: "The snow was falling. Night was falling fast." But the emotion has all evaporated. Now some people will tell you that the second version conveys the same meaning as the first, but it *doesn't*, and it doesn't because it's not telling you anything about the emotions of the speaker—which is far more important than what the weather is outside. So the emotions are intrinsically related to the stress variations.

At a fundamental level, this sounds like Hopkins—the notion that you skillfully vary the accents to express yourself more powerfully.

W. D. SNODGRASS: Absolutely. That's exactly what he was talking about though he called it "counterpointing," which surprises me because he knew a good deal about music. But it *isn't* really counterpointing, it's much more a syncopation, setting up a counter-rhythm, an oppositional friction rhythm. But that's exactly what he's talking about. Another interesting aspect of this is the possibility that meter, in its alternation between function-syllables and meaning-syllables, also involves an alternation from one part of the brain to another. It seems that the function-words are managed in Broca's area and the meaning-words center in Wernicke's area. That may or may not be correct, but it does seem that you can lose one ability while maintaining the other. In PBS's series on the brain, Dr. Norman Geschwind discussed a patient of his, a prominent lawyer in Boston, who'd been in an auto accident. Because of the resultant damage, particularly in Broca's area, he lost the use of function-words. If you told him, "The lion has killed the leopard," he'd understand that one animal was dead, but he wouldn't know which one, because you might have been saying, "The lion has been killed by the leopard."

In your own poetry, you've written in many different forms, but you seem to prefer the ballad stanza. Is that conscious?

W. D. SNODGRASS: Not really. I love ballads, and I sing them, and I translate them. But I wasn't conscious that I'd written a lot in the ballad stanza. When I'm writing, I just try to find something that'll work, and when I find it, I go with it.

After several decades of teaching creative writing, what do you think a teacher can offer to an aspiring poet?

W. D. SNODGRASS: That's a hard question, and I don't have many specific rules about it. But I do believe that you need to do something different for each student. Every student has different needs, and you have to try to do whatever is most appropriate for that individual person. Having said that, I could never jump on my students the way Jarrell jumped on me, but you do whatever you can—given your resources and theirs. I remember that I once taught a class right after another poet, who had the students composing in the most constricted, forced, tiny, and careful poetic lines. So when they came to me, they were ready to explode, and, since I felt they needed it, I'd say to them, "All right, explode!" And they would start doing all kinds of unpredictable and interesting things. So every situation is different. I wouldn't have done that if they hadn't come to me all tensed up and constricted.

Nowadays, the tendency is to start them off with explosions.

W. D. SNODGRASS: Yes, when they have no flammables! I'm afraid that a lot of people have confused cheerleading with teaching, and they end up praising everything. The "Poets in the Schools" program, which I thought was a very good idea when it started out, has tended to encourage the problem. In order to make a living, the teachers began to praise everything that was written in the high schools where they taught; otherwise, they wouldn't be asked back. The end result of this is that when the students finally get to college, they're accustomed to being praised for everything they do. Which is ridiculous. Nowadays, you don't go to school to learn, you go to school to be praised.

What's your opinion of the current American poetry scene? Some people feel it's quite vibrant, while many others feel it's sadly uninspired, even moribund.

W. D. SNODGRASS: I tend to take the negative view. There are definitely a number of poets that I like quite a lot—Donald Hall is wonderful, for example, and so is James Fenton in England. But I don't like very much of the stuff that I see in most of the poetry magazines. It reads like bad translations, and it gives me little pleasure. I seldom find anything I like; occasionally I do. Most of the younger formalists I don't care for very much; it seems to me that they're not really doing very much with it. And I also don't like most of the anti-formalists. But maybe I shouldn't have an opinion at all, since I don't read very much. I read less than almost anybody. I much prefer to go back and re-read Sir Thomas Wyatt, or Herrick, or those older guys. And I definitely don't try to keep up with the literary fashions. I think American literary criticism is unbelievably deplorable. It's hideous. It's full of jargon, and movements, and ideology, and discipleship. It's simply a disgrace, and, given that fact, maybe I shouldn't expect to enjoy most of the poetry that I see. We've really had only two critics, in my opinion: Jarrell and Pound.

Your generation was informed by the New Critics who were serious and talented and thoughtful, and even if one moved away from their premises, as you yourself did, they still took the literature seriously.

W. D. SNODGRASS: Boy, did they! I find that I can still pick up *Understanding Poetry*, the Brooks and Warren text, and leaf through it and find questions that will challenge me. They asked *real* questions about those poems, and ones that led you into a serious consideration of the nature of the poem and what it was really about.

It's a wonderful book.

W. D. SNODGRASS: It taught America how to read, which it needed to learn.

And it still could.

W. D. SNODGRASS: Yes, it could. Every time I pick up that book, it provokes serious thought and feeling—real appreciation.

I'd like to finish up today by reading the moving ending from your long poem, "Heart's Needle," in which a guilt-ridden father, separated from his young daughter by divorce, takes her to the zoo:

> If I loved you, they said I'd leave
>   and find my own affairs.
> Well, once again this April, we've
>   come around to the bears;
>
> punished and cared for, behind bars,
>   the coons on bread and water
> stretch thin black fingers after ours.
>   And you are still my daughter.

Thank you.

W. D. SNODGRASS: Thank you.

JOHN HOLLANDER

John Hollander, recipient of the 1983 Bollingen Poetry Prize, is a distinguished poet, scholar, editor, and teacher. His poetry, written with both vision and the highest technical accomplishment, has secured him, as Vernon Shetley has written in *The New Republic*, "a place as one of the major figures of our moment."

John Hollander was born and raised in New York City where he completed both his A.B. and M.A at Columbia University. Later, he was a junior fellow at Harvard University and eventually received his Ph.D. from Indiana University. He then taught at Yale University for seven years, moving to Hunter College in 1966 for over a decade, and then, since 1977, teaching again at Yale University, currently as the A. Bartlett Giamatti Professor of English.

His many books of poetry include *A Crackling of Thorns*, 1958, chosen by W. H. Auden as the winner of the Yale Younger Poets Award; *The Night Mirror*, 1971; *Spectral Emanations: New and Selected Poems*, 1978; *Selected Poetry*, 1993; and *Figurehead*, 1999. He has also written *Rhyme's Reason: A Guide to English Verse*, 1981; and edited numerous books including *The Oxford Anthology of English Literature*, with Frank Kermode, 1973; *American Poetry: The Nineteenth Century*, Volumes 1 and 2, 1993; *The Gazer's Spirit: Poems Speaking to Silent Works of Art*, 1995; and *Committed to Memory: 100 Best Poems to Memorize*, 1997.

This interview was conducted at the University of the South during the Sewanee Writers' Conference.

You were born in New York City. Did you grow up there?

JOHN HOLLANDER: Yes, I grew up in the city, and I didn't leave it for any length of time except for a visit to Europe at the age of twenty and an earlier summer I spent in California. I was seventeen that summer, and I hitched and took buses west during the vacation. Otherwise I lived completely in New York, going to Columbia and even getting my M.A. there as well. I didn't leave the city to live anywhere else until 1952.

Did you encounter poetry early in your childhood?

JOHN HOLLANDER: I did. My first access to poetry was in songs, and I can still remember a wonderfully illustrated *Chansons de France*. Since my father played the piano, I grew up hearing those songs, looking at the pictures, and trying to put the pictures together with the songs— long before I understood any French. There was also James Weldon Johnson's book of Negro spirituals which I knew very early—when I was about five or six years old. But, of course, the verse that most enthralled me as a child was Robert Louis Stevenson's *A Child's Garden of Verses* and the wonderful A. A. Milne verses. Otherwise, I didn't read that much poetry until eighth grade, but around the fourth grade we started to memorize a lot of verse in school. And most of it was great poetry, although some of it wasn't. I remember memorizing a whole range of verses, like "The Seven Ages of Man" speech from *As You Like It*, a couple of Wordsworth sonnets, and James Hogg's "A Boy's Song"— which was the first poem I ever memorized. Then, in the sixth grade, I had a pre-adolescent crush on a little girl who recited some poems in class, and, later, I asked her to recite them again for me. She did Longfellow's "The Skeleton in Armor" and, even more impressively, "The Lady of Shalott," which absolutely entranced me.

The subject, the sound, or the little girl?

JOHN HOLLANDER: All three! As for sound, my mother once told me a little story about when I was very young, long before I could read. In those days, we listened to radio since TV didn't exist back then, and, one day, I heard a bit of Shakespeare being recited, and it must have impressed me. Then, about a month or so later, I was again listening to the radio, and I called out to my mother who was in another room, "Mommy, Mommy, Shakespeare!" When she came into the room, it was actually someone reading lines from *Dr. Faustus.* I'd simply heard the iambic pentameter and assumed that it was Shakespeare.

Given that your father was a physiologist, were you ever expected to enter the medical profession?

JOHN HOLLANDER: Not really. My mother was a high school English teacher, very literate, witty, and well-educated. She had an M.A. in medieval literature, and there was never a problem with my literary interests.

But didn't you go to the Bronx School of Science?

JOHN HOLLANDER: I did. I commuted from south Manhattan to the west Bronx all through the war. I went there because, at the time, there was nothing equivalent for the humanities, and I'm very grateful for it because I had an excellent scientific education, even if I did bumble at math a little bit.

Then you went to Columbia University as an undergraduate and later received your M.A. there. Did you study with Trilling?

JOHN HOLLANDER: I did, and I learned a great deal from him, but we didn't get along that well at the time. We only became friends years later, in the sixties. We developed this ironic, hedging sort of relationship, but we became very close in the latter part of his life. But back in my college days, I was much more influenced by Mark Van Doren and Moses Hadas. Van Doren was marvelous in the way he took undergraduate writers seriously. He took me seriously as a poet even before I did, and this always meant a great deal to me. In those days, we didn't have creative writing classes, but at Columbia, undergraduate English majors were allowed to take a one-on-one independent study in creative writing with one of the faculty members, and I worked with Mark Van Doren, and he taught poetry wonderfully.

And Moses Hadas?

JOHN HOLLANDER: Well, he, of course, taught classical literature, and I took a wonderful upper-level Humanities course with him called "Colloquium on Great Books." I also took his introductory colloquium in Oriental literature and philosophy which was another extraordinary class. He was always accessible, and I'd often stop by and visit him, and he'd give me advice and kid me about things. Like Van Doren, he always took me seriously, and that was tremendously important to me at the time.

From there, you went to Indiana University for your Ph.D. What attracted you to Indiana?

JOHN HOLLANDER: The first reason was their lucrative teaching assistantships. I'd gone to graduate school with the definite intention of becoming a teacher. Both of my parents were teachers, and even though my father was a physiologist, he also taught doctors at the graduate medical school at Columbia. He had a unique ability for explaining things that always impressed me. I can still remember when I was in the fourth grade, and I'd heard the term "atom," and then my mother, in her everyday conversation, referred to a "molecule" of water. So I decided that an atom must be a minimal unit of something solid, and that a molecule must be a minimal unit of something liquid. That's how I worked it out for myself until I finally asked my father about it one day. I can still remember that it was at breakfast on a Sunday morning, with the early light coming into the room and falling across the table. And he said, "Look, let me explain." Then he took a piece of sugar from the bowl, and he broke the sugar lump in half. "Now I can break this apart, and keep breaking it down, and let's imagine that I keep breaking it down, and breaking it down, until I get something very, very tiny. Finally, there will be something so small that if I were to break it down one more time, it wouldn't be sugar anymore. It would then be a number of different things called carbon and hydrogen and oxygen." So he continued in that vein, making it all perfectly clear, and it was absolutely electrifying for me. I never forgot it, and I've always greatly admired his explanation.

It was very lucid and tangible.

JOHN HOLLANDER: Exactly. And when I got older, and I thought about it, I realized that he surely had twenty different ways to explain what a molecule was, but he chose exactly the right one for me at that time. And that has probably affected my thinking about discourse more than anything else in my life. It made me—after various theoretical follies of my earlier years in teaching—put the highest value on a pragmatic approach to teaching.

Now back to Indiana . . . .

JOHN HOLLANDER: Yes. So I always knew I wanted to teach, hence the digression, but there were no teaching assistantships at Columbia back then. So I checked things out, and I discovered that Indiana University had the highest-paying teaching assistantships in the country. In those days, I.U. was just emerging from being a local cow college, and things were happening very fast. They had a great dean at the time who'd decided to bring the Kenyon School of Letters, founded by John Crowe Ransom and a number of other people, to I.U. That meant that all the literary critics that I'd been reading in *The Kenyon Review, Partisan Review, The Hudson Review, The Sewanee Review,* and *The Southern Review,* were now on the faculty at I.U. People like John Crowe Ransom and Robert Penn Warren, and younger critics and writers like Leslie Fiedler, Irving Howe, Cleanth Brooks, Richard Chase, Delmore Schwartz, and Robert Lowell. All these talented people had clustered around the original Kenyon idea that the traditional philological approach to literature that dominated the universities back then didn't really have a serious interest in literature. It had no more interest in literature than the materialist thugs in English departments have today.

It's very interesting that what's happened over the past ten years has been an unfortunate reversion to another narrow, debilitating, non-humanistic point of view. At any rate, the purpose of the Kenyon School of Letters was to open up literature to all kinds of discourse, and it attracted many of the best writers and critics to Indiana. So this was the other reason that I chose to do my doctoral studies at I.U.

Where was the school before it moved to Indiana? Ohio?

JOHN HOLLANDER: It first began as a summer program at Kenyon, but the school was really amorphous, an administrative entity, until it moved to Bloomington and was integrated with the English Department. Then it became an incredible program, attracting students from all over the country—especially given its high-paying teaching assistantships. The year before I went out there, two people I knew, Stephen Marcus and Hilton Kramer, had gone for a year, come back, and said they hated it. But I decided to go anyway. It was a very interesting time for me in my life, and it was very important educationally. I was able to stop being a New York "hick" and learn about life outside New York City. The second year I was there, I was married, and my wife's family was from Cleveland, and I developed a very interesting and broader perspective on things as a result. At the same time, I was meeting people at school who became very close friends, like Irving Howe and others. It was all quite wonderful for me, and then, just as I was about to start my dissertation, which indeed, was going to be about metrics, I was selected by the Society of Fellows at Harvard, and I went off to spend three years at Harvard, where I came into contact with all sorts of astonishing people like Noam Chomsky, and Don Hall, and so many others. It was a crazy, marvelous conglomeration of people, and I was very fortunate to be part of it.

Then while I was at Harvard, I gradually grew more and more interested in language and linguistics, especially as a result of Harold Lightholm's great course on Anglo-Saxon literature. Originally, my dissertation was going to be about the delineation of fundamental conventions in the history of English metrics. When I'd first read

T. S. Omond's *English Metrists*, it seemed to me just as crazy as theology, because people would use a word like "accent" and then argue endlessly with each other about what it meant. So I wanted to take a fresh look at everything and try to straighten out the confusions. Then, one day, as I was crossing Harvard Yard, I conceived of something I decided to call metremics—using structural linguistics as a model for metrical discourse. So I went back to my room, wrote some pages of notes, numbered the paragraphs in the Vienna School fashion, and even showed them to Chomsky. Then I put them all in a drawer for a few days, intending to spend the next year or so on the project, but when I pulled them out of the drawer a few days later, I asked myself, "What's it good for?" And I concluded, "Nothing." It would have been a very nice little exercise for me, but it wouldn't have yielded any useful knowledge. So, eventually, I abandoned the metrical project and completely changed my dissertation to another topic which became my book called *The Untuning of the Sky*—about music as a subject for poetry.

You were very fortunate that prosody was taken seriously back then.

JOHN HOLLANDER: Yes. And my friend Donald Hall, who'd been at Oxford, was also writing on metrics. So there were a number of people who were very intent on it, but, the truth is, most people back then were literate. If you were studying literature, the language of prosody was considered a basic literary skill. Any English major could recognize what was iambic pentameter and what was tetrameter, and they knew it even before they'd entered college. This doesn't happen anymore. Nowadays, most people don't memorize poetry, and most people never hear any good verse at all. This, of course, relates to what's being taught in the schools—or to what's *not* being taught in the schools.

In the 1800's when McGuffy's books were used all over the country, their companion, Harvey's Grammar, taught sixth graders the fundamentals of prosody.

JOHN HOLLANDER: Quite right. They learned that there was a terminology to identify what they knew from experience. Everyone knew what pentameter was, or what tetrameter was, even if they'd forgotten the terms. But other things besides education have contributed to the problem as well. For example, there's been a tremendous loss in the very useful influence of popular music because the great period of the American standard pop song—which extended into the middle of the rock-and-roll period—was wonderful ear training for writers and readers. The only thing that maintains that now at all is country and western music.

Because of the traditional stanza forms or the rhymes?

JOHN HOLLANDER: Both. But especially the rhymes, although, unfortunately, even their rhymes are beginning to rely more and more heavily on assonance rather than real rhyme. "Shine" and "time," for example, is not really a rhyme. But things are far sloppier in other forms of popular music, so young people arrive at college wanting to write poems, and they don't even know how to rhyme. I once had an interesting talk about this with Steve Sondheim. We were on a committee together, evaluating submitted books and lyrics for grant support. And I remarked to Sondheim that most of these people didn't even know how to rhyme, and he said, "That's right, they all come from rock music. Anyone whose background is in musical theater knows what rhyme is." So if you grew up on the wonderful American musicals, you learned what rhyme was, but young people today don't have that advantage.

And this ties into church music as well. If you talk to Derek Walcott about prosody, he'll always start talking about singing the Methodist hymns in his youth.

JOHN HOLLANDER: Exactly! Absolutely! Hymnody is very important, and look what's happened to that! How it's totally fallen apart. The churches are full of 28th-rate rock groups singing smarmy tunes, and they've thrown away all the great traditional hymns. It's terrible.

Now getting back to your own history, in 1958, W. H. Auden chose your first collection of poetry, A Crackling of Thorns, *for the Yale Younger Poets Award.*

JOHN HOLLANDER

Given the book's wit and remarkable technical skill, had you been greatly influenced by Auden's work?

JOHN HOLLANDER: The earlier poems were not, but in the later ones, Auden is constantly creeping into them all the time. When I first got back the proofs of *A Crackling of Thorns*, I was appalled to see a line in one poem that was absolutely pure Auden, and I had to rewrite it. So, in time, I had to work quite hard to throw off his influence.

Stevens came later?

JOHN HOLLANDER: I'm not sure that Stevens had that much of an influence on me, and I didn't start dealing with him seriously until I'd already written a couple of books, but he was always in my head. He was one of the first modern poets I'd read. But, in truth, I liked Cummings before I liked Stevens, maybe because he was funny. And I even liked some Pound before I liked Stevens. But I still had Stevens in my head from quite early on. My mother had an old anthology called *The New Poetry* from around 1924, and it had the earlier, shorter version of "Sunday Morning," and "Peter Quince," and "Thirteen Ways." So those poems were always reverberating in my head, even though I didn't know exactly what they meant.

Voice is very important in your poetry, and right from the beginning, there's an obvious willingness, like Auden, to try different voices.

JOHN HOLLANDER: Yes, there were always three dominant voices that I had in my head and that I used in my work. Two of them were people I never heard speak, and the third was Auden who I eventually got to know—but only after his voice had already affected me through the poems. The first important influence was George Bernard Shaw, whom I began reading when I was quite young. In the fifth or sixth grade, a friend of mine introduced me to Shaw at school, and I read plays "pleasant" and "unpleasant" and the prefaces.

You were reading those tedious prefaces in the fifth grade?

JOHN HOLLANDER: Some of them. Some of them bored me to death, but I was electrified by the preface to *Saint Joan*. Shaw had a marvelous voice: his wit, his unpredictability, his intelligence, his dialectic, and his sense of "it's never going to be easy to choose sides." So Shaw was my first education in the use of voice. The second was Orwell, and the third was Auden.

Returning to A Crackling of Thorns, *you're now, in my opinion, much too hard on that book and your other early collections before* The Night Mirror. *You've dismissed them as "verse essays" and "epigram-literature," but surely they're more than that as "The Lady's Maid's Song" and "The Great Bear" illustrate. Why are you so dissatisfied with these early poems?*

JOHN HOLLANDER: I'm not really dissatisfied with them. It's just that I came to demand more of myself, and I came to demand more of poetry. But I still like, for example, "The Lady's Maid's Song," which I wrote for the production of a play, and which is, I still think, a very good song of a special kind, given the historical context and everything else. It's quite well put together. It's just that verse is a necessary, but not sufficient, condition for poetry.

Which is the first line of Rhyme's Reason.

JOHN HOLLANDER: That's right. When I was doing the Library of America anthologies, I wanted to call them *Nineteenth Century American Verse*. But they insisted on calling it "poetry" even though there's a lot of stuff in them that's very good verse but not really poetry. Verse is literal, whereas poetry has got to be deeply metaphoric. That's what distinguishes the two, and I didn't understand it for many years. I didn't comprehend what poets meant when they talked about poetry *being* metaphor as opposed to simply having metaphors within it.

I wanted to ask you about that. We all know what metaphors are, but could you elaborate a bit on why you see the poem itself as a metaphor?

JOHN HOLLANDER: When I refer to poetry as metaphor, I prefer to use the more encompassing term "trope" in which *a* is like *b*, but not literally, as you'd have in verse. For example, why is cheese like chocolate? Because they're both edible, and because they both start with "ch." But I daresay, who cares? The act of pointing out the likeness is not really useful or interesting. It's just a true statement. But the minute you suppress the "in that," when you no longer say *a* is like *b* in that . . . , but simply say that *a* is like *b*, then you're heading toward the realm of poetry, toward, at least, the enigma of poetry. And enigma is an essential component of poetry, and the very stuff of poetry is trope.

Most of your poetry, both before and after The Night Mirror, *is quite demanding—allusive, dense, and intellectually probing. Your friend Harold Bloom, who's a great admirer of your work, wrote in his review of* Spectral Emanations *for* The New Republic *that "there seemed almost always to be more knowledge and insight within Hollander than the verse could accommodate." Did you feel that way when you were writing the poems? Did you sense the difficulty of saying all that you'd like to say within a particular poem?*

JOHN HOLLANDER: Well, it isn't that I want to put everything in there, it's just that allusion is discursively natural to me. It's a way to capture different kinds of voices in a short poem. But I know that allusiveness can create difficulties, especially in the present times. For example, I grew up knowing the King James Bible, and knowing that there was a valuable tradition throughout all of English literature of poets echoing phrases from the Bible. But this is a problem nowadays because none of my readers below a certain age will know the Bible, or know what I'm doing when I echo it, and yet all of English and American fiction and poetry up to a certain point is full of this kind of allusion. For me, it's a crucial part of the English language tradition that I can't reject, so the allusiveness is there.

But I'm not questioning the allusiveness, I'm just asking a kind of compositional question. When you're writing your poems, and you're including so many things within the poetry, does it create a difficulty of composition or does it come fairly naturally?

JOHN HOLLANDER: It comes naturally. Totally. All these things, like the allusions, just flow in naturally.

Richmond Lattimore, another admirer of your poetry, admitted to a "pleased incomprehension" when reading much of your work, and you seemed to support this response in your interview with J. D. McClatchy for The American Poetry Review *when you said that "The Night Mirror" was the first poem "that I wrote that I didn't fully understand." Then you went on to say that since "The Head of the Bed, "I don't 'understand' a lot of what I write at first but it doesn't bother me—I expect not to." Could you elaborate on this?*

JOHN HOLLANDER: That simply means that, as a writer, I'm giving incredible attention to certain things about the poem—committing myself to those aspects—and not really worrying about the rest. Now these may be different matters in every poem, but there are always some basic ones that have a kind of natural priority. For example, every poem is going to develop its own ground rules, and any violation of those ground rules is either an error that has to be corrected, or it's so important to the poem that the reader, who's intuited the ground rules, will stop and say, "Why, now?" And that breaking up of the ground rules is the fundamental poetic act of the poem. So when I find that, through carelessness or distraction or something else, I've violated the rules when I shouldn't have, then I go back and rewrite it and correct it. And when I do, the correction will always be poetically better at every level. After a certain point, the poem knows more than you do.

Is that because the underlying structure of the poem has a kind of knowledge as well?

JOHN HOLLANDER: That's a very interesting idea, although it's not exactly what I meant. But the idea that the structure itself has a special knowledge is a wonderful notion, and one that I'd like to pursue sometime. But what I really meant was that having some kind of structural agenda is the means for conjuring up all the other stuff. The silly notion that, "If I just let it all hang out, then I'll be able to get at the deepest things within myself," is quite ridiculous. It's just a bit of romantic mythology—the near-romanticism of high modernism—that by throwing away certain formal conventions, writers will have greater access into themselves. Such people always forget Wordsworth's great sonnet.

"Nuns Fret Not . . ."

JOHN HOLLANDER: Yes, that's right. Sure the sonnet's a small space that you lock yourself into, but it's not a prison. It's a cell, and it's liberating.

Just like the prayer of the nuns, which is actually enhanced by the constriction.

JOHN HOLLANDER: Certainly, and that's what I mean by that.

Your interest in voice, both in your work and criticism, relates to the potential dangers and excesses of first-person poetry. Most of your own poetry, like the twelve "Sonnets for Roseblush," seem excellent examples of a strong and very human voice that successfully mutes the role of the author beyond the voice.

JOHN HOLLANDER: I believe that the only way to learn to write poetry in an appropriate persona is through some kind of dramatic narrative or monologue. If you learn to write poems in which the "I" is not yourself but some fictional person, then you can perhaps not fall into the trap of writing a poem as if it were simply a letter to somebody, or some kind of simple expression of your own feelings. I wrote those particular sonnets as a kind of contemporary equivalent of the artificial literary conventions of Petrarchianism, which purported to be about feelings, but the very concept of "feeling" that it invoked was a literary invention. When I wondered what might be a literary equivalent today, I started thinking about pornography, which deals with a powerful, meaningful act, but which, by its crude conventions, eradicates any depth. So I wrote those somewhat erotic sonnets as contemporary versions of Petrarchian poems.

But they're not pornographic at all. They're very witty and thoughtful. Like the ending of the last sonnet, which wonders why people bother to pursue sexual love:

> *Why then go through with it, when to imagine*
> *What we shall do, what we shall be, is still*
> *The noblest work of all, the sovereign region*
> *Enduring, green, beyond both wish and will?*
> *Why, naked and trembling, act out such old laws?*
> *Because because because because because.*

JOHN HOLLANDER: That's right. I wasn't trying to write pornography; I was just trying to use its conventions. So instead of writing about love-making in an elevated Petrarchian way, I wrote about it in a more direct and erotic manner.

But don't you think your analogy's a bit unfair to Petrarchianism? Certainly, it was artificial, but it still had deeper, serious meanings.

JOHN HOLLANDER: Well, that's an interesting point that can be debated about Petrarchianism. I would agree that there's a lot of substance to it, but it was still highly artificial. It was an inventive, secular mythology that flourished in Italy in city-states that had very, very powerful male rulers—and it was, curiously enough, invented by writers who all had, in some way, both a subservient and subversive relationship to the power of the ruler.

But don't you think that there was also a religious element in that poetry that gave it a depth beyond the conventions?

JOHN HOLLANDER: Yes, but those are in the tropes, not in the basic mythology.

You've been justly praised as one of the most sophisticated and adept users of poetic forms in modern English poetry—a "virtuoso" as Glyn Pursglove once put it. You've written in an extraordinary range of forms—sonnets, the

JOHN HOLLANDER

French forms, sapphics, heroic couplets in "New York City," the wonderful opening tetrameter couplet of "The Four Ages":

> *Terribly unimportant kings*
> *Grimly gave each other rings.*

syllabic thirteeners, In Memoriam stanzas for In Time and Place, *etc.—as well as inventing various forms, including the very popular double-dactyl with Anthony Hecht. Are there any established forms that you haven't used that you would like to try?*

JOHN HOLLANDER: I haven't really thought about it, but not that I can think of. I honestly had no idea that, after a certain point, I was going to fall into writing syllabic verse for such a long time. It started after I wrote a long poem called *Visions from the Ramble*, which was written in loose hexameters. After that, I wanted to get back to short poems, and I felt like I'd forgotten how to write them. So I started experimenting with shaped poems, which were incredibly taxing in certain ways, and yet not quite in accentual/syllabic. Then I gradually found myself being attracted to syllabic verse in Marianne Moore and Auden, and I started doing it, and then my friend Richard Howard started writing syllabics for his second book. I found it to be a marvelous instrument because of the possibilities of various audible rhythms—because of the flexibility.

Did you invent the thirteener?

JOHN HOLLANDER: Yes, I did. I was trying all kinds of syllabic line lengths, and I just fell into it—not by counting or planning, it just happened naturally—and I liked it. I thought to myself, "It's like a sonnet, but it isn't," and I started scribbling more and more, and over the course of two summers, they began accumulating, and I realized what I was doing. I realized that the thirteener was a contemporary alternative to the sonnet—a late modern, post-modern version of the sonnet. And writing all of these poems of thirteen lines with thirteen syllables, I eventually started thinking about "thirteenness" itself and began exploring its numerological significances. Then I drifted back into writing rhymed verse again.

*You once said that syllabics "throw the speaking voice into greater promi-
nence." Why do you feel that's the case?*

JOHN HOLLANDER: Because it elicits so many possibilities. It can be
talky, it can be muttering, it can be whatever you want it to be, especially
in terms of voice.

*In your essay, "O Heavy Verse! The Shopwork of the Workshops," you give an
example of a syllabic sapphic stanza (four lines: eleven, eleven, eleven, and five
syllables), which "you can count but most / Probably will not discern by
ear . . . ." Similarly, in* Rhyme's Reason, *in your example of a syllabic
thirteener, you point out that rhyme can lurk in "its unstressed trees" and
"Moments of audible accent pass across the face / of meditation . . ." but these
are only "moments." This seems to admit, even conceding the fact that the ear
can pick up some kind of pattern with very short lines, that syllabics, despite
their strictures, sacrifice regular rhythm. Is that accurate in your opinion?*

JOHN HOLLANDER: Well, it all depends upon what you mean by
"rhythm." At its most basic, rhythm means regularity of occurrence. In
the Germanic languages, the natural pattern of stressed versus unstressed
syllables becomes the rhythmic alternation—an underlying fabric of
stress alternation. But that's only one kind of rhythm. There's also the
rhythm of syntax, and the rhythm of sentence length, and so on. Dozens
and dozens of other rhythms that are not based on accent. Even in
accentual/syllabic verse, no two lines of, say, iambic pentameter are ever
rhythmically equivalent. They all have different rhythms.

*But they still have a generally regular beat under each of those uniquely-
sounded lines.*

JOHN HOLLANDER: That's right, and that's what distinguishes it from
other kinds of verse rhythms.

*Now I'd like to shift to your teaching of such things in the classroom. What
courses do you teach at Yale?*

JOHN HOLLANDER: When I came back to Yale, I'd never taught a writing course in my life. I preferred teaching literature, and I was very suspicious of writing courses. Over the years, I'd come into contact with many workshops, and most of them had no content and were taught by poor teachers. All they did, in my opinion, was run group therapy sessions without a license. So when I returned to Yale, Robert Penn Warren had retired, and they asked me to take over his verse-writing course, and I said, "Okay, if you let me teach it my way." So that's how it started.

How do you approach things?

JOHN HOLLANDER: Well, we carefully examine poems from the tradition, I make certain points, and then I give them a lot of exercises. Eventually, they begin to write their own poems.

Do you look at their poems in class?

JOHN HOLLANDER: No, I don't. What I have to say about their work is the business of only the author and myself.

Do you put written comments on their poetry sheets, or do you get together with them individually?

JOHN HOLLANDER: Both. I always write detailed comments on their sheets, suggesting things to read, etc. Occasionally, for the benefit of the rest of the class, we'll look at some of their work anonymously. I do this to highlight a characteristic mistake, like, for example, when their pentameters start turning into anapestic tetrameters. You know how easily that can happen! So every semester in the elementary class, I'll take a couple of examples, without identifying the authors, and show them to the class, saying, "You all do this. And I want to show you how you can avoid it or emend it." But mostly in those courses, I'm teaching great poetry and raising all kinds of serious questions. Each class is slightly different from year to year, depending on the students themselves. I have very, very good students. I never take anybody who can't write blank verse that scans, and most of them do it very well. I also prefer people who've read poetry in another language besides English, and the last few years, I've been able to get students who've read poetry in *two* other languages.

In your advanced poetry class, how many students do you usually have?

JOHN HOLLANDER: Usually fifteen, twenty.

Up to twenty?

JOHN HOLLANDER: I try not to have more than eighteen. It's a wonderful class to teach. I just love it!

And what literature courses do you teach?

JOHN HOLLANDER: I teach a lit course every fall, and I've taught Spenser, Milton, seventeenth century poetry, and nineteenth century American poetry. I teach other classes as well, like the graduate course in poetics. Generally, I do whatever the department needs me to do, so my range of courses isn't as broad as I'd like. I'd love to teach a course in children's literature, for example, but I'm not discontent. I learn just as much from teaching *The Faerie Queene* for the twentieth time as I do anything else.

In the first line of your guide to prosody, Rhyme's Reason, *you write, "This is a guide to verse, to the formal structures which are a necessary condition of poetry, but not a sufficient one." Elsewhere, you've pointed out that a familiarity with the forms of poetry is "a necessary skill" even for writing free verse. So why, in your opinion, are traditional forms generally ignored, except for the occasional villanelle or sestina exercise, in the creative writing programs?*

JOHN HOLLANDER: In the first place, I think it's a result of the very poor education in poetry that people have had to begin with.

You mean the teachers?

JOHN HOLLANDER: Yes, the teachers. We talked a bit about this earlier, and we all know that the elementary schools have stopped teaching grammar, and they've stopped requiring memorization, especially of poetry. There also arose the fashionable conviction that to be "modern," poetry had to be free verse, and this was encouraged by ridiculous people like Diane Wakoski saying that to write formal verse was to be a fascist. There were many such stupid people, with loud voices, always making formal matters ideological, which is absurd. There was also that terrible war of the anthologies that took place in the 1960's, during which that silly person Donald Allen anthologized only people who wrote free verse, without regard to anything else, because he knew nothing about poetry. Then there were opposing anthologies that left out everyone who wrote non-metrical verse, and so on. Personally, I always thought the whole "battleground" was completely phony, but the idiotic charge that accentual/syllabic verse was retrograde and "academic" made a big impression and greatly affected the teaching of poetry in this country.

So eventually you wrote Rhyme's Reason?

JOHN HOLLANDER: Yes, but it was a long time in coming. Twenty years ago, I did an anthology with Irving Howe and David Bromwich with the silly title *Literature as Experience*. And when I did a section of terms at the end of the book, just for fun, I decided to write some self-descriptive pieces. Then, several years later, Ellen Graham, who's the editor at Yale Press, saw the pieces and said, "If you do more of these, we'll do a book." So I did, re-writing a lot of the old ones, and that's how it happened.

You once criticized much of contemporary verse as "journalistic." What did you mean by that?

JOHN HOLLANDER: I meant the literal, first-person description of something—as if one is writing a letter to a friend. Even if it was well-done, I never thought that it was really poetry. It was like some kind of moment preserved in verse. It was too literal and unpoetic.

James Dickey had a derogatory term for that; he called it "polaroid" poetry.

JOHN HOLLANDER: Yes, he and I were in complete agreement on that. And on quite a few other things too. I was tremendously fond of him.

As wary as you are of "flabby" free versers and the "rusty irony" of their "heavy" non-poems which you term "clunk," you're equally wary of the "pretentious" "ideology and reductive agenda" of some of the practitioners of the more recent formalism. Yet you're an admirer of a number of the younger poets associated with the movement—Rachel Hadas, for example.

JOHN HOLLANDER: I'm just not interested in "isms." I'm not interested in any kind of ideology about poetry.

But we both know that ideology is, unfortunately, a significant factor in twentieth century verse. You were just discussing the Wakoski-types and all the damage they did. And we also know how hard it's been for young formalists to get their work published.

JOHN HOLLANDER: And you've done something constructive about it. Ten years ago, you said, "I want there to be a respectable magazine that's not going to turn poems down because they're metered or rhymed." Now a lot of imbecile editors for rotten magazines were doing that. Of course, no good editor would ever do such a thing, but there's a lot more bad editors than good, and increasingly so, and for you to say, "Well, here's a magazine that's going to be a refuge for those poets who get turned down simply because their work rhymes," was very admirable. I think your magazine has performed a very important function, and you're doing it without the "ism" stuff.

Thank you. We're trying. Now after your two excellent volumes of American Poetry: The Nineteenth Century *were published by* The Library of America, *the poet Brad Leithauser in* The New York Review of Books, *suggested that, despite all the excellent verse written last century, the volumes illustrate the superiority of the poetry of the twentieth century. I wonder how you feel about such a comparison?*

JOHN HOLLANDER: Well, it's hard to come up with a twentieth century American poet greater than Whitman or Dickinson. It's hard.

Frost is the obvious candidate.

JOHN HOLLANDER: Yes, and I think Frost and Stevens are the very best of the century, but there's something about the originality of Whitman and Dickinson that's astonishing. After Whitman and Dickinson, there are only a few other wonderful poets in the nineteenth century. There's Bryant, and Emerson, and Longfellow, and Poe, and Melville, and the early poetry of Edwin Arlington Robinson. So I would agree that in the twentieth century, there have been more very good poets than in the nineteenth century, and, overall, a lot more truly distinguished verse.

Maybe we could end our discussion today with the last stanza of one of your own distinguished poems, "A Glimpse of Proserpina":

> *We'd met where, as in fields of wars*
> *Forgotten, stones and daisies swarm,*
> *Then turn back, arm in flowers in arm,*
> *And bring them quietly indoors.*

Thank you very much for your time and your poetry.

JOHN HOLLANDER: Thank you.

X. J. KENNEDY

X. J. Kennedy, winner of the Lamont Poetry Prize, is one of the most distinguished and versatile poets in America. As Thomas DePietro points out, Kennedy is "a technical virtuoso who combines metaphysical wit with idiomatic diction." He also may be, as Raymond Oliver suggests, "the funniest poet alive."

X. J. Kennedy was born and raised in Dover, New Jersey. After his undergraduate studies at Seton Hall University, he completed a Masters degree in English at Columbia University. During the Korean War, he served in the U.S. Navy (1951–55). He then continued his graduate studies at the University of Michigan where he won the prestigious Hopwood Prize in Poetry. He later taught at Tufts University in Boston from 1963–79, but in 1979, he resigned his teaching position to become a free-lance writer, producing, sometimes with his wife Dorothy Kennedy, a number of popular university textbooks such as *The Bedford Reader, Introduction to Poetry*, and *Introduction to Fiction*.

His various collections of poetry include *Nude Descending a Staircase: Poems, Song, a Ballad*, 1961, winner of the Lamont Poetry Prize; *Cross Ties: Selected Poems*, 1985; and *Dark Horses: New Poems*, 1992. His numerous books for children include *One Winter Night in August and Other Nonsense Jingles*, 1975; *Knock at a Star: A Child's Introduction to Poetry*, edited with Dorothy Kennedy, 1982; *The Owlstone Crown*, 1983; *Brats*, 1986; and *The Eagle as Wide as the World*, 1997.

This interview was conducted during the Exploring Form and Narrative Poetry Conference at West Chester University in Pennsylvania.

X. J. KENNEDY

You grew up in Dover, New Jersey, and went to Seton Hall and Columbia graduate school. Then you served in the U.S. Navy from 1951–54 during most of the Korean War. How did that come about?

X. J. KENNEDY: I enlisted in the Navy to avoid serving in the infantry. I'd also been reading *Moby Dick*, and I had a rather glamorous view of the sea. I was obligated to sign up for four years, which is a long time, but it was during those years that I really started to write poetry seriously. For about two of those years, I had a rather cushy job as a journalist. I was assigned to cruises on destroyers where I would take pictures of the crew for publication in their hometown newspapers. Fortunately, I could generally finish all my work on the cruise in about two weeks and then spend the rest of the six or eight weeks just keeping out of the way of the working crew. So I had a lot of time on my hands and began working at my verse.

Did you have many books on board?

X. J. KENNEDY: Only what I could fit in the limits of the space I was assigned in my two-foot-wide footlocker. But I did manage to bring a number of books on board—like the collected poems of Yeats.

What was your major at Seton Hall?

X. J. KENNEDY: English.

So you'd never really started writing poetry at either Seton Hall or Columbia?

X. J. KENNEDY: I'd written a little bit, but I never took it very seriously. At Columbia, I read Yeats and Hopkins and Hardy for the first time, and I think that motivated me to try and imitate them.

After your four years in the Navy, you went to the University of Michigan which must have been an exciting place at the time. You once said that you belonged to the "Wolgamot School" of writing—meaning a group of young poets which included Donald Hall and W. D. Snodgrass. Who was John Wolgamot? Was he a professor at Michigan?

X. J. KENNEDY: No, John Barton Wolgamot wasn't a Michigan professor, and, as a matter-of-fact, I never met the man. When we were students at Michigan, my dear friend Keith Waldrop discovered an incredible book in a second-hand store called *In Sarah, Christ, Mencken, Beethoven, There Were Men and Women* by John Barton Wolgamot. This eccentric book was a list of names of famous people strung together by odd phrases like "very titanically" and "very majestically." The book quickly became legendary at Ann Arbor, and whoever touched it automatically became a member of the "Wolgamot Society." Eventually, the name came to be applied to some of us, a group of good friends, who were all interested in writing. One young poet in the group, Donald Hope, published a small chapbook of the Wolgamot poets which included Keith Waldrop, Dallas Wiebe, James Camp, Donald Hall, and W. D. Snodgrass—who was teaching in Detroit at the time, but who used to come over for the readings and get-togethers at Ann Arbor. John Heath Stubbs, who was a visiting professor from England, and for whom I served as a teaching assistant and paper reader, was also included in the anthology.

While you were still teaching at Michigan, you won the university's prestigious Hopwood Prize, and then your first book, Nude Descending a Staircase: Poems, Song, A Ballad, *was published by Doubleday and won the Lamont Poetry Prize. Like your friend W. D. Snodgrass, you had very early success. Was that a good thing? I'm sure it felt like it at the time, but how do you look at it today?*

X. J. KENNEDY: Oh, I wouldn't relive those days any differently! Back then, the Hopwood competition at Michigan was very important to a number of visiting literary agents who would often come to Ann Arbor for the award ceremony. The year I received the prize for poetry, Naomi Burton, who was a literary agent from New York, came to Ann Arbor, liked my work, and took my manuscript of poems back to New York and hawked it around to about a dozen publishers, all of whom turned it down. But then Naomi left her literary agency for an editorial position at Doubleday, and the first book she published was my book of poems. The truth is—I've always been a lucky bastard!

Well, the talent was there, and it's a terrific book. But it's still an amazing story.

X. J. KENNEDY: I was very fortunate.

In that first book and all the ones that followed, you showed a remarkable talent for satire and humor. As a result, your more poignant poems are sometimes overlooked, for example, "Giving in to You," "Celebration After the Death of John Brennan," "Twelve Dead, Hundreds Homeless," and, one of my favorites, "Woman in Rain," in which the narrator recognizes the beauty of a young woman walking through an ugly city environment and realizes that she:

> *Might grace a page or fill a frame.*
> *But then, what planet knows its name.*

Does it ever bother you that your wittier poems draw so much more attention?

X. J. KENNEDY: Well, to be honest, I'm very grateful to *anyone* who takes notice of any of my work, whether it's funny or unfunny. But I'm grateful to hear you point out that there are more serious poems in my books as well.

Many of your serious poems deal with children and the responsibilities of their parents, such as "On a Child Who Lived One Minute," which Wyatt Prunty has called a "little masterpiece"; "Summer Children"; and "One-Night Homecoming," in which a man, visiting his parents at the home where he grew up, realizes that:

> *. . . It's my turn now to fall*
> *Over strewn blocks, stuffed animals on staircases,*
> *My turn to read the writing crayoned on the wall.*

You seem, in Dark Horses, *your most recent collection, to be writing more serious non-satirical poems. Was that a conscious decision?*

X. J. KENNEDY: *Dark Horses* owes much of its shape and tone to John Irwin, the editor of the Johns Hopkins poetry series. Irwin greatly preferred my dead serious poems to my funnier ones, and he discouraged me from putting some of my more frivolous items in the book. So, in a way, the book is a little bit uncharacteristic, but I'm very comfortable with that.

One literary critic has referred to you as a "social historian" for "whom the modern world is dreary and shallow." Others have remarked on your descriptions of "the aridity of the world around" you, and your bemoaning "the bleak state of American culture." Do you feel these are fair characterizations?

X. J. KENNEDY: Well, if at times I'm pessimistic and downcast about the state of American culture, at least I'm not *permanently* depressed. It seems to me that anyone who comments on the American scene will find plenty of absurdity. H. L. Mencken once characterized America as the most entertaining of countries because of all its faults, and maybe there's something to that.

Roger Mitchell in Poetry Magazine *has suggested that, in response to this contemporary vacuity and absurdity, your "comfort is in pointing" it out, "and in crafting those things which baffle the modern world, namely, carefully wrought poems in a recognizable and" what he calls "outmoded manner." Do you see well-crafted poetry as a reaction to modern failings?*

X. J. KENNEDY: I'd be happy to have much of my own work taken that way. But most formal poetry, it seems to me, isn't trying to make political statements or cultural comments so much as it's trying to produce something that satisfies us and makes us sense a certain joy.

It's also frequently said that your work is greatly influenced by the seventeenth century Metaphysicals and their modern proponent, T. S. Eliot. Is that correct?

X. J. KENNEDY: Yes, I was extremely fond of Eliot when I first read him back when I took my Masters at Columbia, and, to this day, I still love his earlier work. I do tend to tune out with the *Four Quartets* and the verse plays, but, yes, he was certainly someone from whom I learned quite a bit. And I did study the Metaphysical poets of the seventeenth century rather intensely at Michigan under a fine professor named John Arthos, and, in a number of my early poems, I tried, quite consciously, to see if it was possible to write metaphysical poems in the twentieth century.

Metaphysical or not, wit in a wide variety of forms is one of the distinguishing and distinguished traits of much of your poetry. This is especially obvious in your many epigrams, such as "Literary Cocktail Party":

> Abuse pours in on all who leave the room,
> Ill nature so abhors a vacuum.

Aside from J. V. Cunningham, who are some of your favorite wits and/or epigrammatists?

X. J. KENNEDY: Besides Cunningham, John Frederick Nims was a master of the epigram. I was very disappointed to see that the Library of America's two-volume anthology of twentieth-century poetry didn't include any of Nims's excellent epigrams. Incidentally, it's still a marvelous anthology, but I miss his epigrams. I also greatly admire the great epigram writers of the seventeenth century, whom I read very closely at Michigan. What's that little poem that everyone points to as the finest epigram in the English language? The one by Sir John Harington:

> Treason doth never prosper: what's the reason?
> For if it prosper, none dare call it treason.

One could die happy in heaven having written those two lines.

Did you know J. V. Cunningham?

X. J. KENNEDY: I met Cunningham only once—when I served as a juror for the Brandeis University Arts Award. Cunningham was chairman of the jury, and it was a hilarious occasion. He was such a dear man, and you had to respect a man of his sour integrity. So a bunch of us were sitting around trying to decide which poet should deserve the $10,000, or whatever the prize was, and the jury also included Rolfe Humphries, George P. Elliott, Richmond Lattimore, and Denise Levertov—who had a cold and was communicating with the rest of us by telephone. Cunningham kept trying to sway the jurors to a formalist poet, and Levertov, via her telephone connection, kept trying to give the prize to some wild Olsonite, so we ended up giving the prize to yet another poet—who, as it turned out, was the only nominee that everyone on the jury had actually read! That was my only meeting with Cunningham in person, but he did contribute an epigram to the magazine that Dorothy and I ran for a few years in the early seventies, *Counter/Measures*.

Aside from your witty epigrams, you've written some of the most famous bawdy poems of recent times, like "Flagellant's Song" and the much-anthologized "In a Prominent Bar in Secaucus One Day." Where did the latter poem come from?

X. J. KENNEDY: Well, that poem accumulated by bits and pieces for a couple of years. John Heath Stubbs, whom I'd assisted as a paper grader at Michigan, had written a poem about an old whore with the refrain, "For after death there's a judgment due," and that might have been in the back of my mind when I started my own poem. Anyway, after I'd fooled around with bits and pieces of it for several years, I spent a summer at home in Dover, New Jersey. I was all alone, with nothing to do except tool over my poetry, and suddenly all the pieces came together, and the character emerged to speak her lines. It was a wonderful experience when the poem finished itself that way. I bawled with thankfulness because it was such an emotional release. Since then, the poem has been included in a number of anthologies of light verse, and every time it's printed as light verse, I think to myself, "Isn't that poem quite serious too?" At least, it made *me* weep.

Well, it's both. But it's easy to see why it would appear in anthologies of humorous verse, given its rollicking rhythm, the strength of her voice, and some of the silly things she says.

X. J. KENNEDY: That's right.

I wanted to ask you about your excellent translations which have occasionally appeared in your collections and also in your little book of French translations entitled French Leave. *Do you enjoy translating?*

X. J. KENNEDY: Yes! Don't we all wish we had more time to do translations? And more years left to do them in? I've loved translating poems in so far as I've been able to do it. It's a game-like challenge that I very much enjoy. Recently, at David Slavitt's request, I translated—or maybe I should say "Englished"—a new version of Aristophanes' *Lysistrada*. I really don't know Greek, so I had to work with books of crib notes, and to look at about sixteen other translations.

How did you handle the Spartan dialect?

Like all translators who wrestle with *Lysistrada*, I had to face the problem of which English dialect the Spartans should speak. Apparently, in the original, Aristophanes had them speak some very un-Athenian yokel language, so one translator, for example, decided to have them speak with a Russian accent. Others have had them speak like hillbillies. In the old Loeb Library version, they use a Scottish dialect. So I tried to think what would be the most vulgar dialect to the American ear, and I settled on Brooklynese.

Back in 1972, with your wife Dorothy, you established a unique and rather rebellious poetry journal called Counter/Measures *which published only metrical, formal poetry. Was there much hostility back then?*

X. J. KENNEDY: We got very little nasty backlash. A few poets thought that we'd gone off the deep end to limit the magazine to rhyme and meter. And I think my friend Don Hall disapproved of us for that reason, but on the whole we received a warm, even enthusiastic, reception. Dorothy and I had actually hoped that we wouldn't get a great flood of manuscripts to consider for the magazine because we were doing it with very little time and using our own pocket money, but we got a great influx of manuscripts—and this was at a time when rhyme and meter were in the doghouse. In those days, if you sent a sonnet off to most respectable magazines, it would boomerang back to you very quickly. But it turned out that there were scores of poets out there who were glad to have such a market, and we got an enormous volume of mail. In the three issues we put out, we published about 200 different poets, and some of them were people whom I'd never thought of as formalists before, like Louis Zukofsky, and Leslie Fiedler, and a great number more.

Did you enjoy the editing?

X. J. KENNEDY: Very much. It was a great deal of fun and very revealing. We were greatly heartened to see how many poets were still devoted to the old formalities. Our only disappointment was that we'd hoped the magazine would showcase some people who were doing bold, different, and experimental things with rhyme and meter, but I can't say that we really unearthed much material of that kind. Have you at *The Formalist?*

Not very much, but maybe that says something very positive about the stability and strength of the old forms. It's hard to improve on the sonnet.

X. J. KENNEDY: That's right.

So Counter/Measures *lasted three years. Was it the work that wore you both out and made you discontinue the magazine at that point?*

X. J. KENNEDY: Actually, we really quit the magazine because we ran into a number of personal problems. My parents' health was failing, and

I had to contribute much more time to their support, so, eventually, the magazine just got to be too much—both financially and time-wise.

In your own poetry, you've written in an extraordinary variety of forms— sonnets, elegies, couplets, the French forms, even limericks—are there any that you prefer?

X. J. KENNEDY: I love them all, and that isn't merely "la dee da." Also, I don't think I ever choose a form first and then go ahead and write a poem in that format. For me, the impulse to write the poem comes first, and then, as the poem materializes, it decides what form it wants to take. So if you're writing a poem that's about twelve lines of iambic pentameter, and it looks as if it'll wrap itself up very shortly, you start to think, "Hmmm, maybe this should be a sonnet." So, in general, I don't have any favorite forms as such. Whatever form the poem wants to choose for itself is fine with me.

You've always been very wary of excessive "ego" in poetry. You once said, "What I like is song and balladry; the freedom of not having to express myself." You've also claimed that, "Writing in rhythm and rhyme, a poet is involved in an enormous, meaningful game, not under his ego's control." Could you discuss this a bit?

X. J. KENNEDY: Well, it seems to me that when you write in meter and rhyme you erect obstacles between yourself and so-called "self-expression." I'm especially thinking of all the undergraduate poets I've worked with, or talked to, because when they first try writing in rhyme, they're appalled because they're unable to say what they wanted to say. So I try to explain to them that being unable to say exactly what our tight, little intellects want to say, is a great advantage—and that by coping with the arbitrary restrictions of form, we can be led forward on a very curious and exciting voyage of discovery. Very often, the best poems are those that shape themselves unexpectedly. When you write in rhyme, it's as if you're walking across a series of stepping stones into the darkness, and you can't really see what's at the far end of the stepping stones. So you're led onward, often to say things that surprise and astonish you. As Rolfe Humphries once put it, rhyme leads you to say much better things than you could have thought of all by yourself. And that's also, I believe, one of the ways in which form prevents us from waxing too personal. Nowadays, many poets write in free verse, and many of them have nothing to prevent them from gassing on cozily about their own little personal concerns. But rhyme and meter stand in the way of that kind of self-absorption, or, at least, they make it more difficult. As W. D. Snodgrass has pointed out, the process of shaping a poem in a rhymed stanza can often force you to find out what you really want to say through the process of laboriously overcoming obstacles.

Related to this subject, a number of critics consider your striking poem "The Self-Exposed" as an attack on the so-called Confessional school of poetry. Did you see it that way when you wrote it?

X. J. KENNEDY: No, not at all. I wrote that particular poem about an off-beat character who feels the urge to parade his nudity to unsuspecting people on a railroad station platform. It was one of several poems in which I was trying to understand some lonely outcast of society. I didn't see the poem as attacking confessional poetry or anything else.

But it is about self-exposure—the urge to expose parts of one's self that are not considered appropriate.

X. J. KENNEDY: That's right, and I don't mind critics finding something in a poem that I didn't know was there—some further depth perhaps. So I'm very grateful for that, even though it wasn't my intention.

In 1979, you made the important decision to give up your teaching post at Tufts University and work as a free-lance writer. Since then, you've edited a number of very popular university texts—some with Dorothy—such as An Introduction to Poetry *and* An Introduction to Fiction. *Wasn't this a rather risky move at the time? To give up your teaching job to make your living off of textbooks?*

X. J. KENNEDY: It was rather risky. But Dorothy encouraged me to take a chance—she's always been braver and more adventurous than I am. For a little while, it was hard to do without the regular paycheck from the University, and we ran up lines of credit on our credit cards, but before long we found ourselves better off than we had been before. This was partially because a publisher who needed a rhetorical reader put together quickly came to Dorothy and me and asked us to assemble a textbook called *The Bedford Reader* which he needed in six weeks. Since I was now a free agent and no longer teaching, we were able to do it by the deadline, and this led to an expansion of our textbook base. So, in time, everything worked out just fine.

How do you feel about the amount of time you can devote to your own poetry, vis-à-vis the editing? It's hard enough to find time when you're teaching full time, but you do get the summers off.

X. J. KENNEDY: Well, even when I was teaching, I was doing textbooks as well, so the change really didn't limit my ability to write verse. I should also mention, however, that I loved teaching at Tufts, and I was treated very well there. After I left, I missed the students and my colleagues quite a bit. But in the end, it was a good move, in my opinion, and eventually I had more time to write than ever before.

You've also found time to write a variety of popular books of children's verse, and a number of those poems were included in Cross Ties: Selected Poems. *Your children's verses are extraordinary exercises in outrageous nonsense, clever playfulness, and flamboyant sound.*

> *With walloping tails, the whales off Wales*
> *Whack waves to wicked whitecaps.*

How did you get started writing for such a young audience?

X. J. KENNEDY: I actually started writing verse for kids back before I was ever a father. I think I was fired up by the fact that back around the late fifties a number of very good poets were writing verse for children. John Ciardi and Randall Jerrell and William Jay Smith and others. And I read their work and I thought, "What fun! I'll try some myself." So I wrote about a dozen or so poems that I imagined children might like to read, but I didn't know what you did with such poems once you'd written them. I didn't know who'd have any interest in publishing them. So when I came to do *Nude Descending a Staircase*, my first book, I happened to include a couple of my poems for children, and I titled them, "For Children If They'll Take Them." But I wasn't sure if they would! Then, by another stroke of exceptional luck, these poems came to the attention of the children's poet and anthologist Myra Cohn Livingston, and she included one of my little poems in one of her anthologies, and she also wrote to me and asked me if I had any other poems for children. So I sent her the rest of my unpublished work, and she showed them to the great children's book editor Margaret McElderry. Margaret liked the samples, and she wrote to me and said, "Have you got enough to make a whole book?" Wow! What an incredible event that was! To have a New York publisher write to you and request a book of poems! I was stunned. So I wrote back and said, "Well, I don't have enough right now, but if you really mean it, I'll see what I can do." So I was put to the task of writing more verse for children, and six months or so later, I sent Margaret the manuscript which became my first children's book, *One Winter Night in August*, which came out in 1975. That began a 25-year-long relationship with Margaret McElderry which was one of those dream-like relationships— where you have a publisher who'll publish anything you want to publish. Over the years, Margaret brought out a dozen of my books for children. She's now in her mid-eighties, and though she still works at Simon and Schuster, which now has her imprint, she's less involved in actually directing the choice of manuscripts these days, so I think I'm about at the end of my great long run with Margaret McElderry. Anyway, she was a wonderful editor of the old, tough, blue-pencil school and very encouraging. She did the *Brats* books, and she did my two novels for children, *The Owlstone Crown* and *The Eagle as Wide as the World*.

X. J. KENNEDY

I remember in your introduction to the original Brats *book, you told the story about how your own young son wrote that clever little poem about the electric blanket.*

X. J. KENNEDY: That's right. He wrote the best of the Brats poems when he was twelve-years-old. Dorothy and I were shopping for bedding in a department store, and our son, Josh, was with us and very bored at the time. Since I'd been reciting some of the Brats poems to him, and he'd figured out how to do it, he decided to entertain himself in that boring department store by coming up with his own Brats poem—which he wrote right there on the spot.

> Stupid little Lucy Wankett
> Washed her automatic blanket
> While the thing was still plugged in.
> Notify her next of kin.

The poem was subsequently published by Robert Wallace in one of his *Light Year* anthologies, to my great pride and joy.

Given your remarkable productivity as a poet, editor, and writer of children's books, I wonder if you ever have blank periods? You seem to imply this in your poem "In a Dry Season":

> *Descend, O Muse. Bestow, ungracious slattern.*
> *Quit circling Boston in a holding pattern.*

X. J. KENNEDY: I often go long periods without writing any verse because I get distracted by the other things in my life—for example, our recent move out of the town that we'd lived in for thirty years and subsequently establishing a new home elsewhere. But whenever I get some free time on my hands, I'm always ready to write. Ideas flow in—and impulses flow in—and I always have far more plans for things to write, both poetry and prose, than I'll ever have time to write. So I don't have

"droughts" myself, but it can certainly happen, of course. I remember
W. S. Merwin saying that whenever he has a dry spell, he translates.

*You once described yourself as "one of an endangered species." Are you
heartened by the number of younger poets today who are taking rhyme
and rhythm more seriously, or do you still feel that formal poetry is on
the "endangered list"?*

X. J. KENNEDY: Well, it's certainly healthier these days than it was
back in 1972 when we started *Counter/Measures*. The existence of a
magazine like *The Formalist* and the existence of the West Chester Form
and Narrative Conference are clear signs of blooming health, it seems to
me. Also, there are many excellent young poets now appearing with
their first volumes of poetry—poets like A. E. Stallings, for example.
This is cause for great good cheer to me. While it's still probably the
case that poets who write in rhyme and meter remain a minority, they're
certainly a healthy and impressive minority.

*You've written in a number of poems about the "po biz," as Louis Simpson
once described it, and your poem "Reading Trip" is an uncompromising
satire about the "scene." How do you feel about it today?*

X. J. KENNEDY: Since we're here at the West Chester Poetry Conference,
I should first point out that this is the most harmonious assembling of
poets I've ever seen. People are here not because they're interested in
advancing their reputations; they're here because they truly love formal
poetry. Regarding "po biz," as Louis Simpson once called it, he was
referring to the process of going out and giving readings and going
through a whole process of familiar steps: travel, cocktails, book sign-
ings, meeting people, etc. I have nothing against it as long as the poet
can survive its demands. Some people handle it very well, returning
home in good health. But others, as you know, have found such reading
trips occasions to get wildly drunk, solicit sex, and fall prey to the very
mistaken notion that they're some kind of literary deities. So there are

real dangers, I think, in the "po biz," but for the poet who can keep his or her eye on the more important business of writing poetry, such reading tours can be a good way to meet people and get one's work around.

The last poem in Dark Horses, *"Ambition," raises a crucial question about the methodology of the writer/artist. In the month of October, the narrator, a writer, wonders:*

> . . . *Was I wrong*
> *To have clung to my workdesk the summer long,*
> *scratching out, striving? . . .*

How do you feel about this?

X. J. KENNEDY: Well, if one can look back and still sense what one was saying while writing the poem, I suspect that "Ambition" is dealing with the dichotomy of "willing" yourself to write, versus just being open to whatever inspiration or impulse may come. The poem sees the poet as rather envying other people who will accept what the wind bestows, who'll write nothing but what's given by the muse, as opposed to people like him who dig in their roots and strive and toil at their work desks—trying to write poetry deliberately. In the end, I'm rather torn about it, but I think Randall Jerrell's right when he says that there has to be some deliberate striving in one's attempt to write poetry. Jerrell points out that in Michelangelo's famous vision of creation, Adam is given the divine spark, but to receive it, he has to extend his forefinger.

What are you working on now?

X. J. KENNEDY: I'm trying to put together a new collection of the verse that I've written since *Dark Horses,* and this has involved retooling a number of poems that have already been published. For me, it often seems that when a poem is first printed, it's just another stage in its development towards whatever it's going to become. So I've been looking over these poems and trying to get them in the best possible shape. I must admit that the realization that many of the poems that I've published in magazines aren't really worth reprinting is always a painful fact to face. It may be, as Delmore Schwartz once said, that the wisest course is to write as much as possible and to print as little as you can.

Your poems have always been extraordinarily well-crafted, but the poems in Dark Horses *seem to build more consciously toward the final line or lines. For example, "Woman in Rain," "Twelve Dead, Hundreds Homeless," "For Jed," "To the Writers Forbidden to Write," and "Veterinarian," which ends, "She murmurs words to soothe the languageless." Do you have the sense that you've developed a heightened sense of closure?*

X. J. KENNEDY: Well, you're probably right. I've always liked poems with loud closures, following the lead of Yeats who said that a poem should click shut like a closing box. The last line of a poem is terribly important; it's what the reader is going to take away with him. On the other hand, the first line is terribly important too, because if it's no good, the reader might not keep on reading. Someone—I can't remember whom—once said that there are "first" line poems that start out magnificently well and then get worse as they go along, and there are "last" line poems that build up to excellence even though they might have started out mediocrely. I guess what we all want to do is write poems that are both first and last line poems, and not so bad in between.

I'd like to finish up today by citing the last six lines from your excellent quatrain poem "To the Writers Forbidden to Write," which is not only a tribute to all politically oppressed writers but also to the fundamental power of literature itself:

You start awake when telephones
Clang from the floor above your flat

X. J. KENNEDY

As though the light of day could bring
The clocklike latch, unlatch of arms
While in a thousand basement rooms
Your thoughts explode like fire alarms.

Thanks very much.

X. J. KENNEDY: Thank you, Bill.

INDEX

www.ingramcontent.com/pod-product-compliance
Lightning Source LLC
Chambersburg PA
CBHW060344030726
47497CB00003B/585